£2.50
SCHOO
1221

EAST SUSSEX SCHOOLS LIBRARY SERVICE	
12-Dec-2008	PETERS
1201235	

The Living Coast

An Aerial View of Britain's Shoreline

First published 2008

LAST REFUGE Ltd.

Photography © **Adrian Warren** and **Dae Sasitorn**
Text © **Christopher Somerville**

This book was designed and produced by
Last Refuge Ltd.
Batch Farm, Panborough, near Wells, Somerset, BA5 1PN, UK, tel: (44) (0) 1934 712556
e-mail: info@lastrefuge.co.uk, web: www.lastrefuge.co.uk

Designers:
Dae Sasitorn
Will Brett

Front cover: *Beachy Head*
Back cover: *St Ives, Beach and Rocks near Bude, Groyne at Prestatyn, Harlech Castle, Muckle Roe, Brough of Deerness, Tres Ness & Cata Sand, Barrisdale Bay, Mudeford Spit and Hengistbury Head, The Needles, Rumps Head*
Previous Page: *Pagham Harbour*

All photographs in this book are available for publication or as prints from www.lastrefuge.co.uk

ISBN: 978-09558666-0-9

All rights reserved. No part of this publication may be reproduced, stored in a retrieval system, or transmitted, in any form or by any means, electronic, mechanical, photocopying, recording or otherwise, without the prior permission of the copyright holders.

Printed and bound by NPE Print Communications, Singapore

The Living Coast

An Aerial View of Britain's Shoreline

Photography by Adrian Warren & Dae Sasitorn

Text by Christopher Somerville

LAST REFUGE

Great ship

We will set topgallants and flying stu'nsails, and
will square north away for Unst before
a screaming Scillies westerly. We will slip
the black Crebinicks, Gilstone and Gorregan,
the Haycocks and the Hellweathers;
come up that long harsh jaw of Cornish shore,
Blackapit and Crackington under our lee,
round Bight-a-Doubleyou, round Madbrain Sands,
the English and the Welsh Stones of
ill-repute, Severn tides and bridge ties.

We will con the creep, the sideways
inching up eastern tideways,
the Essex shore, the creeks and crooks, rays
and guts, runnels, channels, swales and swatchways
of Foulness, of Dengie Flat and Buxey Sand,
Deadman's Island, Bedlam's Bottom, Hangman's Point –
Trimingham, Gimingham, the Eye of Cley,
Salthouse and the green saltings grey
with salt crustings.
Then Inner Knock and Outer Knock at the open
door of the Wash, half sand, half tide
and mud, wholly mud in blue whalebacks –
Friskney Flats, Boston Deeps – the gloom of the Deeps.

Hard a-port there for the great sands,
the ten-mile tides, the forty-mile strands
where cocklers and cabin boys sleep;
the old salt pans of Salters Bank,
of Out Marsh and In Marsh, of
Fishnet, of Fluke, of Shoulder and Point of Lune.

And it's on for Scotland shore, for otherness -
craigs for rocks, carregs and stanes for stones:
Yellow Craig, Limpet Craig, the Bell and the Black Stane.
Seduction of lumpen names, of friction -
Butter Lump, Clashfarland Point,
Craig Nabbin, Skelmorlie, Gourock and Greenock,
the kyles and the sea lochs
and the isles.

We will haul our wind between
orchid sands of Mingulay, stony tombs of Orkney;
go about among Norse names for
black Shetland borders: Bogligarth's Geo,
Tang of Noustigarth, Trinks O' Clave –
for thrashing sea and bitten-out cave,
Whilkie Stack, Swinga Tain,
a swinging sword, a plunging bow to
torch a fiddle, fire a longship.

Up on Unst we will beach in Burrafirth
and climb the long back of Hermaness to
stare north over the canted blades, the full stops
of Vesta Skerry, Rumblings, Tipta Skerry,
of Muckle Flugga and the granitic hummock
Out Stack and the Arctic ice, ominous, oncoming –
at the forefoot of the great ship, Britain.

Christopher Somerville, 2008

North east coast of Hoy at Quoyness, Bay of Quoys, Orkney
N 58°54'23.1" W 3°18'37.8" Grid Ref: HY246028 Map Ref: 12 B7

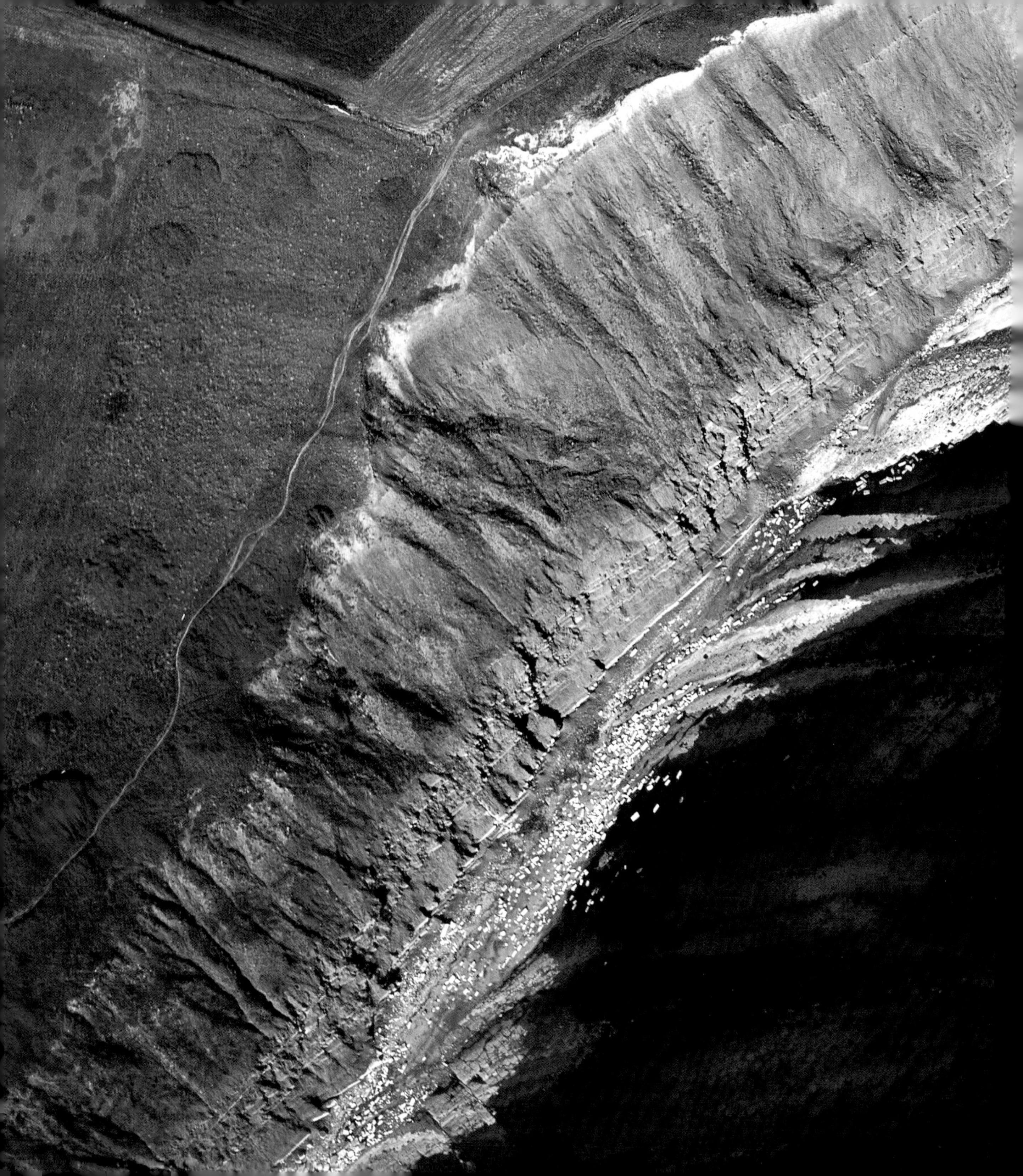

CONTENTS

Foreword

Flying to produce the aerial photographs in this book has been immensely rewarding. Over the years and over many different projects, our trusty Cessna 182 has become an old friend. We have flown in it, from our little grass strip in Somerset, as far as Africa to the south and northwards to the northernmost tip of Shetland, and out west over the cold North Atlantic to the remote St Kilda archipelago. Over mountain ranges, over ocean and high over thick blankets of cloud, its single engine has never faltered.

Following the British coastline has taken us on some epic flights over countless stunning, dramatic landscapes. Whenever the light is right we are ready to go again, for a flight that may last five hours or so. Before take-off we ensure the cows are safely cleared from our runway, then, with systems checked, camera ready, maps at hand, and eager engine warm and tugging impatiently at the brakes, we finally open the throttle and gather speed. As the nose lifts, the fields, trees and the world below recede into miniature. Over towns and motorways we cast sympathetic looks at the traffic jams far below, and speed on towards the coast. It is not far. Approaching the sea the horizon widens, with green fields and rolling landscape gradually left behind. Below, the water is a shimmering silver and blue, but between land and sea is that fascinating fringe, the coast. It might be sand or pebble, cliff or mudflat, river estuary or harbour, lonely cottage, quiet village or gaudy resort town – for a small group of islands, Britain's coast has a richness in variety that would be difficult to match anywhere else – an exotic geological cocktail of ancient rocks and sediments pushed and squeezed together by unimaginable tectonic forces.

Everywhere the coast has a story to tell, for it is constantly changing, the rocks battered and shaped by waves, sand or shingle heaped by powerful currents, with silt and mud dumped by rivers as they meet the sea. Exposed in cross-section, the geology offers clues to events long forgotten, and to what future nature might bring. The coast is a focus for living too, exploited by people since earliest times for defence or refuge, a location for trade and industry, a place to set sail on voyages of exploration, a base for fishing fleets, merchantmen, naval vessels, or just somewhere to be enjoyed for relaxation and pleasure, it is a living, dynamic landscape. Looking at the coastline from the air puts everything into perspective, not only making sense of the geology and the locations chosen for human exploitation, but also allowing a visual appreciation in a more abstract sense.

An aerial perspective on its own however is an incomplete story. By chance, we met Christopher Somerville who has walked, explored and written about the British coast for some 30 years. His powers of observation and poetic mind lend a unique edge to his writing. For him, this project has been an opportunity to see his well-trodden paths from an unfamiliar, aerial perspective. For us, his wonderful text has enabled a more satisfying interpretation of all those memorable flights. The resulting combination offers a 3-dimensional view of our extraordinary coastline.

Adrian Warren & Dae Sasitorn
Somerset, August 2008

Mudflats at Wigtown Bay, Dumfries and Galloway
N 54°51'39.7" W 4°23'22.8" Grid Ref: NX467544 Map Ref: 6 E2

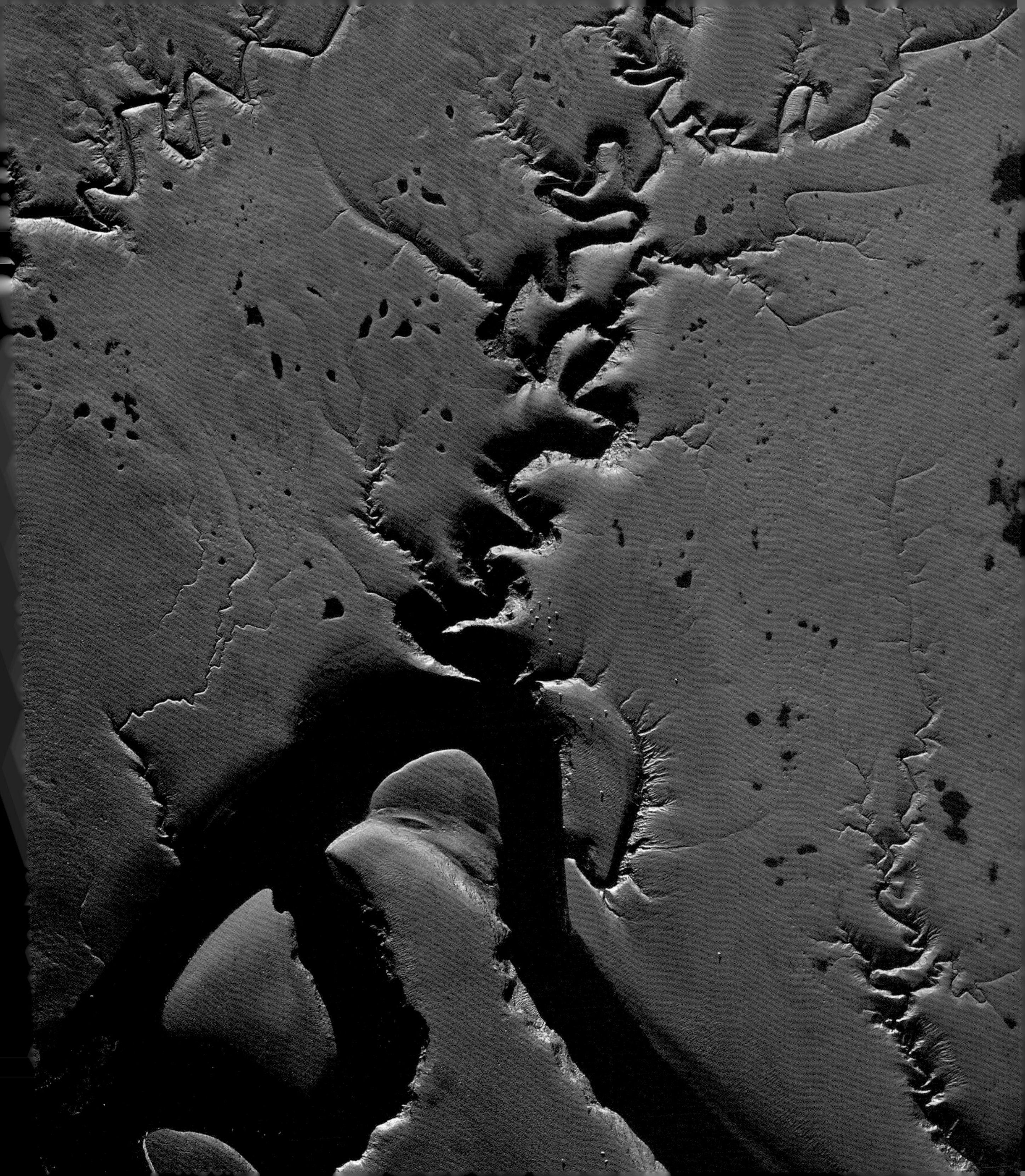

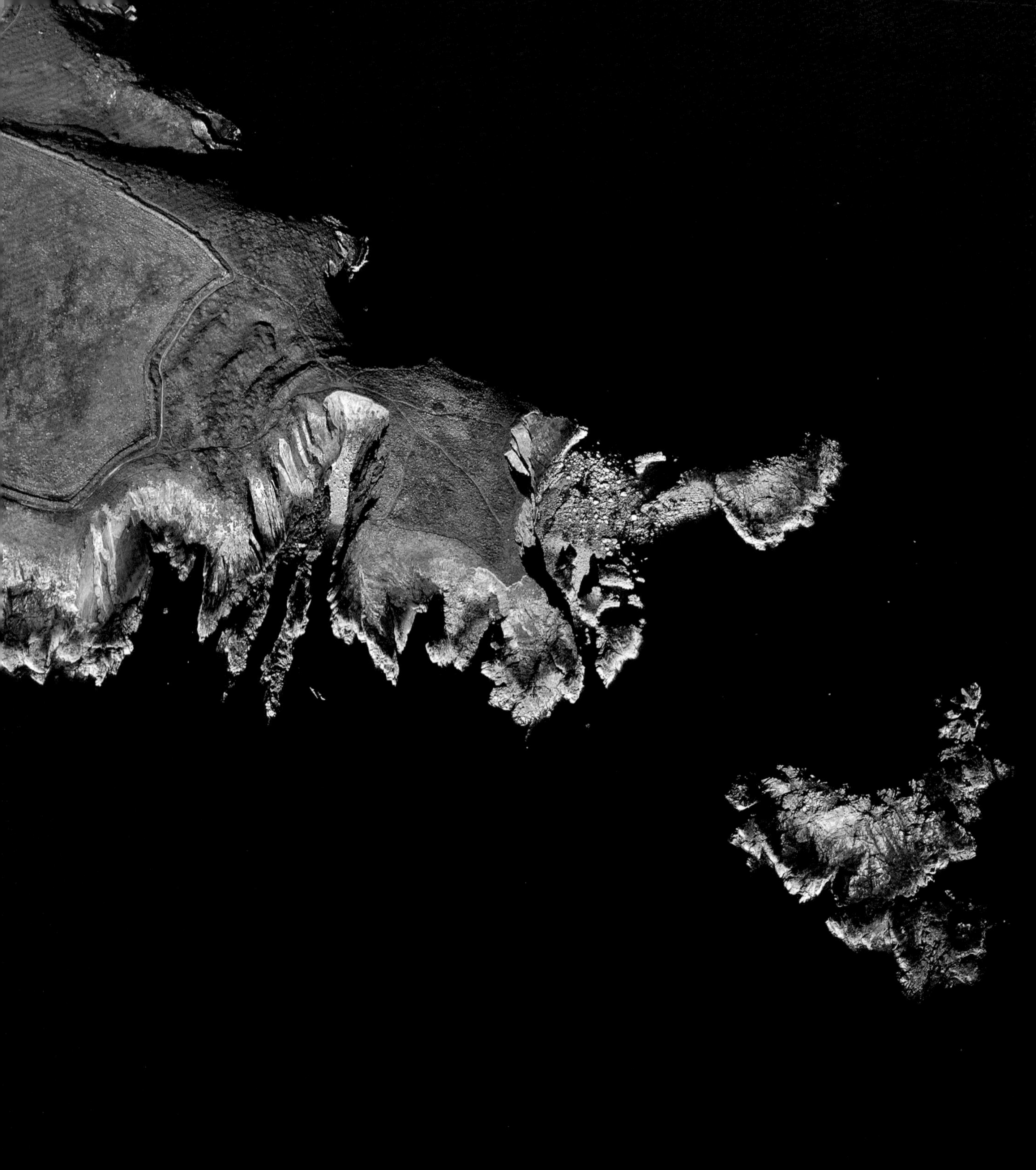

Introduction

Swooping around the coasts of Britain in their bird-like little aeroplane, Dae Sasitorn and Adrian Warren have captured the string of quite remarkable images which inspired me to write this book. I have been exploring and writing about the margins of these bewitching islands for most of my life. Tide-smoothed slobs of Wexford, wave-hammered geos of Shetland, sandy coves of Llŷn, sea banks of Lincolnshire and mudflats of Essex - the more remote and overlooked the nooks and crannies of the coast, the better I have liked conjuring them up in prose or poetry. There is profound beauty in the interplay of tide and shore, no matter where it may be. I'll never forget waking up in a home-coming plane just as we crossed the mighty East Coast estuary of The Wash on an ebb tide, and looking down in stunned delight at the gleaming, fractured collage of mazy creeks and channels, and the vast arched backs of the sandbanks that from 20,000 feet seemed a fleet of leviathans ponderously heaving themselves clear of seas of molten glass.

Well-known or obscure, I always suspected that other places I knew at ground level would look as astounding as this from a gull's-eye viewpoint - the great South Devon sandspit of Dawlish Warren, for example. I was already aware, from my own visits over the years, of the spit's contrasting zones of sea, sand, shingle, scrub, heath and mudflats, its many and varied colours, and its remarkable hooked shape lying across the mouth of the Exe estuary. But seeing Dawlish Warren with the magic eye in the sky has lent it a completely and stunningly new aspect. Here are no bird songs, no wave splash or wind hum to distract from the pure appreciation of the eyes alone – the brilliant greens and rich chocolate duns set against one another, the almost palpable textures of smooth mud, bushy heath and wiry scrub, and the plastic, free-flowing form of the thick collar of sand that enwraps the island of dunes at the head of the spit. Now I have savoured Dawlish Warren from this god-like perspective I will see it for ever more, above all else, as a masterpiece of Nature the artist, that supreme sculptor of natural materials.

Our coasts are, for their small compass, the richest and the most sensationally beautiful on this planet. A trip round the coasts of Britain by air unrolls a fabulous ribbon of juxtaposed colours and textures, of ancient, wildly bent and contorted layers; of deep-cut clefts, dug out of iron-hard cliffs by unimaginable forces, next to wide swathes of estuarine mud and sands moulded with more than human subtlety by the sea. Into all this is inserted the extraordinary maritime history of these islands, from uncultivated wilderness through Roman and Danish invasion, medieval and Industrial Revolution prosperity, imperial omnipotence and retreat into a more modest rôle in the world. Castles, docks, boatyards, lookouts, lighthouse towers and gun platforms, breakwaters and quays: they stand out from the air, signs and symbols of an island people in contact and conflict with all around them.

We love our coasts. We live by them if we can; we holiday there; we fight tooth and nail to keep the paths open and the views uncluttered. Those views have truly been opened up for me through the peerless artistry of Dae and Adrian. Because of them I will relish all the more the lap of spring floodwater along the Severn Estuary, the fruity summer tang of baked mud in the salt marshes of Burry Inlet, the whistle of autumn gales on the cliffs of Dunnottar, and the yelping of the pinkfoot geese as they cross Bob Hall's Sand against the green and pink sunrise of a frozen winter's day.

Caerfai Camp Cliff Fort and Penpleidiau, Pembrokeshire

N 51°52'04.0" W 5°15'08.2" Grid Ref: SM762238 Map Ref: 4 C11

Ancient Land
Land's End to Morte Point

The south-westernmost tip of Britain dips into the Atlantic sea like a bather's leg. The delicately arched toe of ancient Penwith seems poised to step away into the blue. Such images come irresistibly to mind in England's favourite seaside holiday paradise of west Cornwall. All seems fair and favourable, a blend of magically beautiful coasts, beach villages bursting with photogenic charm, a climate so mild that sub-tropical gardens flourish, and a rich treasury of myths and mysteries that lie thick on the moors and hills, in each secret cove and under every rock-pool stone.

Yet a glance at the coastal landscape of Penwith, the West Country's most westerly extremity, and on up the long northward-trending coast of North Cornwall and Devon, shows the steely fist beneath this most velvet-seeming of gloves. The coast of Cornwall and Devon is ancient – Penwith is composed of granite some 300 million years old, while much of the rest is made up of old red sandstones and upper carboniferous sediments that are even older. It all makes for a hard land of thin soils that are difficult to farm, craggy cliffs full of copper and tin to attract and endanger miners, steep little sandy-floored coves ideal for hiding contraband but tricky for launching a fishing boat into oncoming waves, rocks and reefs hiding just below the sea's surface in wait for unwary or fogbound mariners. And the sea itself, the big rollers driving onshore unbridled after a passage of 3,000 miles across the open North Atlantic, is a furious element around the peninsula.

The mining landscape of these cliffs has been designated a UNESCO World Heritage Site, and no wonder – the mining and mine engineering heritage of Cornwall and West Devon seems printed in the DNA of the local people. Even today, with the mineral industry dormant these past ten years, you can meet ex-miners not much past the prime of life who are delighted to talk and show you round the eerie, atmospheric 'wheals' or works whose ruins lie scattered all along the cliffs and moors of western Cornwall, many in the gaunt shadow of a roofless engine house and the tall, admonitory finger of a chimney lifted heavenwards.

Phoenician tin-traders sailed to Cornwall from the Mediterranean two thousand years ago – Joseph of Arimathea may have been one, and some stories say that he brought his young nephew Jesus with him. And did those feet ...? Something about the remoteness, the mistiness and other-worldliness of the Cornish coast seems to attract tales and myths. Did Arthur, the Once and Future King, begin his life at sea-girt Tintagel Castle on its lonely neck of rock? Legend has it that the arch-mage Merlin snatched the baby king from the waves as he came floating ashore – or was that Saint Piran, drifting to land aboard the millstone which had been tied round his neck to drown him on the orders of an ill-disposed Irish chieftain?

Whatever the truth of these splendid and illogical fables, hard archaeological evidence tells us of the struggles of our ancestors to survive, let alone to thrive, in these harsh western lands. Stone and Bronze Age people built themselves round houses and mysterious underground passages lined with stone slabs; they erected stone circles and stone-built, turf-domed tombs across the moors. Some of their Iron Age descendants went seaward, settling at easily-defended, cliff-encircled lookouts such as the coastal promontories of Gurnard's Head in Penwith and Rumps Point further north, where they dug ditches and mounded ramparts to keep enemies at bay while they farmed tiny pocket handkerchiefs of walled fields. Much of the land was sour, its acid soil, manured with seaweed, sand and excrement, fit only for grazing.

Levant tin and copper mine, Cornwall *N 50°09'09.6" W 5°41'10.2" Grid Ref: SW368346 Map Ref: 1 B11*

Stark and functional, the buildings of the Levant tin and copper mine perch at the edge of their granite cliff plateau a few miles out of Land's End on the north coast of Cornwall's most westerly region, Penwith. For all the myth and mystery of western Cornwall it is these ruined engine houses and chimneys that characterise the hard, uncompromising landscape and livelihoods of Penwith.

Gurnard's Head, Cornwall *N 50°11'33.9" W 5°35'56.8" Grid Ref: SW432387 Map Ref: 1 B11*

Long stretches of the Penwith coast are devoid of human inhabitants these days. On the outer crest of Gurnard's Head, a defiant fist of granite thrust into the Atlantic, Iron Age farmers toughed it out 2,000 years ago in the promontory fort of Trereen Dinas – a harsh life in a harsh land.

Ancient Land
Land's End to Morte Point

Medieval agriculturalists discovered how to burn limestone in hot kilns and extract an alkaline powder which would sweeten the fields. Their stone-built kilns, many in ruins, still dot beaches and coves of the West Country such as Buck's Mills in North Devon, anywhere where limestone and coal could be landed from a coasting vessel.

Their modern counterparts, the present-day farmers of the Cornish and Devon coasts, have more chemicals, more science and machine technology at their disposal than those ancestral farmers ever dreamed of. Their neat fields, still mostly used for grazing cattle and sheep, run to the edges of cliffs whose rocky faces plunge to the beach. You would never dream, looking at the mild appearance of the countryside, that beneath those agreeable green pastures lie rocks crazily tumbled, twisted, canted and bent. Only when you view the cliffs from the beach, or a boat, or by proxy from the little light aeroplane of Adrian Warren and Dae Sasitorn via their stunning photographs that embellish this book – the vees and crescents of crushed and squashed rock strata around Hartland Point, the upended dragon's teeth near Bude, the wave-hollowed caves and the sea-carved buttresses – do you begin to appreciate the extraordinary violence of the tectonic plate collisions, the submarine explosions and volcanic boilings that coalesced to shape the ancient land of Britain's extreme west.

As for the human settlements of this coast, those that were not dictated by mining or farming were brought into being by the need to catch fish. The far west possesses one of the toughest, roughest and least sheltered coastlines in Britain. Anywhere up a creek or river (Instow and Boscastle), round the sheltering bend of an estuary (Bude and Padstow) or tucked between two headlands (Port Isaac and Croyde) might serve as a fishing haven. Port Isaac is a fine example, with the old houses all snugged down out of the wind behind the quay, built strong and simple, with great breakwaters added later to stun the force of the waves. During the 19th century Port Isaac, in common with almost every other coastal village, began to expand along its flanking clifftops and beaches, putting out houses the likes of which the poor village fishermen could only dream of occupying. For this was the boom era of the seaside resort, and Cornwall had exactly what middle-class holidaymakers were after: romantically rugged scenery, clean seas, fresh food straight out of the ocean, and sandy beaches to perambulate on and bathe from. Myth-laden Cornwall was thrillingly remote, too, and exclusive because of it - though not for long, once the railways had extended their tentacles to the very extremities of the peninsula. Just about every seaside village follows this easily discerned pattern: an old and crowded centre near the harbour, a thin spread of fine Victorian villas along the bay, then a rash of 1930s houses further inland, and, where the surrounding land is not too steep, a spatter of large new developments pushing the outskirts further and further inland.

Times have changed, and the tempo of West Country holidays has changed with them. The village of Rock, opposite Padstow on the Camel estuary, is so much a well-heeled Londoners' boating resort that some have taken to calling it 'Islington-on-Sea'. Newquay is a surfer's heaven, a place to catch the hedonistic club scene as much as the big waves. Yet we still bring our children to dig the sand, explore the rock pools and swim in the sea – timeless, innocent delights. And the ever-increasing popularity of the truly wonderful and uplifting South West Coast Path, a National Trail that hugs these cliffs and shores for 500 miles, is witness enough to the enduring pleasures of this incomparable coastline – fresh clean air, warm sunshine, a sense of being away from it all, and the glories of those cliff-edged, sea-encircled views.

St Ives, Cornwall *N 50°13′05.3″ W 5°28′39.0″ Grid Ref: SW520411 Map Ref: 1 C11*

St Ives lies curled around its three beaches, the old fishing quarter crowded close to the harbour with its sturdy granite breakwaters. In the foreground swells the green headland known as The Island, with the ancient sea-mark of St Nicholas's Chapel at its summit. Before the coastguard station was built on the eastern brow of The Island, the chapel did duty in Georgian times as a lookout for Excise officers engaged in a long, bitter war with local smugglers.

Pentire and Newquay, Cornwall *N 50°24'31.4" W 5°06'33.9" Grid Ref: SW792612 Map Ref: 1 E9*

A glorious panorama over contrasting North Cornwall coastal landscapes - in the foreground the ribbed tidal sands of wild Crantock Beach; behind them, and the long built-up headland of Pentire, the perfect surfing scoop of Fistral Bay; beyond that the sprawl of Newquay, a resort town expanded by the railway to fill the cliffs around another surf-pounded crescent of sand, leading to a line of cliffs diminishing to vanishing point.

Towan Head, Cornwall *N 50°25'28.9" W 5°05'56.1" Grid Ref: SW800629 Map Ref: 1 E9*

The half-moon coves just east of Newquay, bitten by the sea out of old red sandstone cliffs, are clearly seen from Towan Head, another of those characteristic promontory headlands of North Cornwall. The giant red wedding-cake of the Headland Hotel forms a splendid, Gothic introduction to the headland, whose lush green turf is founded on lime-rich windblown sand.

Bedruthan Steps, Cornwall *N 50°29'07.8" W 5°02'04.3" Grid Ref: SW848695 Map Ref: 1 E9*

Bedruthan Steps are a line of weathered and wave-beaten sea stacks separated from the old sandstone of the mainland coast by the constant action of the sea on the weaker rock between the Steps and their parent cliffs. Fossils found here include a rare pteraspid, a primitive armoured fish with a tremendous nose spike that lived some 395 million years ago.

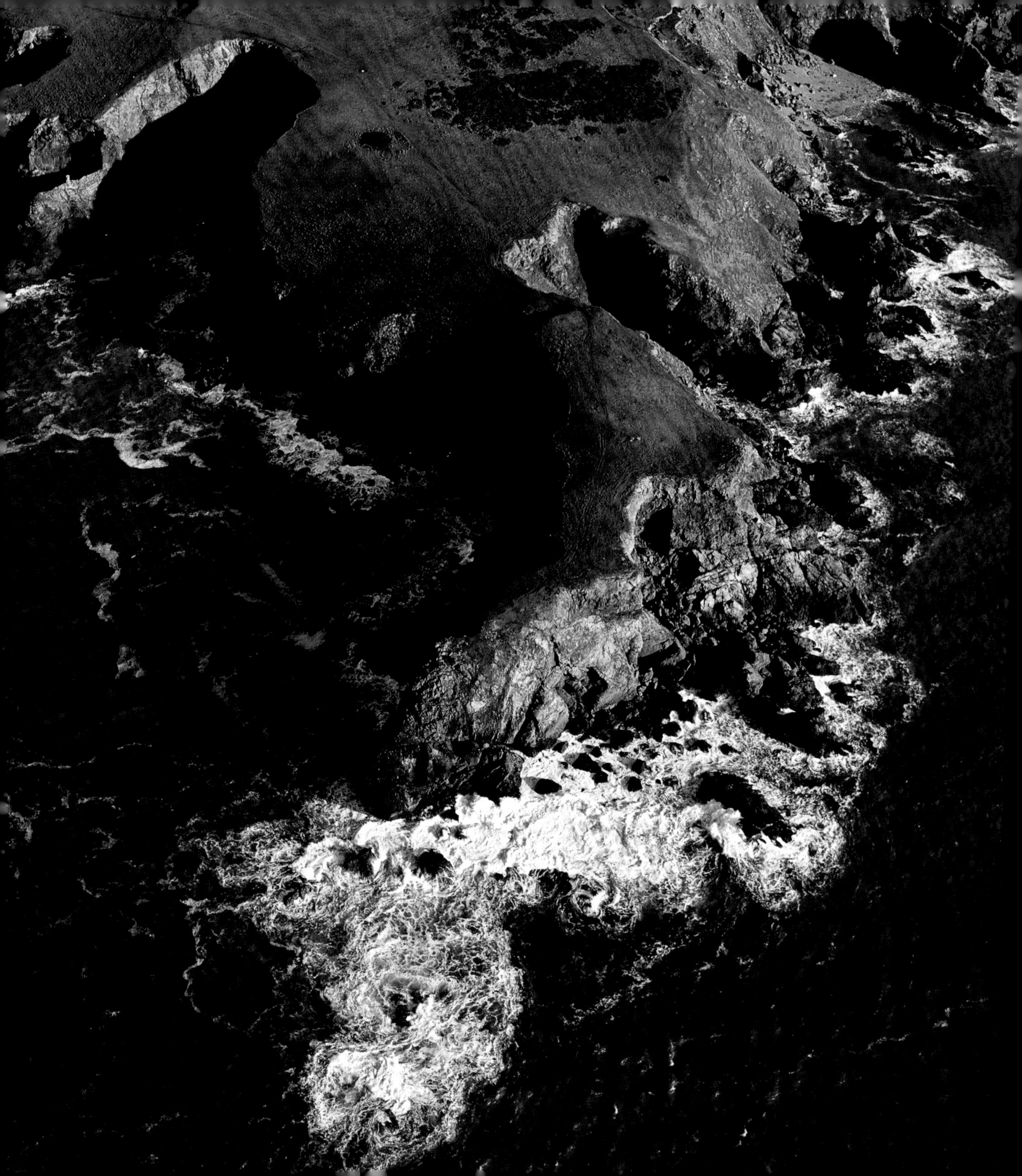

Park Head, Cornwall (left)

N 50°29'51.9" W 5°02'36.7"
Grid Ref: SW843709 Map Ref: 1 E9

Just north of Bedruthan Steps, the twisted snout of Park Head sticks well out westward into the sea. It's an exciting walk from the South West Coast Path across the narrow neck of the promontory and out onto the Head among the hummocks of Bronze Age burial mounds, flanked by the deep, shadowy clefts of Mackerel Cove (seen on the right) and High Cove.

Trevose Head, Cornwall

N 50°32'57.5" W 5°02'06.6"
Grid Ref: SW851766 Map Ref: 1 E8

Trevose Head is a lump of hard volcanic basalt, left sticking out boldly into the sea while the softer cliffs of Devonian sandstone surrounding it have been gradually eaten back by the Atlantic waves. The lighthouse was built in 1847 in response to a number of terrible shipwrecks on the promontory. Trevose Head, though, remained a deadly obstacle in fog until a mighty 36-foot-long foghorn, with a frog-like mouth 18 feet wide, was installed in 1913 to warn off shipping.

Camel Estuary, Cornwall

N 50°34'01.1" W 4°56'48.1"
Grid Ref: SW914783 Map Ref: 1 F8

The broad expanse of North Cornwall's pastoral hinterland, a patchwork of small hedged fields, shows to advantage in this fine view of the estuary of the River Camel winding seawards from Padstow. The estuary waters wrinkle over the sandbank of Doom Bar, site of many shipwrecks. On the far bank the green dome of Brea Hill rises over the diminutive church of St Enodoc in its walled graveyard, resting place of Poet Laureate Sir John Betjeman (1906-84).

Polzeath, Cornwall

N 50°34'25.9" W 4°54'54.8"
Grid Ref: SW937790 Map Ref: 1 F8

A calm day at Polzeath, one of Cornwall's most agreeable small resorts, with the beach well packed with sunbathers and a Kelly's Ice Cream van no doubt on its way to its usual station out on the sands. Polzeath Bay, long and narrow and facing north-west, is a different prospect in a stiff onshore wind when Atlantic breakers roll in one behind another, topped with lines of ecstatic surfers.

Rumps Point, Cornwall (right)

N 50°35'36.4" W 4°55'14.4"
Grid Ref: SW934812 Map Ref: 1 F8

Across the neck of Rumps Point run a series of deep grooves, the scars of a network of defensive walls and ditches thrown up there by the Iron Age farmers who inhabited the promontory from the 4th century BC for the next five hundred years. The faint circles of their hut foundations lie in the turf of the more easterly headland (seen on the left). With the isthmus walled off and steep cliffs on all sides, the people of Rumps Point could feel as secure as anyone in those uncertain times.

Port Isaac, Cornwall

N 50°35'32.0" W 4°49'56.6"
Grid Ref: SW996808 Map Ref: 1 F8

Though newer buildings have sprawled along the inlet over the course of the 20th century, it is the tight huddle of the old fishing village of Port Isaac that draws the eye. Stone-built cottages, public houses, shops and fishermen's stores lie close around the harbour along constricted lanes – one of the narrowest is known as Squeezeebelly Alley.

Tintagel, Cornwall *N 50°40'08.5" W 4°45'43.7" Grid Ref: SX049891 Map Ref: 1 G8*

Here is the place for hopeless romantics to idle and dream of King Arthur. The mainland is separated from the promontory known as The Island by a sea-cut chasm, whose abutting cliffs carry the dramatic ruins of the early medieval Tintagel Castle – the Lower Walls on the landward side, the Upper Walls on The Island. Was the Once and Future King conceived in the castle, or was he born here? Or was he rescued as a castaway baby by Merlin, and nurtured in the sea cave under the stronghold that still carries the master magician's name?

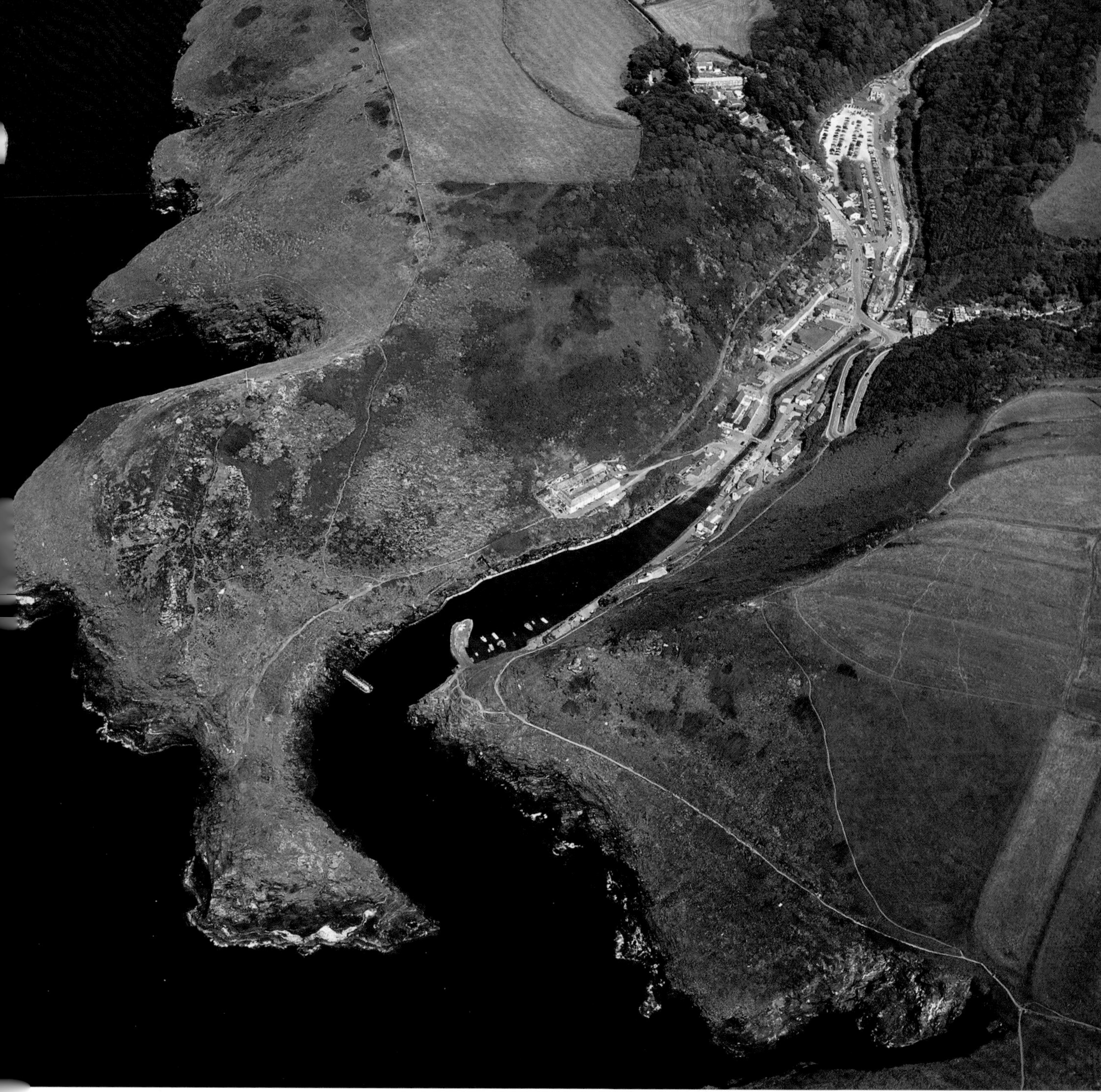

Boscastle, Cornwall *N 50°41'29.5" W 4°41'51.5" Grid Ref: SX096915 Map Ref: 1 G8*

The notorious Boscastle flood of 16 August 2004 will not soon be forgotten in the village. Five hours of torrential rain sent a terrifying flash flood down the epically named River Jordan, tearing down houses and walls as it burst through Boscastle. Miraculously, no-one was killed or badly hurt. The damaged structures have been rebuilt and the flood defences strengthened. Given the layout of Boscastle, with houses crammed along the brink of a river in a narrow, deep and steep-sided limestone valley, it is rather remarkable that flooding on this scale had not been seen here before.

Crackington Haven, Cornwall *N 50°44'30.5" W 4°38'05.2" Grid Ref: SX142969 Map Ref: 1 G7*

Like neighbouring Boscastle (page 25), Crackington Haven lies at the foot of a long, confined and winding valley. It, too, suffered damage in the rainstorm flood of 16 August 2004. The sheltered beach, pebbly at high tide with sand exposed at the ebb, was once a landing place for coal and lime fertiliser from South Wales. Hemmed in by tall cliffs, shut off from landward communications, Crackington Haven stayed undeveloped, tiny and remote.

Bude, Cornwall *N 50°49'49.8" W 4°33'01.8" Grid Ref: SS205065 Map Ref: 1 H7*

Bude owed its development as a harbour to the carboniferous sandstone that underlies it. The snake-like shape of the Bude Canal, built in the 1820s, can be seen in the centre of the picture; lime-rich sand was taken from the beaches and transported inland up the canal to fertilise the acid farmlands. The Victorians supplied Bude with a railway late in the 19th century, and the sandy beaches made it a popular resort for a few decades. But it never really experienced a boom time, and remains a small-scale haven on a rugged coast.

Beach and rocks, near Bude, Cornwall

N 50°48'29.9" W 4°33'23.7"
Grid Ref: SS200041 Map Ref: 1 H7 (above left)

N 50°50'36.8" W 4°33'24.4"
Grid Ref: SS201080 Map Ref: 1 H7 (right)

N 50°51'20.7" W 4°33'26.3"
Grid Ref: SS202094 Map Ref: 1 H6 (below left)

The coast of North Cornwall faces due west into the Atlantic swell, and the waves never cease from pounding and sucking at the cliffs. The effect of this constant, steady erosion are superbly illustrated here along the coast near Bude, where narrow beds of carboniferous limestone were squeezed, folded and hoisted by tectonic plate collisions from their original horizontal position to a vertical stance some 300 million years ago. Ground down by the Atlantic to beach level, they form countless close-packed scars of razor-edged rock pavement.

Lower Sharpnose Point, Cornwall *N 50°53'10.0" W 4°34'02.8" Grid Ref: SS195128 Map Ref: 1 H6*

At the aptly named Lower Sharpnose Point, a few miles south of the Cornwall-North Devon border, sea erosion has sculpted the tilted rock strata into remarkable, widely separated ribs. Softer layers of rock have been nibbled back by the waves, leaving the harder depositions standing proud of the main body of the cliff like sturdy buttresses.

Hartland Point, Devon *N 51°01'19.1" W 4°31'31.6" Grid Ref: SS230278 Map Ref: 1 H5*

Hartland Point marks the realignment of the North Devon coast from south-north to west-east. The tides off this sharp right-angle of cliffs are turbulent, the winds fierce and the reefs many. The lighthouse, built in 1874, was continually undermined by the waves until a sea wall was built to protect it. Geological upheavals hundreds of millions of years old are recorded in the wildly tilted and contorted strata of the cliffs. Inland, the rolling farmland and fields conceal all this ancient subterranean violence.

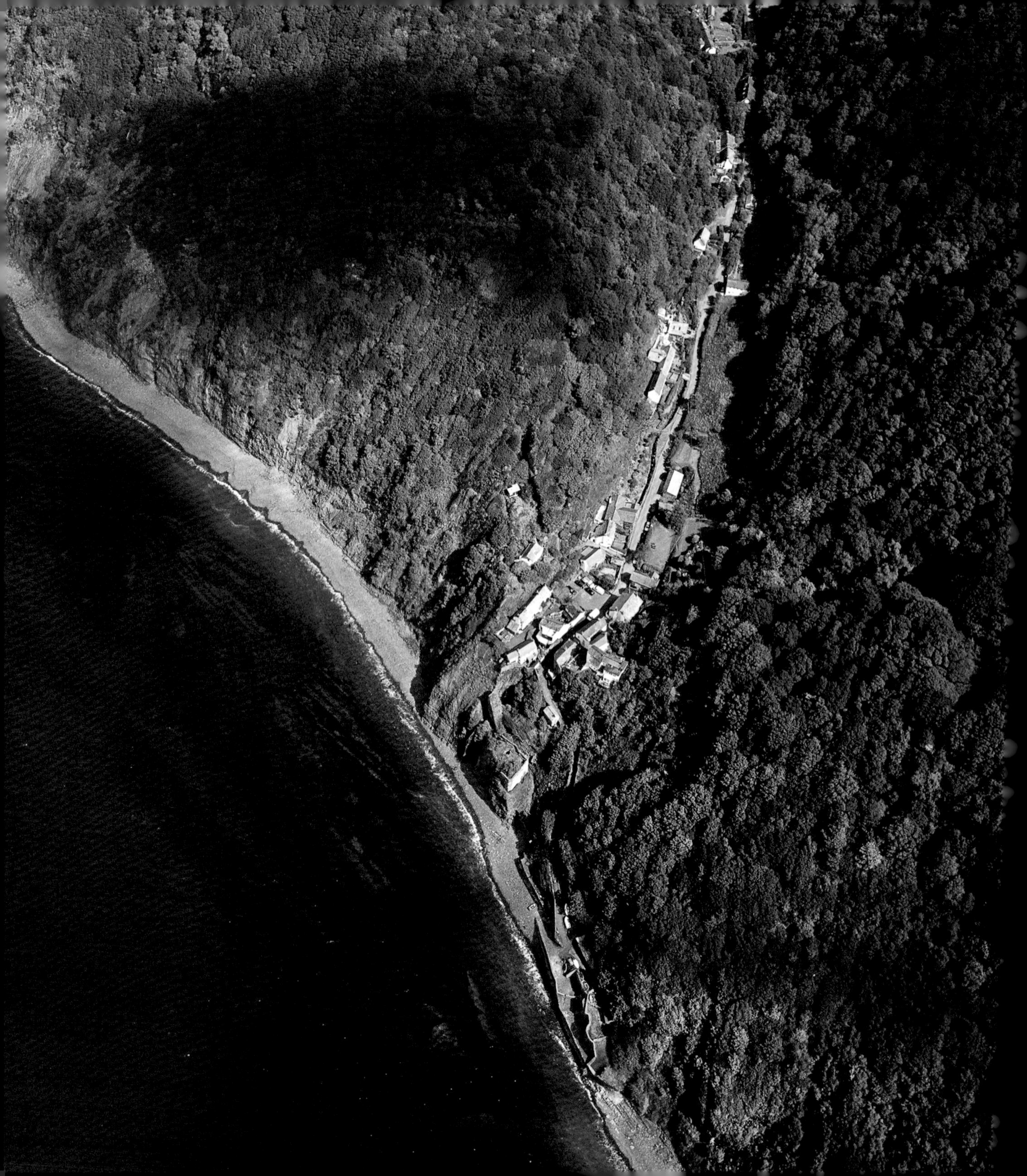

Buck's Mills, Devon (left)

N 50°59'18.6" W 4°20'43.9"
Grid Ref: SS355236 Map Ref: 1 I5

The North Devon coast east of Clovelly is steep and narrow. At Buck's Mills a slender, thread-like valley has been carved by the river that rushes down through Buck's Wood, fast enough to power a mill which once ground corn here. Fishing and lime-burning were the shore hamlet's other chief occupations; limestone was burned to produce alkaline fertiliser in two kilns, East Kiln (the green-topped square of stone in the centre of the picture) and West Kiln, whose wall lies just along the beach.

Appledore, Devon

N 51°03'19.6" W 4°11'32.2"
Grid Ref: SS465307 Map Ref: 1 J5

The imprint of a vanished shipyard indents the shore at Appledore (**above right**) – the long scoop of the building dock, the ladder-like launching ramps. The North Devon village on its rounded, seaward-facing crescent of coast at the mouth of the Two Rivers has been a boat-building centre for hundreds of years. Though one main yard (**below right**) still remains in operation, the much-lamented Hinks's Boatyard is no more than a scar in the shoreline.

Instow, Devon *N 51°03'14.9" W 4°10'51.7" Grid Ref: SS472306 Map Ref: 1 J5*

Instow lies opposite Appledore at the mouth of the Two Rivers, the Torridge (seen on the left here), and the Taw towards the top of the photograph. The trackbed of the disused Bideford Extension Railway (closed in 1982), arrowing into the village from the north, now carries the Tarka Trail long-distance path. In the distance two stark old jetties and a large area of scarred ground show where the old coal-fired East Yelland power station once loomed over the estuary.

Torridge Bridge, Devon *N 51°01'46.8" W 4°12'05.1" Grid Ref: SS457279 Map Ref: 1 I5*

Bideford Long Bridge, a 13th-century structure of 24 arches, offered the most seaward crossing of the River Torridge right up until 1987, when the Torridge Bridge was opened a couple of miles downriver. Combining practicality and a slender beauty, the new cantilever bridge relieved the chronic congestion around the ancient Long Bridge by carrying Bideford's A39 bypass road nearly a hundred feet above the Torridge in three graceful spans.

Two Rivers Estuary, Devon *N 51°04'46.9" W 4°13'57.5" Grid Ref: SS437335 Map Ref: 1 I5*

Anyone who has read Henry Williamson's great nature novels *Tarka The Otter* and *Salar The Salmon* will recognise the setting: the twin rivers of Torridge and Taw mingling in their mighty west-facing estuary. The tides rush and surge around the sandbank of Zulu Bank (on the right), forming feathery fans of agitated water which seethe and roar their way along the tideway.

Croyde Beach and Downend Point, Croyde, Devon *N 51°07'27.6" W 4°14'33.3" Grid Ref: SS432385 Map Ref: 1 I4*

The striations of millions of close-packed geological strata, tilted on end and reduced to stubs by the sea, show to stunning effect around the surfers' paradise beach of Croyde. Though the skirt of worn-down rock acts as a natural defence for the land against the ocean, the Atlantic never ceases its blind work of attrition, grinding rock to sand for the sea wind to heap into dunes.

Woolacombe Sand, Devon *N 51°10'18.8" W 4°12'43.0" Grid Ref: SS455437 Map Ref: 1 I4*

A classic peregrine's-eye view of Woolacombe Sand on a glorious day – two miles of firm, tawny sands, bookended by the long headland of Morte Point. Here the West Country coast finally ceases its northward trend and turns decisively east for its long inland run up the Bristol Channel.

Morte Point, Devon *N 51°11'16.9" W 4°13'50.3" Grid Ref: SS442456 Map Ref: 1 I4*

The blunt otter's snout of Morte Point, topped with a crest of sharp bare rock, shoves out west into the Atlantic, with the Morte Stone off its tip as a final full stop to the far south-west corner of Britain. Here at the turning point of the North Devon coast one bids goodbye to the ancient land of the west, and looks east to spy out the start of the next adventure of exploration along the shores of the mighty Severn Sea.

The Mighty Severn
Ilfracombe to Taf Estuary

Turning the shank of the West Country peninsula at the Morte Stone, you are in sheltered water. It may not feel like it, especially in one of those black winter north-westerlies that come howling in from the open Atlantic; but within a matter of a mile or two the Welsh shore, up to now a rumour below the northern horizon, becomes a matter of fact on the skyline, and the knowledge of being between the slowly closing jaws of the Severn Estuary, walking along the sea margin of one country with the other growing ever nearer, is borne in on you.

Two factors combine to give the Severn Estuary – and the Bristol Channel into which it debouches – its special character: the tremendously high tide range in the narrowing inlet, and the extraordinary mineral wealth hidden in the hills inland. The former is mainly the preserve of the southern or English shore, the latter of the northern or Welsh coast. There are ores of iron in the Brendon Hills, of lead and silver on Mendip, but exploitation of these along the Devon or Somerset coasts and their export through the southern Severn ports never approached a fraction of the industrial activity that took place across the water. A glance at the aerial photographs of the West Country shore shows narrow pebbly beaches, steep cliffs and tiny, difficult harbours on treacherously rocky bays, prone to drying out at low tide. Marsh and mud replace the rock as the estuary turns from east to north-east on its progress inland. The sea level in the channel can rise and fall forty feet in a single tide, and on low spring tides the harbours are left bereft of water.

Across on the Welsh side of the estuary, accidents of geography provided more harbours that retained their water. And for those that did not, the immense wealth generated by the coal seams and the mineral ores of the South Wales Valleys gave 19th-century landowners the power and means to develop such extensive, self-sealing dock systems as those at Newport, Cardiff, Barry and Swansea. The Marquesses of Bute in particular were very big players indeed in Victorian Cardiff; they owned the Bute Town docks through which all the coal and iron wealth of the South Wales Valleys went pouring out to feed the industrial Moloch of the British Empire. When the coal industry collapsed late in the 20th century, recession and depression hit the Cardiff docklands; the Tiger Bay area became one of the most shabbily depressed places in Europe. But around the turn of the second millennium something approaching £2.5 billion in public and private money was poured into the downtown areas once collectively known as Tiger Bay. Hundreds of acres of swish new housing, forests of yacht masts, ponytail cafés and 'leisure villages' sprang up. They stand alongside grand Gothic temples to Victorian commerce such as the Pierhead building and the mini-Versailles of the Coal and Shipping Exchange. Recent architectural giants around Cardiff Bay include St David's Hotel with its towering glass atrium, and the eco-friendly Senedd (Welsh Assembly) building opened in 2006. One can only marvel at the extraordinary hymn to optimism that is Cardiff Bay; an optimism reflected in the parallel revamping of Swansea's run-down docklands.

Lundy, Devon *N 51°10'29.0" W 4°40'12.9" Grid Ref: SS134451 Map Ref: 1 G4*

A dream cloud when glimpsed on the misty sea horizon from the Exmoor heights, Lundy close up becomes a hard, blocky bar of granite, green-topped and defiant among its Atlantic tide-rips. Lying eleven miles from land in the outer mouth of the Bristol Channel, this little cliff-buttressed 'world in the water' carries a tiny village, a scatter of holiday houses, a brace of lighthouses, and the remotest pub in the West Country, the admirable Marisco Tavern where wild goat and grasshopper gateau are highlights of the menu.

Bull Point, Devon *N 51°11'57.2" W 4°12'02.7" Grid Ref: SS463468 Map Ref: 1 I4*

The lighthouse on the ragged headland of Bull Point, lying north and east of the Morte Stone, warns shipping off that deadly little reef and the nearby Rockham Shoal with a beam that carries 24 nautical miles out to sea. Not that the cliffs hereabouts are as solid and adamantine as they look. In 1972 a great chunk cracked and tumbled into the sea, taking much of the lighthouse's fog signal station and engine house with it.

The Mighty Severn
Ilfracombe to Taf Estuary

A tidal inlet of the width and length of the Severn Estuary was always going to see enormous, wealth-creating traffic of goods and people. It was also a potential route for sea-borne invaders. Iron Age lookouts and Roman military sentries kept watch on the channel from hill forts they established along the Exmoor heights, while the headlands, promontories and estuary islets all saw strongholds established down the centuries. Invasion scares prompted two notable flurries of fortification in succeeding centuries. In the 1860s, fears that the French Emperor Napoleon III, great-nephew of Napoleon Bonaparte, was planning to invade Britain prompted a programme of military construction along the estuary. Forts, barracks and gun emplacements were positioned on the headlands of Brean Down on the English coast and on Lavernock Point opposite in Wales, and also on the twin mid-channel islands of Steep Holm and Flat Holm. The guns sited on Flat Holm were rifled muzzle-loaders mounted in special deep pits on splendid contraptions known as 'Moncreiff Disappearing Gun Carriages'. These were supposed to lower the gun out of sight and danger by folding down into the pit after firing, though they were never called into action to prove their efficacy. Eighty years after the hysteria of the French invasion scare, the Second World War brought real and immediate threat of invasion by Hitler's Germany. Once again the headlands and islands were garrisoned and fortified; once more the dreaded incursion never materialised. Explorers among the islands and out on the promontories and cliffs of the Severn Estuary will find rusting guns, crumbling gunpits, tumbled barracks and weed-grown pillboxes still in situ, even today.

It is vigilance of a different kind that is needed nowadays along the estuary shores. Developers are hungry for the shores around resorts such as Penarth and Minehead, along the undervalued marshlands downriver of the Second Severn Bridge. The muddy tidal inlet of Cardiff Bay which provided food and shelter for millions of over-wintering wildfowl has been tidied away in the name of progress and development. What huge changes would occur if the often-mooted 10-mile-long Severn Barrage between Brean Down and Lavernock Point, supposedly capable of generating five percent of the UK's electricity needs, were ever actually built, are a matter of debate. But the creation of a vast brackish lake upriver of the barrage, and the abolition of the tidal sweep from that point inland, would irrevocably alter the character of the tideway that inspired the Welsh national poet Dylan Thomas and the supreme English nature writer Henry Williamson – the giant, restless, untamed organism that is the Severn Estuary.

Capstone Point, Ilfracombe, Devon *N 51°12'43.9" W 4°07'16.0" Grid Ref: SS519480 Map Ref: 1 J4*

The North Devon resort of Ilfracombe is founded on hard slate, fractured and folded some 300 million years ago. Its guardian promontory of Capstone Point pokes defiantly out among the waves. This is a favourite spot for seawatchers to come in hopes of spotting two creatures that are often seen around the Point – harbour porpoise and bottle-nosed dolphins.

Widmouth Head and Watermouth, Devon *N 51°13'02.6" W 4°04'33.5" Grid Ref: SS551485 Map Ref: 1 J4*

The long promontory of Widmouth Head is one of the strongholds of coastal heath, an increasingly rare habitat. Widmouth Head lies separated from the mainland by the curious, square-ended inlet of Watermouth, which was scooped out in dramatic fashion at the end of the last Ice Age, some 10,000 years ago, by the scouring power of a river of meltwater bursting free from its restraining ice.

Little Hangman (above) and Great Hangman (right), Devon

N 51°12'52.3" W 4°01'37.5" Grid Ref: SS585481 Map Ref: 1 J4 (above) *N 51°13'03.7" W 4°00'08.0" Grid Ref: SS603484 Map Ref: 1 K4 (right)*

The propensity of the old sandstones of the North Devon coast to weather into softer, more rounded shapes than the slates and limestones further west is well displayed at Hangman Cliffs. The sloping frontage of Great Hangman, the tallest sea cliff face in England, curves 800 feet down into the water. One mile to the west, its sister cliff of Little Hangman, nearly a hundred feet lower, is reckoned to be the marker for the western boundary of Exmoor's coast.

Lynmouth and Lynton, Devon *N 51°13'53.2" W 3°49'49.8" Grid Ref: SS723496 Map Ref: 1 K3*

Lynton sits perched at the edge of the North Devon cliffs, 500 feet above its sister village of Lynmouth on the shore below. A fan of grey pebbly debris spreads across the beach at the mouth of the West Lyn River, testimony to the scouring power of the water as it tumbles down from the heights of Exmoor through a narrow valley. In August 1952 that power turned deadly as the rain-swollen West Lyn, sweeping huge boulders along, punched like a giant fist through Lynmouth at dead of night. Thirty-four people drowned, and the village was wrecked.

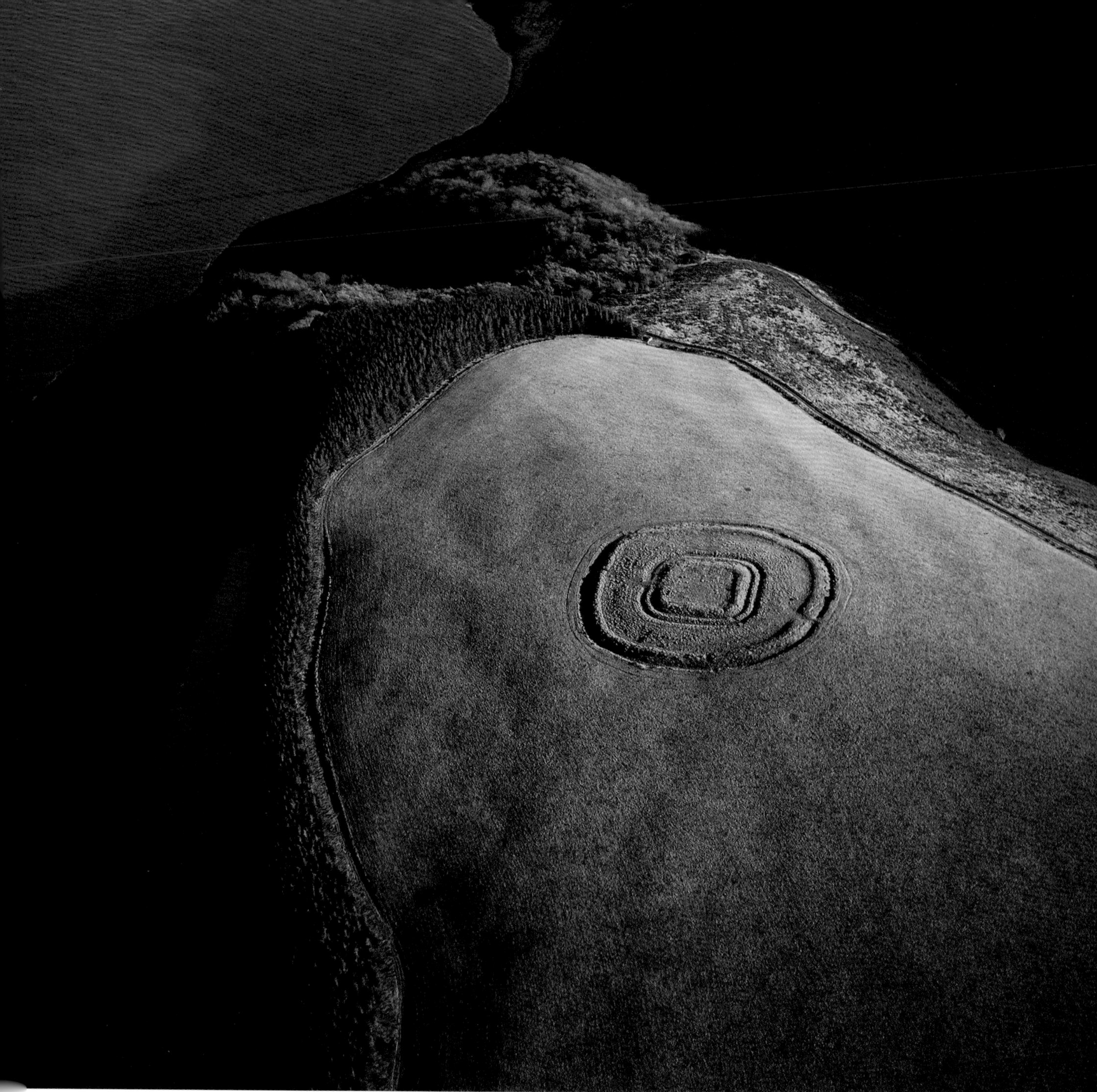

Old Burrow Roman Fortlet, Brendon Hills, Exmoor *N 51°13'49.1" W 3°44'15.0" Grid Ref: SS788493 Map Ref: 1 L3*

This very fine fort, square-built by Roman soldiers under tight discipline around AD 60, probably contained several barrack huts inside a tall palisaded wall defended by a double ring of ramparts, It was one of a pair of small hilltop strongholds built on the Exmoor coast – the other was further west at Martinhoe – shortly after the Romans arrived in Britain, at a time when they still felt the need to keep a sharp eye on comings and goings in the Bristol Channel.

Minehead, Somerset *N 51°12'20.0" W 3°27'57.8" Grid Ref: SS977462 Map Ref: 1 M4*

The layout of Minehead reflects the stages of its development - a tumble of unregulated houses along narrow lanes in the shelter of North Hill around the original fishing and trading harbour, then a rash of more deliberately planned streets behind the village as the holiday resort grew during the Victorian boom era, and finally the enclave of Butlins holiday camp dominating the beach itself behind the shoreline, complete with that unmistakable symbol of the 1990s, the peaked plastic 'tent' roof.

Watchet Harbour, Somerset *N 51°11'00.1" W 3°19'44.1" Grid Ref: ST072435 Map Ref: 2 A4*

Harbours along the southern shore of the Bristol Channel have always suffered from access problems, well illustrated in this view of Watchet as the tide ebbs. At low water the outer harbour, enlarged in the 19th century to export iron ore from the Brendon Hills behind the port, dries out completely; while the 250-berth marina within its walls, opened at the start of the new millennium, is inaccessible from the sea until the tide is well on the turn.

Kilve Beach, Somerset *N 51°11'30.1" W 3°13'56.7" Grid Ref: ST140443 Map Ref: 2 B4*

The coast as tapestry: Kilve Beach on a falling tide. Hundreds of alternate layers of limestone and oil shale, canted at up to 30° some 200 million years ago, form low cliffs packed with ammonites and other fossils. Seen from beach level they look striking; viewed from a seagull's stance, as here, the scars they form along the shore combine sensationally with the patchwork of the fields and the chocolate smoothness of the Severn Estuary.

Brean Down, Somerset *N 51°19'37.8" W 3°01'49.6" Grid Ref: ST283592 Map Ref: 2 C3*

An outlier of the Mendip Hills, the limestone whaleback of Brean Down enters the Severn Estuary just south of Weston-super-Mare. When French invasion was feared during the 1860s a fort was built at the seaward tip to guard the approaches to Cardiff and Bristol. During the Second World War, experimental weapons were tried out here - often with unlooked-for results. The splendidly-named 'Expendable Noise-maker' deviated by 90° from its intended course, landed in a local farmer's chicken-run and blew it up around his ears.

Flat Holm *N 51°22'39.5" W 3°07'14.2" Grid Ref: ST222649 Map Ref: 2 B3*

Five miles out from Barry Docks on the Welsh side of the Severn Estuary rises the low-lying island of Flat Holm, guardian of an old farmhouse, a foghorn station, a former cholera isolation hospital and many military installations. Gun-pits scar the cliffs, amid the nests of thousands of lesser black-backed gulls. From this tiny island, in May 1897, Guglielmo Marconi sent the world's first wireless message to be transmitted across water - the somewhat prosaic phrase 'Are you ready?'

Second Crossing Severn Bridge *N 51°34'21.2" W 2°41'38.3" Grid Ref: ST520862 Map Ref: 2 D1*

The Severn Estuary was first spanned between England and Wales in 1966, upstream of Bristol. But this pioneering Severn Bridge proved inadequate for modern volumes of traffic. So in 1996 a second bridge was opened some four miles downriver – a beautiful and graceful design in which some see the sails of a ship breasting the tides, others the strings of a Welsh harp eternally strummed by the estuary wind.

Caldicot Castle, Monmouthshire *N 51°35'35.2" W 2°44'32.3" Grid Ref: ST487885 Map Ref: 2 D1*

Just upstream of the Second Crossing bridge, Caldicot Castle stands on the Welsh bank of the Severn Estuary – such an excellent lookout position over the river that the Romans built a fort here, and the Normans followed suit a thousand years later. With its drum-shaped keep and walls three yards thick, Caldicot would have been a hard nut to crack, and even more so after the addition of its curtain wall and great 14th-century gatehouse. Yet the domestic rooms within the walls, with their generous fireplaces, private lavatories and – unheard-of luxury – bathing tub, tell of lives carried comfortably on even in the shadow of strife.

Cardiff *N 51°27'14.2" W 3°10'12.0" Grid Ref: ST188734 Map Ref: 2 B2*

The old and the new lie starkly contrasted along the waterfront of the Welsh capital: derelict docks rendered redundant by the collapse of the South Wales coal and mineral industries, derelict communities that went with the docks; and a vast spread of new housing, light entertainment complexes, hotels and retail outlets that replaced them when Cardiff Bay was redeveloped and given a huge facelift in the 1990s. Near the centre of the photograph stands the great redbrick and terracotta temple to Victorian commerce, the Pierhead Building.

Caravan Park, Porthcawl, Bridgend *N 51°28'44.8" W 3°41'09.0" Grid Ref: SS830769 Map Ref: 4 K14*

West of Cardiff and Barry, Glamorgan possesses a beautiful coastline, a virtually unspoiled stretch of estuarine cliffs, rock pavements, coves and beaches protected from development under the title of Glamorgan Heritage Coast. Then comes Porthcawl, and its caravan sprawl ...

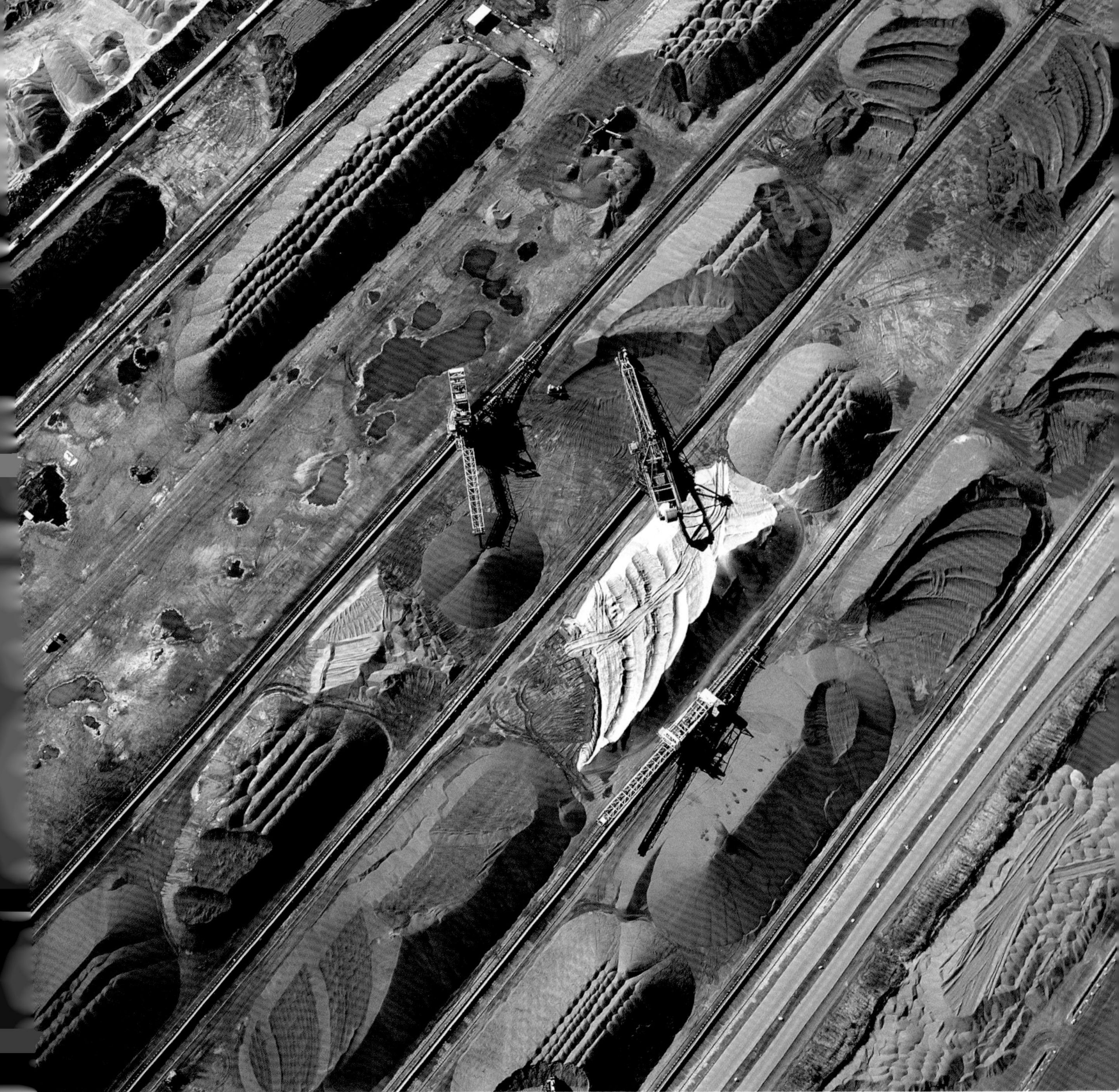

Iron ore, Steelworks, Port Talbot *N 51°34'40.9" W 3°47'22.4" Grid Ref: SS761881 Map Ref: 4 J13*

There has been ironworking of some kind at Port Talbot for over a hundred years. Like a man-made range of hills, the heaps of iron ore at Port Talbot steelworks rise from the parallel 'valleys' of trackway separating them. Their size can be appreciated by comparison with the giant conveyor gantries that disgorge material onto their summits. A clear evening shows the heaps to best advantage, with the setting sun bathing them in fiery orange, rich purple and slate grey.

Swansea *N 51°36'37.4" W 3°55'34.8" Grid Ref: SS667919 Map Ref: 4 J13*

A hundred years ago Swansea was 'Copperopolis', one of the most industrial towns in the world, with the ores of copper, zinc, tin, iron, steel and lead being processed nearby and their products exported through the docks. As with Cardiff, when heavy industry collapsed towards the end of the 20th century, so did the life of the dockside. Since then the newly designated Maritime Quarter has been refurbished, smartened and revitalized with a clutch of excellent industrial and maritime museums.

Mumbles Head, Gower Peninsula *N 51°34'00.6" W 3°58'15.3" Grid Ref: SS635872 Map Ref: 4 I13*

How the Mumbles – twin limestone islets guarding the southern headland of Mumbles Bay – got their curious title is a matter of much speculation. The best guess is that their rounded shapes caught the eye of Norman strangers, who named them 'Les Mamelles', The Breasts. The lighthouse on Mumbles Head was built in 1794. When the great French invasion scare started in 1860, the tower was fortified with the massive drum-shaped stronghold that still surrounds its southern flank.

Oxwich Bay, Gower Peninsula *N 51°34'12.3" W 4°06'44.1" Grid Ref: SS537878 Map Ref: 4 I13*

The first of the Gower Peninsula's large sandy bays as you go west from Swansea, Oxwich Bay is a beauty. The bay has something for everyone, and plenty of it: lazily snaking waters and long pools, a mile-long beach of firm, pristine sand, sheltered and safe bathing, and the giant flower-spattered sand dunes of Oxwich Burrows lying behind the beach, preserved as a National Nature Reserve for the delight of walkers, amateur botanists and bird watchers.

Paviland Cliffs, Gower Peninsula *N 51°32'56.9" W 4°15'14.8" Grid Ref: SS439858 Map Ref: 4 H13*

The limestone strata of Gower's cliffs lie slanted at 45° as the coast nears the south-west tip of the peninsula just seaward of Paviland Manor. The sea has eaten large caves in these faulted ramparts, and it was in one of these in 1823 that the Rev. William Buckley excavated a headless skeleton, covered in red ochre, which he imagined to be that of a prostitute who had served the nearby Roman garrison. Later scientific study established the corpse of the 'Red Lady of Paviland' as that of a sturdy, well-proportioned man, ceremonially prepared for burial, who died some 26,000 years ago.

Worm's Head, Gower Peninsula *N 51°33'53.4" W 4°19'53.2" Grid Ref: SS385877 Map Ref: 4 H13*

From the sea at high tide the disjointed segments of the Worm's Head promontory resemble the humpy spine and head of a sea serpent with blunt rocky nose and pale stratified grin, swimming from the mainland towards you. Low water reveals bladed rock causeways between the various sections of this remarkable landmark, named 'Wurm' or 'dragon' by Norse adventurers for whom sea monsters were a fact of the sailor's life.

Rhossili Bay, Gower Peninsula *N 51°34'47.7" W 4°17'25.2" Grid Ref: SS415893 Map Ref: 4 H13*

A peerless curve of beautiful sand three miles long, Rhossili Beach lies beyond Worm's Head in the shadow of Rhossili Down. A footpath crosses the 630-ft summit of the down, a truly tremendous viewpoint over some 50 miles of sea, coast and countryside. The Norsemen who named Worm's Head must have thought it a view worthy of the noble dead, for here in the face of wind and sea they built the quartzite ring tombs of Sweyn's Howes.

Mudflats on Loughor Estuary *N 51°37'37.6" W 4°13'30.2" Grid Ref: SS461944 Map Ref: 4 I12*

The great mudflat inlet of Loughor or Burry Inlet on the north shore of Gower was enthusiastically planted with cordgrass or spartina in the 1930s, in hopes of reclaiming it for grazing. Now vast extents of salt marsh cover much of the estuary, grazed by hardy sheep and crazed into a million wriggles of muddy creeklet.

Taf Estuary, Carmarthenshire *N 51°45'14.8" W 4°24'59.3" Grid Ref: SN334089 Map Ref: 4 G12*

Three rivers meet in confluence in the mouth of the Taf Estuary – Taf itself, Tywi and Gwendraeth. The scouring power and energy of these sandbank-moulding waters is mesmerising. So thought the Swansea boy Dylan Thomas when he set up home in the Boathouse at Laugharne above the estuary. Wales's national poet, who died in 1953 of a 'massive insult to the brain' exacerbated by drink, had the great tideway in view from the garage shed where he wrote *Under Milk Wood*.

Wild Wales
Tenby to Anglesey

The west coast of Wales is dominated by the great seventy-mile arc of Cardigan Bay, hollowed out by the sea between the hard volcanic rocks of its outstretched headlands, St David's Head to the south and the Llŷn Peninsula to the north. Behind the coastline the hinterland of West Wales rises into the formidable Cambrian Mountain chain, a barrier to land communication with the rest of Britain so effective in times past that the west retained its Welsh language, culture and mindset to a remarkable degree. The travelling impulse seems to have been outwards across the sea; ferry services to Ireland from Fishguard and Holyhead, adventurers like bold Prince Madog launching themselves from tiny bays such as Borth-y-Gest to seek new worlds beyond the ocean.

Seafaring has always brought its dangers. The west shore of Wales bristles with sharp headlands, toothed reefs, lonely islets, rocks and rip tides. Shipwreck haunts this coast. For many centuries warning lights have been maintained to alert vessels to danger, with the heyday of lighthouse building in the 19th century. Finding crews for the towers never proved a problem; the romance of the job, and its appeal to practical, tough-natured men, saw to that, even though some of these West Wales stations – the South Bishop rock out beyond Ramsey Island, for example – were among the loneliest off the coasts of Britain. Isolation was a way of life, too, for dwellers on the many small islands of West Wales. From early Christian hermits and their monkish successors, through pirates and soldiers, warreners and farmers, to idealists and dreamers such as Ronald Lockley of Skokholm Island, the islands have seduced, challenged and tested their human inhabitants. Outlines of hermit cells, monastic ruins, shells of barracks and forts, tumbledown field walls and abandoned farmhouses all speak of the vigorous history of these tiny slips of land in the sea, now mostly inhabited by conservation wardens, hordes of rabbits and millions of seabirds.

West Wales is a land apart, walled in by its mountains. But however tough the land barrier, water will find its way through. Ice Age meltwaters carved out deep valleys such as that between Dinas Island and the mainland; mountain-born rivers snake down to Cardigan Bay in the splendid estuaries of the Teifi at Cardigan, Dyfi at Aberdyfi and Mawddach at Barmouth. Smaller streams have cut a path to the sea between narrow headlands where the Atlantic attacks the granitic cliffs and tiny fishing and quarrying villages have established themselves. Anywhere with a stretch of sand was

Tenby, Pembrokeshire *N 51°40'16.6" W 4°41'35.3" Grid Ref: SN139004 Map Ref: 4 F12*

The sight of Tenby's seafront hotels and houses perched at the edge of their rocky cliff is a spectacular one. A glance shows exactly why this small Pembrokeshire resort has proved so enduringly popular. It boasts four fine beaches – the long strands of South and North Beach (left and right respectively in this view), Harbour beach (hidden behind the grass-topped promontory of Castle Hill), and Castle Beach in the centre. From here at low tide you can walk out to St Catherine's Island (in the foreground) on whose rocky back squats a square-built fort, constructed in 1870 against a French invasion that never came.

St Margaret's Island, Pembrokeshire *N 51°38'33.9" W 4°43'02.3" Grid Ref: SS121973 Map Ref: 4 F12*

An outlier of Caldey Island a couple of miles off Tenby, tiny St Margaret's Island is itself split into two. A square field, walled in stone, is the main feature of the larger portion; the smaller holds the ruin of a quarrymen's barracks, converted from a former chapel. The island's limestone was quarried until the mid-19th century; then St Margaret's was left to the black-backed gulls, the puffins and shags and guillemots that thrive in this lonely outpost today.

Wild Wales
Tenby to Anglesey

fair game for the tourist industry once the railways had sneaked round the mountains in mid-Victorian times, and West Wales boasts some fine resorts - Newport, New Quay, Aberystwyth, Aberdyfi, Barmouth, Criccieth.

History lies stamped on the headlands and rock outcrops in the form of castles built by the Welsh against the English, or vice versa. Strife between the two nations ricocheted for the best part of 400 years until it petered out after Owain Glyndŵr's brilliant but abortive rebellion at the turn of the 15th century. Mighty coastal strongholds bear witness to this long international struggle, especially those castles built by the English at Harlech, Caernarfon and Beaumaris towards the end of the 13th century as part of King Edward I's 'Iron Ring' of fortresses intended to hem in and overawe the rebels of West Wales. By ordering the native rulers of Wales to pay homage, and hunting and executing those who would not, Edward aimed to bring the whole Welsh nation to heel under an English Prince of Wales installed by the English crown. The year of 1282 saw the execution of the last true prince of the Welsh, Llywelyn the Last; and a short while later King Edward announced that he had chosen as nominee for Prince of Wales a prince who had been born in Wales and could speak not one word of English. The Welsh, believing this candidate to be one of their native royalty, agreed to accept him without opposition. They were not best pleased when the new Prince of Wales turned out to be King Edward I's own son and heir – a baby, newly born in Caernarfon Castle.

The scars of former industries – slate and granite quarrying in particular – are still seen on many a headland and cliff-top. Modern industry rumbles on in South Pembrokeshire, where oil and gas tankers discharge their loads into the refineries and storage silos around Milford Haven. Along the coast of West Wales you can still find quaysides stacked with crab pots and fishing nets. But it is mostly the leisure industry that holds sway here today: beach and sea sports, sea bathing and walking the coast paths, along with the timeless pleasures of contemplation, of delight in the subtleties of nature as artist among the forms and colours of the great estuary waters and sandbanks, or of idling on a headland or out on an island shore, gazing seaward in hopes of seeing a porpoise break the waves in an arc of gleaming purple.

Milford Haven, Pembrokeshire *N 51°41'05.4" W 5°01'37.6" Grid Ref: SM908028 Map Ref: 4 D12*

Not exactly a thing of beauty – but Milford Haven imports, refines, stores and sends on its way about 20% of the UK's fossil fuel oil, not to mention the LNG or Liquefied Natural Gas that the biggest port in Wales will soon be handling, to the tune of one-third of Britain's needs.

Jetties and Oil Tankers at Popton Point, Milford Haven, Pembrokeshire *N 51°41'49.1" W 5°02'54.3" Grid Ref: SM894042 Map Ref: 4 D12*

It is the deep water in the more seaward section of the 22-mile-long inlet of Milford Haven that enables huge supertankers to moor up next to their jetties. But there are dangers, not only from explosions but also the potential ecological disasters resulting from oil spills. In the worst to date, 73,000 tonnes of crude oil leaked from the *Sea Empress* after she ran aground in 15 February 1996, polluting well over 100 miles of South Wales's coastline and killing thousands of seabirds.

Stack Rock Fort, Milford Haven

N 51°42'08.8" W 5°05'31.6"
Grid Ref: SM864049 Map Ref: 4 D12

Stack Rock lies in Milford Haven, right in the middle of the fairway, a formidable obstacle to be given a wide berth – especially, the British Admiralty hoped, by any French invasion ship rash or lucky enough to have escaped destruction by the guns of the batteries on headlands further seaward. In case any enemy should get this far up the anchorage, Stack Rock Fort was built on the islet in the 1860s and filled with guns – a cramped, lonely, claustrophobic prison for the unfortunate men of its garrison.

Fort Hubberstone (left)

N 51°42'29.4" W 5°03'20.4"
Grid Ref: SM890055 Map Ref: 4 D12

The Victorian defensive stronghold of Fort Hubberstone lies half sunk in the heather of the headland above Gelliswick Bay as if emerging from a cushion of purple velvet. Well fortified with cannon, the fort was built in 1863 to guard the naval dockyard at Milford Haven. The semi-circular barracks at the upper end held 250 men, waiting endlessly for a French invasion that was never to materialise. Among young soldiers, Fort Hubberstone in its bleak isolation was not the most popular of postings.

Fort Popton, Milford Haven

N 51°41'34.5" W 5°02'52.8"
Grid Ref: SM894038 Map Ref: 4 D12

Fort Popton lies opposite Fort Hubberstone, and was built at the same time to present a formidable Scylla and Charybdis to any potential attacker through the narrows of Milford Haven. A garrison of 240 men under the command of ten officers was maintained in Fort Popton's barracks for some years after the 19th-century French invasion scare was at its height, and the old fort on its isolated but strategically well-sited promontory was re-fortified during the Second World War.

Skomer, Pembrokeshire *N 51°44'07.0" W 5°17'36.4" Grid Ref: SM727092 Map Ref: 4 C11*

Lying in Broad Sound off the south-west tip of Pembrokeshire, the island of Skomer measures less than 2 miles long. Though derelict farm buildings remain and the outlines of field walls can be made out, residential farming ceased there in 1950, and the island has become the world's most important outpost for breeding manx shearwaters. More than 100,000 of the burrow-dwelling seabirds nest and breed on Skomer each summer, sharing the hollowed-out turf with up to 25,000 rabbits.

Ramsey, Pembrokeshire *N 51°51'41.9" W 5°20'16.7" Grid Ref: SM703234 Map Ref: 4 C10*

The crab's claw hook of St David's Head is usually taken to be the most westerly point of Wales, but ragged-edged Ramsey lies even further west. This bird reserve island, now administered by the RSPB, was farmed for centuries against the odds – storms scoured the crops and could cut off the farmer and his family for weeks at a time, while the notorious tides of Ramsey Sound, seething through the Bitches reef immediately opposite the farmhouse and landing slip, were a constant hazard for the small boats of the islanders.

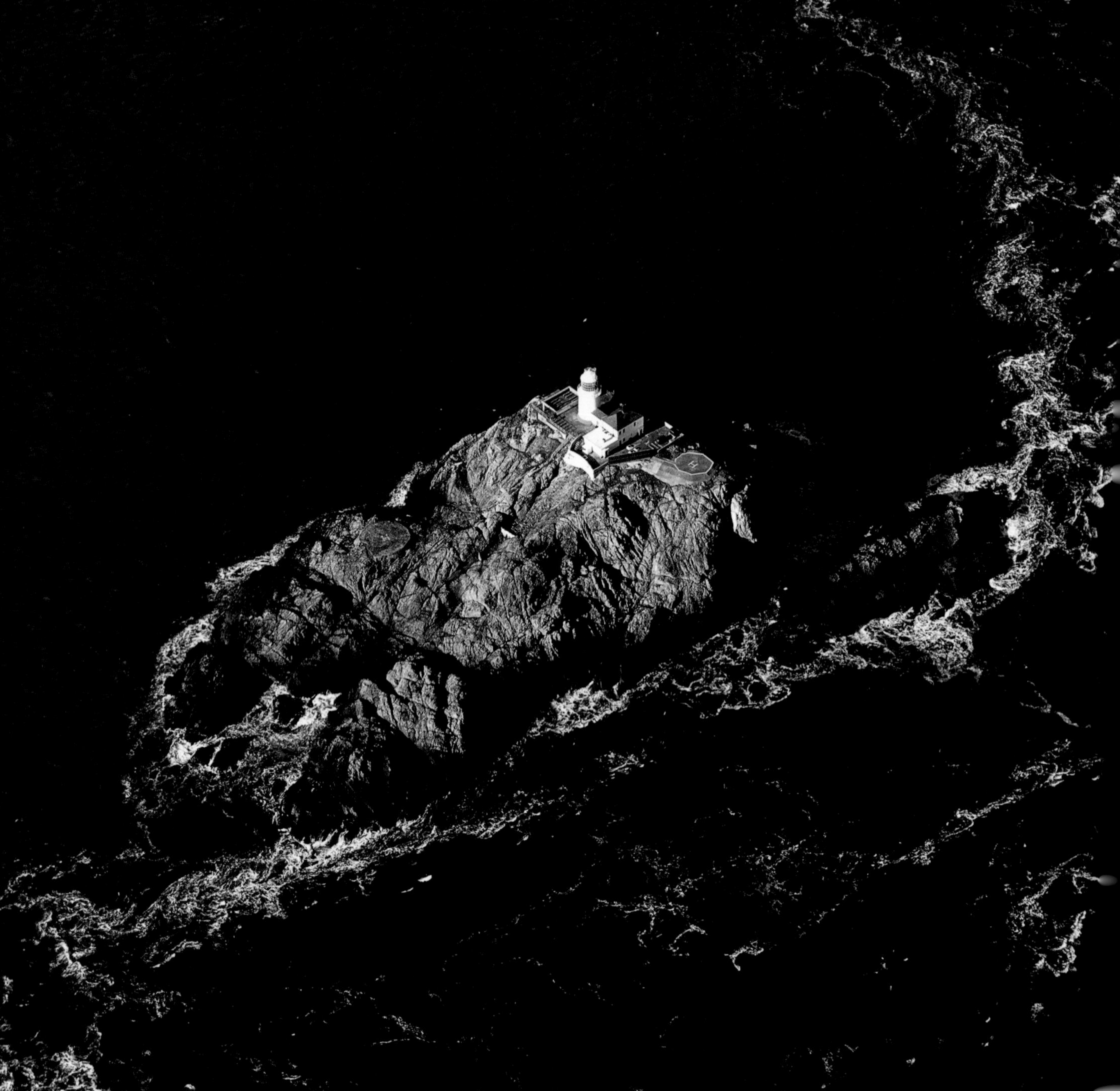

South Bishop Lighthouse, Pembrokeshire *N 51°51'05.6" W 5°24'42.3" Grid Ref: SM651225 Map Ref: 4 C11*

Norsemen named this naked hump of rock 'Emsger', Em's Skerry, but the most southerly of the loose scattering of Bishop Rocks in the sea west of Ramsey is better known today as South Bishop. After centuries of shipwrecks around the archipelago the stumpy South Bishop lighthouse was built on the rock in 1839, one of the loneliest posts that Trinity House ever established off the shores of Britain. The light was automated in 1983.

Carreg Rhoson and Maen Rhoson, Bishops and Clerks, Pembrokeshire *N 51°52'45.5" W 5°23'19.4" Grid Ref: SM669255 Map Ref: 4 C10*

West again from Ramsey a bench of Bishops, assisted by a well-drilled school of Clerks, presides over a wide marine diocese. These little Bishops and Clerks, a line of islets forming a helpful aid to navigation when sighted in fair weather, have been the cause of countless shipwrecks down the years at night or in fogs or blinding storms.

Porthgain, Pembrokeshire

N 51°56'54.5" W 5°10'54.9"
Grid Ref: SM814326 Map Ref: 4 D10

The coastal village of Porthgain, a few miles north-east of St David's Head, lies in a narrow cleft below a headland extensively quarried around the turn of the 20th century for the hard granite rock that makes excellent roadstone. The solid jaws of Porthgain harbour's breakwaters, warding off the winter storm waves that drive into this north-facing inlet, protected not only the fishing fleet, but also the stone transporting vessels. The brick-built 'bins' or silos where the quarried and chipped granite was stored can still be seen around Porthgain's quay.

Abercastle, Pembrokeshire

N 51°57'36.1" W 5°07'38.6"
Grid Ref: SM852337 Map Ref: 4 D10

The tiny Pembrokeshire harbour of Abercastle had its moment of fame on 12 August 1876, when an exhausted man fetched up in the harbour in a 20-ft-long fishing dory. He had to be carried from his boat to the pub because his limbs were no longer working, and no wonder – this 30-year-old Swedish-born adventurer, Alfred Johnson, had just made the first single-handed, 3,000-mile crossing of the Atlantic Ocean. He had set off solo from Nova Scotia on 25 June in order to celebrate the centenary of the American Declaration of Independence, and to fulfil a boast he'd made to friends. 'I made that trip,' confessed "Centennial" Johnson later, 'because I was a damned fool, just like they said.'

Strumble Head and Lighthouse, Pembrokeshire (right)

N 52°01'46.8" W 5°04'25.9"
Grid Ref: SM892413 Map Ref: 4 D9

The rugged promontory of Strumble Head, a danger to shipping down the ages, stands into the sea a little west of the port of Fishguard. Its lighthouse occupies the hump-backed rock of Ynys Meicel, St Michael's Isle. The chasm between islet and mainland is narrow enough to be spanned by a short footbridge, from which you look down on a ferocious tide-race sluicing through the narrows. The hardships and hazards of building the lighthouse (completed in 1908) are all too easy to picture - every component had to be winched or slung across this dizzying gap.

Bryn Henllan and Dinas Island, Pembrokeshire (left)

N 52°01'13.1" W 4°54'37.9"
Grid Ref: SN004398 Map Ref: 4 E9

This spectacular view looks east towards Newport along the deep-carved cleft of Cwm Dewi, St David's Valley. You can clearly see how meltwaters, rushing west from glacier-blocked Newport Bay at the end of the last Ice Age some 10,000 years ago, trenched out the curving valley between the mainland and Dinas Island (really a promontory) whose landward flank rises to the left. Rising sea levels in the near future might well complete the severance.

Aberystwyth, Ceredigion

N 52°24'32.4" W 4°05'16.9"
Grid Ref: SN581811 Map Ref: 4 I7

Lying at the very heart of the vast sweep of Cardigan Bay, cut off until modern times by the Cambrian Mountains at its back, Aberystwyth developed as an early medieval garrison town around its mighty stone castle. The English-built stronghold still dominates the seafront; the town, thanks to the insularity imposed by its former isolation, has become the capital of Welsh-speaking western Wales, a seat of national learning and culture.

Barmouth, Gwynedd

N 52°42'54.2" W 4°03'09.5"
Grid Ref: SH614150 Map Ref: 4 I4

Great swathes of sand, spread at the wide mouth of the River Mawddach where it tumbles into Cardigan Bay, guaranteed the success of Barmouth as a seaside resort. At the back of the town rise steep slopes with beautiful, poetic names - Carreg Gribin, the Rocky Crest; Craig y Gigfran, Raven's Rock; Fron Felen, Golden Breast; Dinas Oleu, the Fortress of Light.

Harlech Castle, Gwynedd *N 52°51'36.0" W 4°06'33.3" Grid Ref: SH581313 Map Ref: 4 I3*

One of King Edward I's 'Iron Ring' of intimidating strongholds, Harlech Castle was built on a 200-ft cliff. The sea came further inland in those days, so the fortress could be supplied directly by ship. Harlech saw a tremendous amount of action. A garrison of 37 men defied a long siege by Madog ap Llywelyn in 1294-5. Owain Glyndŵr captured the castle in 1404 by starving its defenders, and made Harlech his base until the King's men recaptured it four years later. During the Wars of the Roses Harlech Castle was a Lancastrian stronghold, and withstood an 8-year siege until Lord Herbert of Raglan finally took it for the House of York in 1468 – a heroic resistance which inspired the defiant battle song of the Welsh, 'Men of Harlech':

'See! They now are flying! Dead are heaped with dying!
Over might hath triumphed right, our land to foes denying;
Upon their soil we never sought them; love of conquest hither brought them –
But this lesson we have taught them: "Cambria ne'er can yield!"'

River Dwyryd, Gwynedd *N 52°54'50.0" W 4°04'55.7" Grid Ref: SH601372 Map Ref: 4 I3*

Nature as sculptress and subtle colourist – the opalescent waters of the River Dwyryd gleam like shot silk as they flow past Portmeirion, before mingling with those of sister River Glaslyn, to skirt the sands of Traeth Bach, the 'little beach', and drain into Tremadog Bay between Snowdonia and the Llŷn Peninsula. These waters are not quite as pristine as they appear - full of minerals and metals from the hills, some of them have passed through the Trawsfynydd reservoir to cool the nuclear power station there.

Criccieth Castle, Gwynedd *N 52°54'56.4" W 4°13'57.5" Grid Ref: SH500377 Map Ref: 4 I3*

Dominating a promontory that juts south into Tremadog Bay, Criccieth Castle with its towering, forbidding gateway predates most other English castles in this part of Wales. Many think it was actually a Welsh construction, a stronghold patterned on English examples but erected against the oppressor. Experts seem unsure, but most likely it was Llywelyn the Great, Prince of Gwynedd and ruler of Wales, who started the castle early in the 13th century. Certainly it was in the hands of the English by 1280, and there is no doubt who destroyed it – Owain Glyndŵr, the last native-born Prince of Wales, who had it pulled to pieces during his great rebellion more than a century later.

Pwllheli Harbour, Gwynedd *N 52°53'02.1" W 4°23'57.4" Grid Ref: SH387345 Map Ref: 4 H3*

Isolated on a remote peninsula only five miles wide, Pwllheli's good fortune lies in its geography. Its saltwater basin provided the little town on the south coast of the Lŷn Peninsula with livelihoods based around shipbuilding, fishing and the coasting trade; and when these began to fade in the face of competition from elsewhere, Pwllheli's sandy beaches proved just what seaside holidaymakers were looking for.

Caernarfon Castle, Gwynedd *N 53°08'20.3" W 4°16'39.0" Grid Ref: SH478626 Map Ref: 4 H1*

The old town of Caernarfon, belted tight inside a girdle of stone walls, huddles up next to the mighty stronghold of Caernarfon Castle. The strongest link in the chain of castles known as the Iron Ring, Caernarfon Castle was built from 1283 onwards, on the orders of King Edward I, to command the narrow Menai Strait between mainland Wales and the Isle of Anglesey. The fortress was created, as Daniel Defoe crisply summed it up, 'to curb and reduce the wild people of the mountains.'

Menai Strait and Bridges *N 53°13'12.4" W 4°09'46.5" Grid Ref: SH557714 Map Ref: 6 F15*

This breathtaking view runs south-west down the Menai Strait, with the coast of the Isle of Anglesey on the right looking across the narrow waterway to the mainland shore. Narrow the Strait may be, but its currents and sucking sands are deadly. Thomas Telford's suspension bridge of 1826 (in the foreground) was built to carry road travellers on their way to the port of Holyhead and the Irish ferries; Robert Stephenson's innovative tubular Britannia Bridge of 1850 did the same for railway passengers.

Dulas Bay, Anglesey

N 53°22'29.5" W 4°16'32.3"
Grid Ref: SH487889 Map Ref: 6 E14

On the north-east coast of Anglesey, another stunning instance of nature as abstract artist. Afon Goch, the Red River, winds seaward, its flow moulded by the obstruction of a headland to create the wide Traeth Dulas behind the river mouth. Out on the shore Craig y Sais, the Saxon's Rock, divides Traeth Bach, the Little Beach lying in front of the headland, from the cliff-encircled Traeth Ora. Some say Traeth Ora signifies Beach of the Fortified Landing Place; others that 'Ora' is a foreign word, harking back to some Italian seafarers who fetched up here around 1750 after a shipwreck.

Puffin Island, Anglesey

N 53°19'13.4" W 4°01'21.0"
Grid Ref: SH654823 Map Ref: 6 F14

Puffin Island lies off the easternmost tip of Anglesey. The turbulent sound between the island and Penmon Point, guarded by a lighthouse since 1838, formed a very notorious hazard to shipping in the days of sail. The puffins of Puffin Island suffered for almost a century after a bizarre episode in 1907 when brown rats deserted a sinking Dutch ship, invaded the island and proceeded to devastate the eggs and chicks of the ground-nesting seabirds. In 1998 a very thorough cull of the rats restored the previous status quo, and puffin numbers are slowly recovering.

Beaumaris Castle, Anglesey (right)

N 53°15'53.6" W 4°05'22.7"
Grid Ref: SH607762 Map Ref: 6 F14

The 'castle of the beautiful marsh', built from 1295 onwards but never completed, was the last in King Edward I's 'Iron Ring' of eight castles that hemmed the wild Welsh into their mountains. It was also the most technically advanced, a theoretically impregnable stronghold with four miles of defences, sixteen massive bastions in the high outer walls, inner walls even higher with even stouter towers, and any number of traps and obstacles in wait for attackers. Today, lit up by sunshine in silent ruin, Beaumaris seems a fairy-tale castle.

Sand, Marsh and Mudflat
North Wales to Solway Firth

From the Dee Estuary, where North Wales meets Merseyside, it is over 150 miles as the peregrine flies to the Scottish border along the Solway Firth, and in all that distance there is scarcely a sea cliff worth the name. Only along the West Cumbrian coast do the cliffs rise more than house high, and then it's for no more than a dozen miles or so. This is a coast dominated by Irish sea and English sand. The sea advances on the flood tide across sands up to ten miles wide from low to high water mark. Margins of mudflats and salt marshes spread along the river mouths where they broaden into the sea - Dee and Mersey, Wyre and Ribble, Lune and Duddon, along with the intermingling of lesser rivers that form the great estuaries of Morecambe Bay, Esk and Solway Firth.

This giant sweep of tidal sands is the longest and broadest in the British Isles. It has made access a matter of difficulty, for seafarers to the land, for landlubbers to the seas. Deepwater ports and coastal anchorages for big vessels are rare here. Yet raw materials - cotton, spices, New World fruit – had to be landed. Inland industry, too, from crude ores of iron mined in the Cumbrian hills to the Lancashire mill town textiles that clothed the 19th-century world, demanded a means of onward transport for its goods long before the arrival of reliable roads and railways. The sea was the only viable highway back then. There were coal mines and chemical works on the West Cumbrian cliffs, ironworks at Barrow-in-Furness and Millom, and later steelworks at Shotton on the Dee estuary and a great oil refinery on the River Mersey at Stanlow. Human ingenuity was thoroughly called into play, building canals and locks and basins, dredging silt from choked waterways, digging and re-digging channels through the muds and sands. Fishermen went out deep-sea in trawlers from Fleetwood, or down the centuries developed specialised methods of fishing shallow tideways: cockling, fluking, whammelling, cart-shanking, haaf-netting.

What caused so many trade and communications problems was meat and drink to the tourist trade, of course. Sand was exactly what every holidaymaker wanted. Once the railways had crawled across the coastal plains to Llandudno and Rhyl, Southport, Blackpool and Morecambe, the former resorts of well-heeled gentry became available to anyone who could stump up the price of a cheap ticket. Piers sprouted seaward, ornate towers climbed skyward, funfairs settled

Sand, Marsh and Mudflat
North Wales to Solway Firth

along the shores and B&B landladies laid down immutable rules of behaviour for their guests. There was a hundred-year honeymoon with the faithful captive populace of the great Northern factory towns; then came the 1970s and cheap flights to guaranteed Mediterranean sun and vino, making the Great Sands resorts feel - and look - tired and jaded. They are still casting round for what to do next.

The seemingly unexceptional ranges of sand dunes that run for so many miles behind this coast are a haven for threatened wildlife. Red squirrels thrive at Formby Point, in pinewoods not yet invaded by their American native grey cousins who have driven them back to the margins almost everywhere else in England. Natterjack toads breed among the sandhills of the Sefton Coast of Lancashire, as they do a hundred miles north in Cumbria on the dunes of Eskmeals and Drigg. Green-flanked sand lizards, another rare and endangered species, lie out on the warm dry dunes and patches of coastal heath. The dunes, rich in orchids and other lime-loving plants, are part of a complex eco-system of intertidal foreshore, saltings and grassy grazing marshes that together make up a Ramsar wetland of international importance, and a Special Protection Area for birds. Avocets raise chicks in the RSPB's Marshside Reserve in the Ribble Estuary; lapwings flicker in black-and-white clouds over the dunes; pinkfooted and greylag geese overwinter on the coast.

Islands lie among the sands, blobs of rock reachable on foot with an eye on the tides: Hilbre with its bird observatory and historic telegraph station, Roa with a handful of much-sought-after houses, Piel Island where you can drink with a King and receive a knighthood at his hands. This is a landscape for romantics. The purity of the headwaters of the River Duddon inspired William Wordsworth to more than 30 sonnets in the early 19th century. As the following century drew to a close the Duddon's estuary, now gritty and polluted by ironworks slag, could still draw poetic magic from Lakeland's other supreme poet, Norman Nicholson. But you don't need to be a poet, only to have a spark of poetry inside you, to find magic in the purple and ochre of a Lune mouth sandbank stained by an incoming tide, or the sinuations of sea-going water towards nightfall at the moment where gold turns to silver in the tide stream of the Solway Firth.

Conwy Castle *N 53°16'48.8" W 3°49'26.2" Grid Ref: SH785775 Map Ref: 6 G*

Conwy Castle was one of the Iron Ring of forts established by King Edward I at the end of the 13th century to cow and impress the populace of Nort Wales. Eight massive drum towers defended the outer walls. Not that Conwy was impregnable: in 1401 a couple of Owain Glyndŵr's cousins tricke their way cheekily into the castle and captured it during the Great Rebellion. Conwy Castle lies squeezed up against three neighbouring bridges that spa the narrows of the River Conwy: Robert Stephenson's castellated railway bridge of 1846, the road bridge of 1958, and pinched between them Thom Telford's 327-ft suspension bridge of 1822-6, originally a roadway but now open only to pedestrians, still suspended from its original chain links.

Great Orme's Head, Conwy *N 53°20'05.0" W 3°51'39.0" Grid Ref: SH762836 Map Ref: 6 G14*

The massive, bulbous extrusion of Great Orme's Head pokes out north-west into the sea to form the western flank of Llandudno Bay. A lumpy mass of limestone, the headland was named 'ormr' (dragon) by Norse sailors who saw in it – as they did in the Worm's Head promontory on the Gower Peninsula (page 64) – the shape of a sea serpent with slender neck and outstretched head.

Great Orme Copper Mine, Conwy (left)

N 53°19'49.2" W 3°51'14.7"
Grid Ref: SH766831 Map Ref: 6 G14

A gannet's-eye view of the lumps and bumps left by copper mining on Great Orme's Head, an industry stretching back to the time before the secret of smelting iron was imported into Britain. In that era copper was King, its ores essential for blending with tin to produce bronze, the most effective metal then available. A labyrinth of tunnels, dug by miners with tools of bone and flint between 3,000 and 4,000 years ago, ramifies for 5 miles through the limestone of the Great Orme's Head promontory - the largest such ancient mine system in the world. On the tunnel walls are graffiti left by miners through the millennia; up top, visitors have taken to making their own marks for the edification of passing seagulls and light plane pilots.

Llandudno, Conwy

N 53°19'31.0" W 3°49'40.2"
Grid Ref: SH784825 Map Ref: 6 G14

Looking west across the narrow neck of the Great Orme's Head peninsula and on along the mountainous coast of north-west Wales to the distant shore of the Isle of Anglesey. Across the isthmus lies Llandudno, a Victorian seaside resort planned and purpose-built along gridded streets. Llandudno blossomed after its railway station was opened in 1858. Twenty years later the splendid 1,234-ft pier was opened, setting the seal on the town's position as the premier resort in North Wales.

Rhyl, Denbighshire

N 53°19'27.9" W 3°29'24.2"
Grid Ref: SJ009819 Map Ref: 6 I14

In contrast to the elegance and picturesqueness of Llandudno on its curving bay between the Great and Little Orme's Head promontories, the neighbouring resorts of Rhyl and Prestatyn stand on a flat, windy littoral. Not that their exposed position inhibited their 19th-century development as seaside resorts, for they look seaward over the most extensive beach in North Wales, a stretch of sand nearly ten miles long. Hard times hit Rhyl towards the end of the 20th century; British holidaymakers preferred cheap flights to the sun, and much of the resort became derelict. Now regeneration is slowly getting under way.

Groyne, Prestatyn, Denbighshire *N 53°20'40.6" W 3°24'37.9" Grid Ref: SJ062840 Map Ref: 6 I14*

The superb beach that fronts Rhyl and Prestatyn was the catalyst for the twin towns' development as seaside resorts, but it comes with its own liabilities. The problem with all those straight miles of sand, a windy environment and a vigorous offshore current is the tendency of the beach to shift and to allow sea incursions. Hence the installation of a variety of beach defences over the years, such as this hammerhead Groyne at Prestatyn – a practical instrument at ground level, a sculptural art installation from the air.

Flint Castle, Flintshire *N 53°15'07.5" W 3°07'48.6" Grid Ref: SJ247734 Map Ref: 6 K15*

Flint Castle, built in 1277 to dominate the Dee Estuary, was the first of King Edward I's Iron Ring of castles built with the purpose of subduing the upstart Welsh. Beside the moat bridge stands the enormous cylindrical donjon, a structure unique among British castles, detached from the main body of the fortress and intended as a place of last retreat for hard-pressed defenders. In August 1399 Flint Castle was the scene of the surrender of King Richard II to his usurper Henry Bolingbroke. Even Richard's greyhound, legend says, deserted the king and sidled off to lick the hand of Bolingbroke.

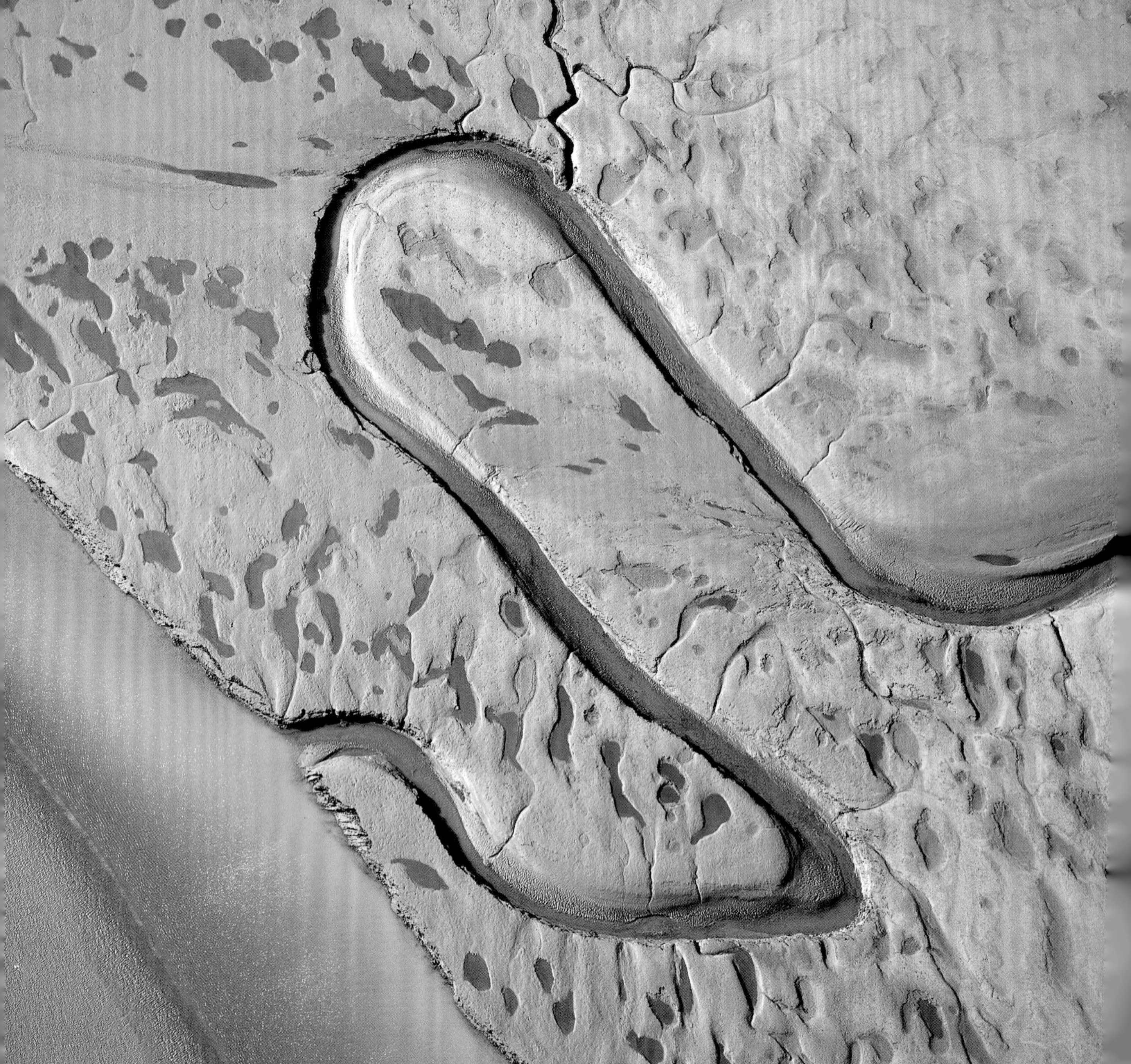

Mudflats, Dee Estuary, Cheshire & Flintshire *N 53°18'56.5" W 3°08'14.4" Grid Ref: SJ243807 Map Ref: 6 K14*

Where the River Dee broadens to the sea, innumerable rivers and streams add their tribute of silt in slabs of glutinous mud through which creeks and gutters make their snaky way to the estuary. The soft yet resistant texture, the smoothly and subtly curved structure of a mud flat absorbs the inward push of the sea, so that it reaches the high tide line with much of its destructive force spent. As summer advances and the flow of the rivers is reduced, so the mud banks of the Dee Estuary begin to dry out. The miniature canyons of the creeks cease to glint with water, and the narrow threads of the gutters harden to become dark cracks in the algae-smothered face of the mud. Over the flats hangs a strong smell, part salt, part river, part decaying vegetation – the smell of summer in the estuary.

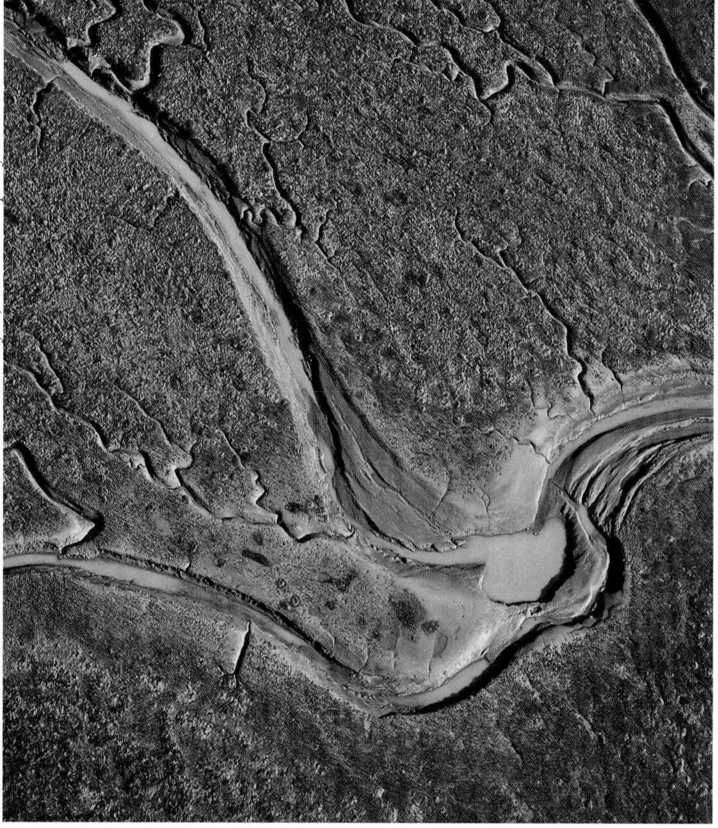

N 53°17'18.4" W 3°05'31.6" Grid Ref: SJ291727 Map Ref: 6 K14

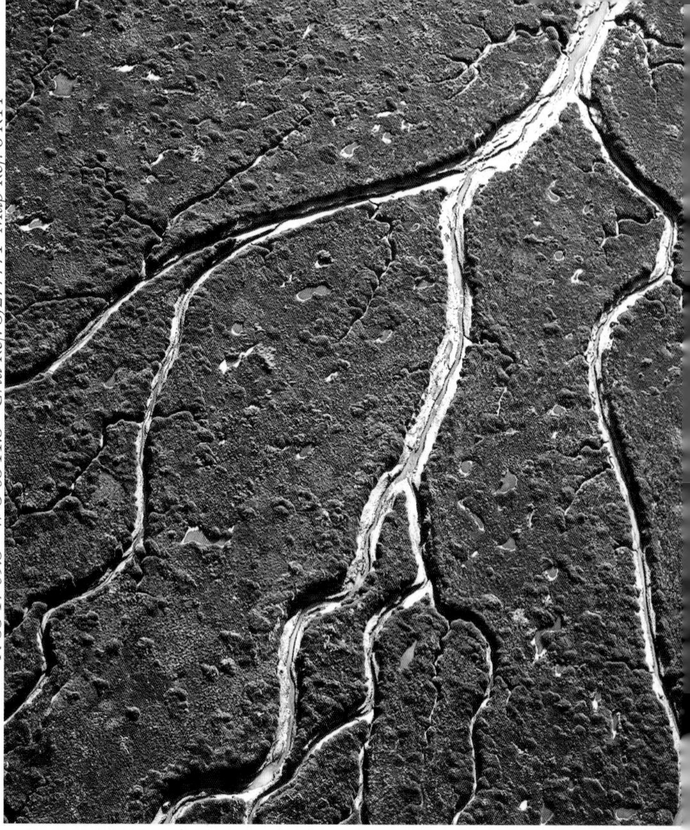

N 53°17'09.5" W 3°05'11.5" Grid Ref: SJ277771 Map Ref: 6 K14

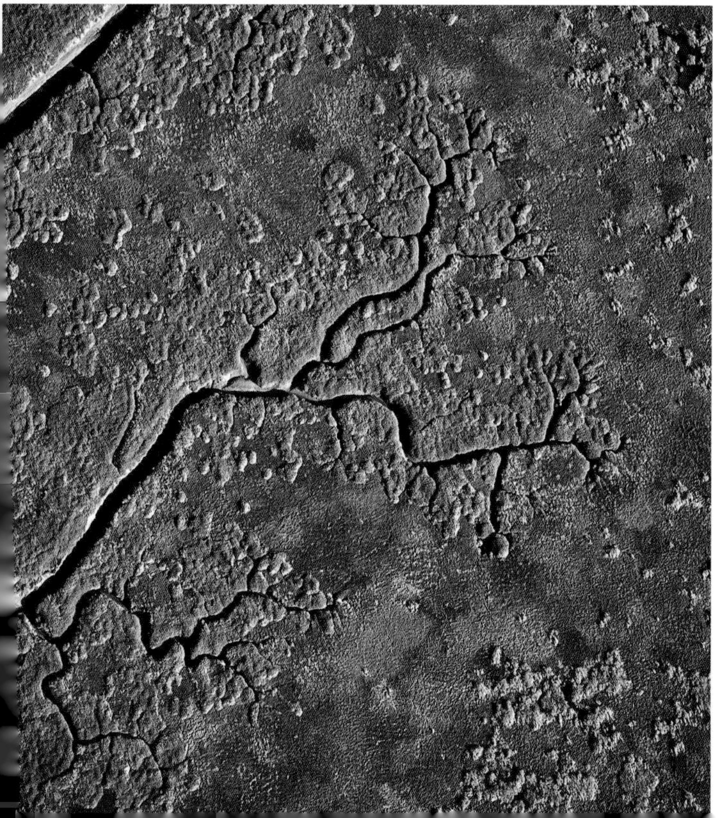

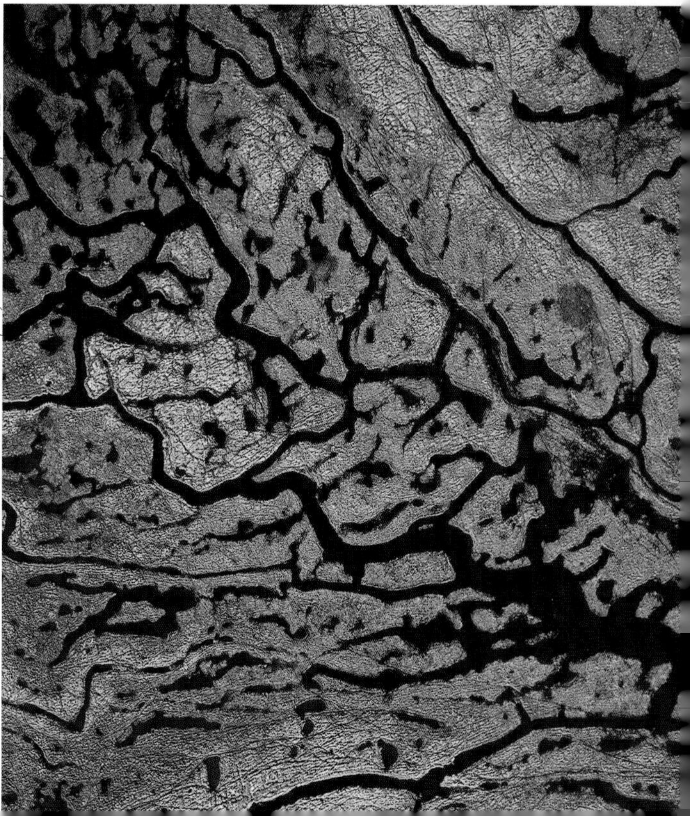

N 53°15'44.9" W 3°04'02.6" Grid Ref: SJ289745 Map Ref: 6 K14

Ribble Estuary, Lancashire *N 53°42'30.3" W 2°56'54.4" Grid Ref: SD375240 Map Ref: 6 K11*

The River Ribble winds down from the Lancashire moors and enters the Irish Sea amid a vast confusion of sand and mudflats between ragged fringes of salt marsh. On a flood tide the wriggling channels through the banks and marshes fill with water; at the lowest ebb the edge of the sea is five miles from land, and the sands with their uncountable millions of invertebrates become an enormous larder for hundreds of thousands of seabirds.

Blackpool, Lancashire *N 53°48'57.3" W 3°03'19.5" Grid Ref: SD306360 Map Ref: 6 K10*

Three hundred years ago Blackpool was a muddy hollow by the shore. A century later, it was a fashionable holiday hideaway for well-to-do persons. When the railway arrived in the mid-19th century, Blackpool with its famous Tower and Golden Mile became the premier seaside resort for the factory and mill hands of the industrial North. Today, it is still a popular centre for its conference venues, casinos and theme parks.

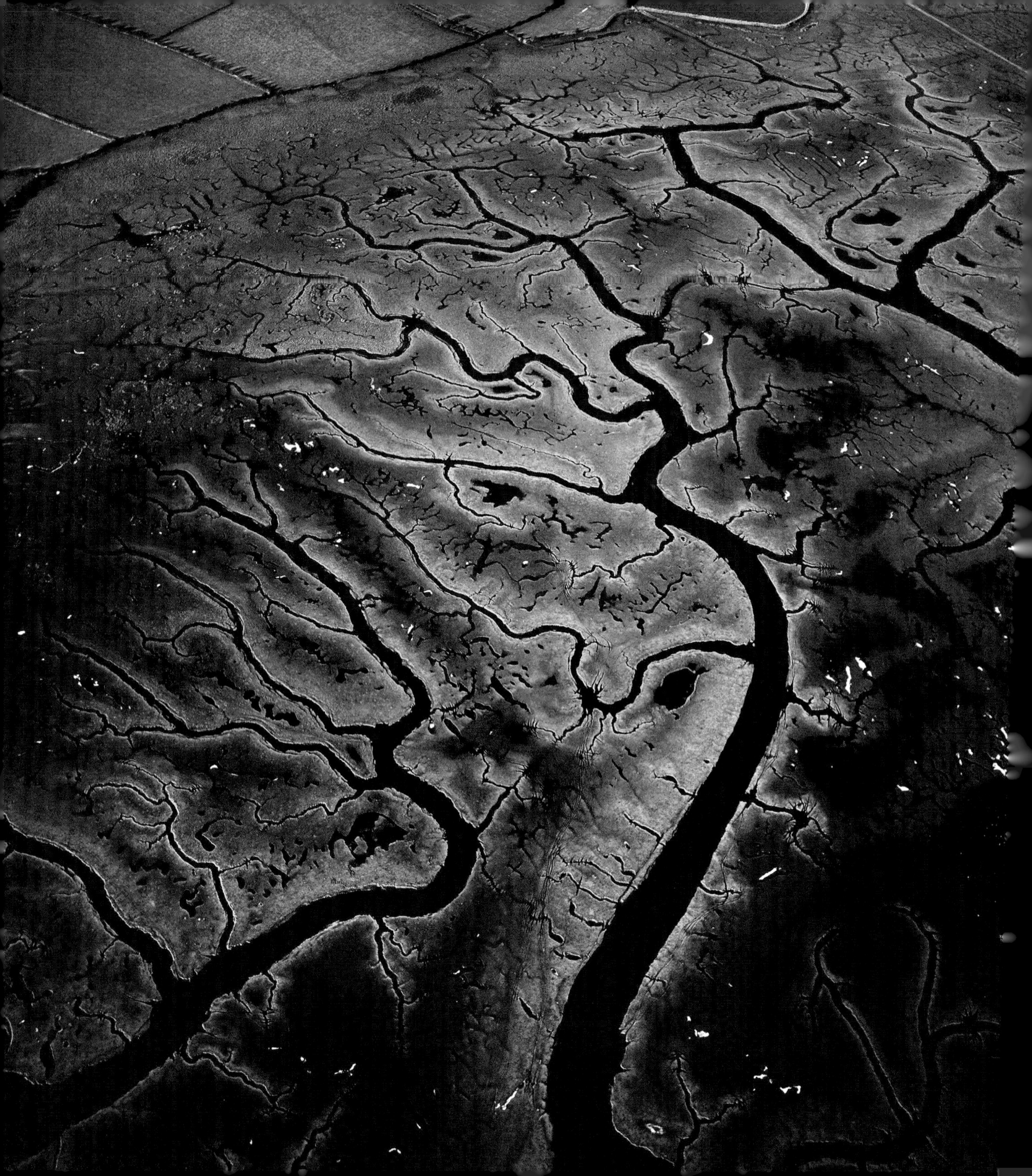

Mudflats, Lune Estuary, Lancashire (left)

N 54°01'26.1" W 2°50'22.8"
Grid Ref: SD451590 Map Ref: 6 L9

A wonderful image of the marshes and mudflats that line the estuary of the River Lune downstream of the city and former port of Lancaster. In the late 17th century, with transatlantic trade opening up and the broad Lune providing a navigable waterway to Lancaster from the Irish Sea, the city grew prosperous despite its position six miles inland. Then, just as ships were growing bigger and wider, the whole system silted up. The mudflats grew and spread, the Lune became a narrow and shallow channel, and Lancaster was left high and dry.

Morecambe, Lancashire

N 54°04'27.2" W 2°52'39.6"
Grid Ref: SD427646 Map Ref: 6 L8

Morecambe sprawls along its bay, with the peaked fells of the Lake District a tantalising prospect on the north-west horizon. The town is another former seaside playground, now looking for a way to reinvent itself. The answer to its problems may lie on its seaward doorstep; for Morecambe Bay, a big arc of sea at high tide, dries on the ebb to uncover over 100 square miles of sands thronged with birds. The town of Morecambe aims to become a base for naturalists, adventure walkers and bird-watchers in the bay.

Roa Island, Cumbria

N 54°04'27.2" W 3°10'28.0"
Grid Ref: SD233649 Map Ref: 6 J8

Roa Island owes its hard-edged, sculptural shape to the sea defences which stabilise this little causeway community out in the bay south of Barrow-in-Furness. The causeway was built in 1846 by banker John Smith, who had bought Roa Island in hopes of developing it into a resort and shipping station. A more enjoyable way to reach Roa is to walk the mile out across the sands at low tide, as the sea withdraws southward and the majority of the bay dries out.

Piel Island, Cumbria *N 54°03'48.5" W 3°10'27.8" Grid Ref: SD232637 Map Ref: 6 J9*

Off the southern tip of Roa Island lies the teardrop outline of Piel Island. Its stern castle was built in the 14th century by the monks of Furness Abbey to deter pirates. In 1487 ten-year-old Lambert Simnel, puppet Pretender to the throne of England, was landed here as a first step on a march to London which would end with his backers beheaded or imprisoned, and Simnel himself installed as a humble spit-turner in King Henry VII's kitchen. The white-washed Ship Inn is still open for business, its successive landlords dignified with the grand title of 'King of Piel', its customers gaining the dignity of a knighthood simply by sitting in a ceremonial chair.

Barrow-in-Furness and Walney Island, Cumbria *N 54°06'26.9" W 3°14'39.2" Grid Ref: SD188687 Map Ref: 6 J8*

The slender arc of Walney Island was a seaward extension of the mainland until some ten thousand years ago, at the end of the last Ice Age, when a glacier in the Duddon Estuary to the north released meltwaters of such ferocity that they gouged out the channel that now separates Walney from Barrow-in-Furness. Barrow grew as a planned town, an iron-working centre, a place of gritty, rust-red industry, still carried on these days in the shipyard that builds nuclear submarines – its giant sheds dominate the waterfront near the Walney Island bridge.

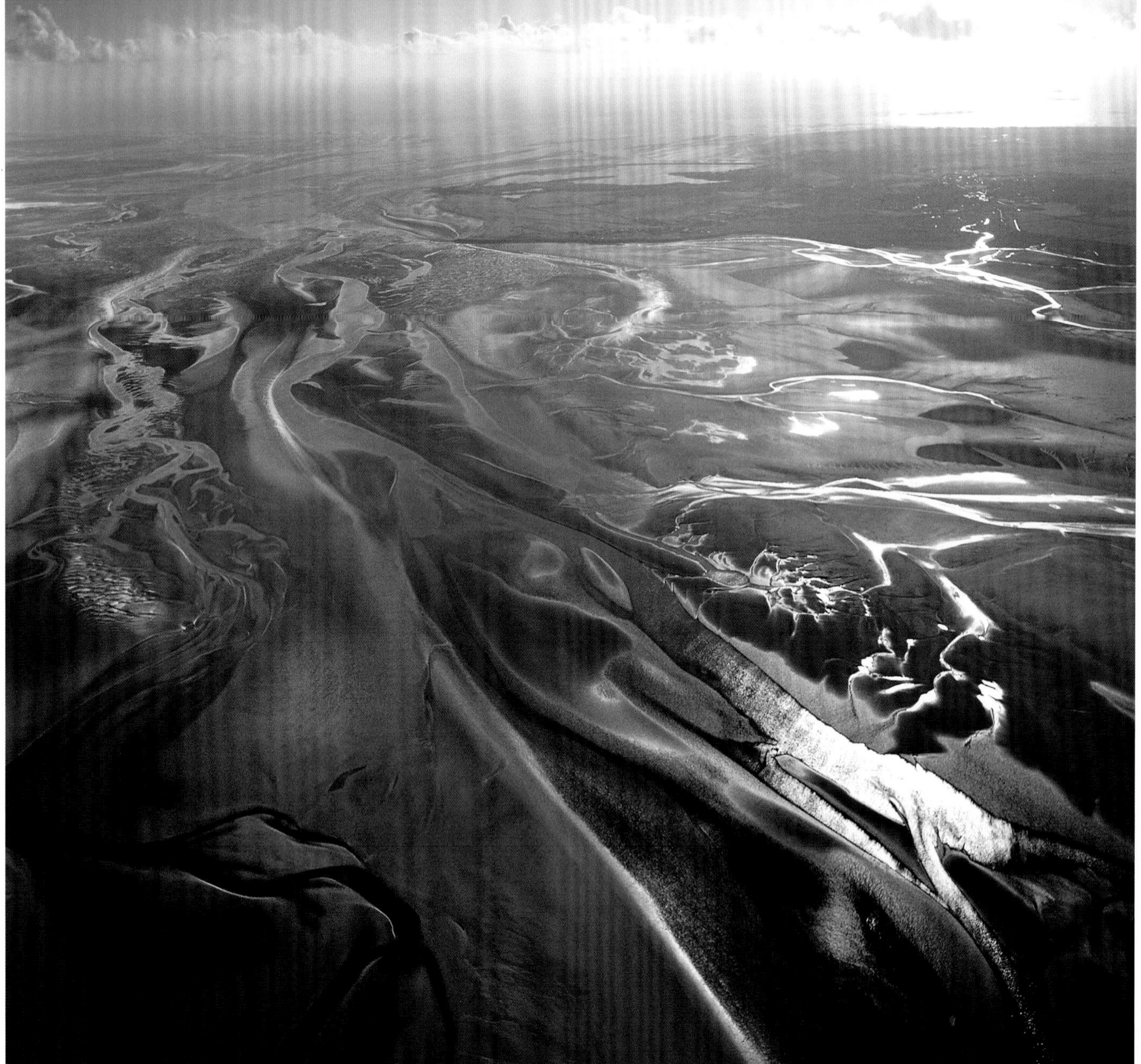

Duddon Estuary, Cumbria

N 54°13'29.0" W 3°13'08.5" Grid Ref: SD206817 Map Ref: 6 K7

Not hurled precipitous from steep to steep;
Lingering no more 'mid flower-enamelled lands
And blooming thickets; nor by rocky bands
Held; but in radiant progress toward the Deep
Where mightiest rivers into powerless sleep
Sink, and forget their nature--'now' expands
Majestic Duddon, over smooth flat sands
Gliding in silence with unfettered sweep!

Beneath an ampler sky a region wide
Is opened round him:--hamlets, towers, and towns,
And blue-topped hills, behold him from afar;
In stately mien to sovereign Thames allied
Spreading his bosom under Kentish downs,
With commerce freighted, or triumphant war.

River Duddon Sonnet XXXII, William Wordsworth, 1818

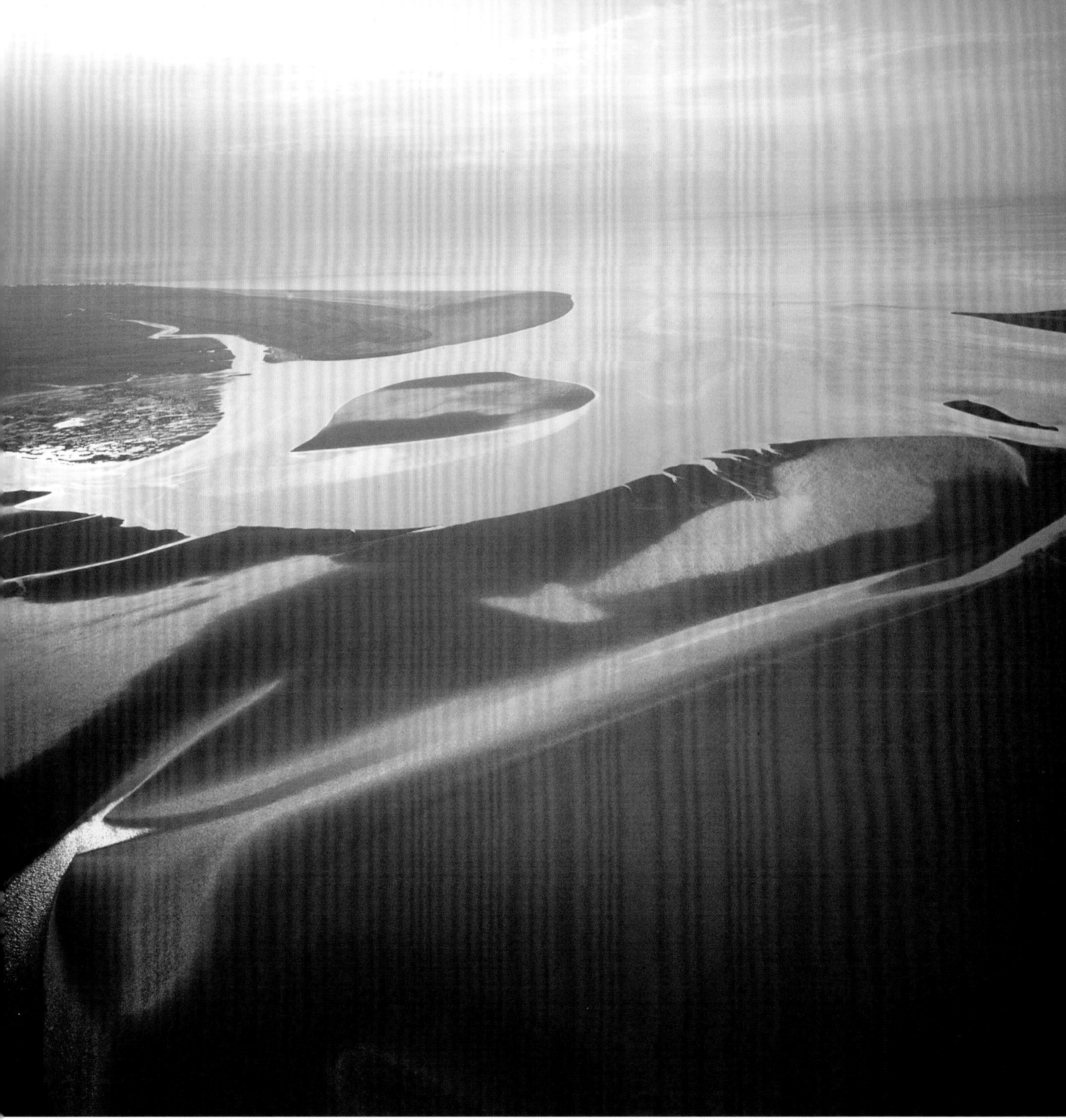

Solway Firth at Grune Point, Cumbria *N 54°53'47.9" W 3°19'35.9" Grid Ref: NY150566 Map Ref: 6 J2*

Celestial beauties of the Solway Firth: evening light, its effects magnified by the giant mirror of open water lying below, pours across the firth to flood the sandbanks and mudflats with a refracted luminescence as fiery and blinding as molten gold.

River Esk, Solway Firth *N 54°59'02.4" W 3°03'02.2" Grid Ref: NY329660 Map Ref: 6 K2*

The River Esk snakes lazily into the broad tideway of the Solway Firth on the Scottish Border. Today the flanks of the estuary are green and pastoral, but during the First World War the lonely miles of the north bank (on the right in the picture) were covered with the buildings of the giant Moorside munitions factory, a complex that measured 9 miles long and 2 miles wide. Thirty thousand men and women were employed making what Sir Arthur Conan Doyle dubbed 'the devils' porridge' - cordite RDB, an explosive mixture of guncotton and nitro-glycerine used in bullets and shells, which the female workers mixed by hand. It stained the skin bright yellow – hence the women's nickname of 'Moorside Canaries'.

Caerlaverock Castle, Dumfries and Galloway *N 54°58'21.6" W 3°31'24.0" Grid Ref: NY026653 Map Ref: 6 I2*

Caerlaverock Castle, built by the Maxwells in 1270 on a triangular plan half a mile inland of the Solway Firth, enjoyed its full share of burnings, demolishings, sieges, hangings and slaughter. In AD 1300, King Edward I arrived outside the walls with 87 knights and 3,000 men. The king's giant siege engines lobbed huge stone balls over the walls until Caerlaverock's sixty-strong garrison surrendered. Many were hanged on the spot for their defiance. By the 17th century the Auld Enemies' antagonism had simmered down to the point where Lord Nithsdale felt it was safe to build a 'dainty fabrick', a three-storey mansion with wonderful allegorical carvings, inside the structure of the old stronghold.

Highlands and Islands
Argyll to Sutherland and Inner Hebrides

The west of Scotland is a stern place constantly at war with the Atlantic, its mainland coast cut deeply into ragged sea lochs. Communications are difficult, livelihoods tricky, communities small and self-reliant. North of the holiday resorts of the Firth of Clyde, the focus shifts to tiny, practical towns with a sober purpose – the three chief ferry ports of Oban, Mallaig and Kyle of Lochalsh, the planned fishing settlements of Ullapool and Inverlochy. This is a tough coast; it is the most beautiful in Britain, too. Wonderful beaches of pristine white sand lie between massively rugged headlands, their water shelving through bottle-green and turquoise to indigo, deep and deadly cold to swim in. Mountains of ancient rock rise to towering peaks. The glens lie empty, their grandeur immense, their former life drained by clearances and economic emigration.

Out west are scattered the isles of the Inner Hebrides, formed mostly in titanic volcanic upheavals that saw molten sheets of outflung lava cooling to become layers of basalt hundreds of feet thick. Now weathered and sea-worn to outlandish spires, hummocks and ledges, they offer a fairy-tale vista to the sailor or beach-walker – Fingal's Cave in the flanks of Staffa, the cliffs of Trotternish on the Isle of Skye, the Dutchman's Cap on the western horizon like a surfacing submarine. Tales lie as thick on these islands as orchids on *machair*: Robinson Crusoe's great-grandson as a lighthouse keeper in the Sound of Mull, lovelorn Lachlan Lubanach Maclean kidnapping his future father-in-law the Lord of the Isles, Flora MacDonald bravely defying her inquisitors in the dungeons of Dunstaffnage Castle.

Of all the West Coast tales there is none so seductive as the one about the handsome young prince in danger, and the simple island girl who rowed him over the sea to Skye. Everywhere in the Highlands and Islands lies the shadow of Charles Edward Stuart, the fugitive Young Pretender who roamed these braes and crossed these sounds in the summer of 1646, during the five months he and his faithful companions spent as hunted men 'in the heather' after the Battle of Culloden. Bonnie Prince Charlie left a fine scent of romance behind him when he sailed away from Loch nan Uamh on 20 September 1646 – a whiff of self-delusional arrogance, too, and a trail of dead men, mourning families, burned villages and broken livelihoods.

Highlands and Islands
Argyll to Sutherland and Inner Hebrides

Along with all the glories of these landscapes, the romance and the wide open spaces, this is a coast of grim castles, of bloody clan feuding, of back-stabbing and screaming charges and unending strife. To appreciate the depth of such bitter enmity, and to contrast it with the breathtaking beauty everywhere the eye rests today, one has only to hear the words of Iain Lom, 'Bald John', poet of Clan MacDonald, as he savagely celebrates the MacDonald victory in 1645 at the Battle of Inverlochy:

Early Sunday morning I climbed the brae above the
castle of Inverlochy. I saw the army drawn up for battle,
and victory in the field was with Clan Donald.
The most pleasing news, every time it was announced
about the wry-mouthed Campbells, was that every company
of them as they came along had their heads battered with
sword blows.
Were you familiar with Goirtean Odhar? Well was
it manured, not with the dung of sheep or goats, but by the
blood of Campbells after it congealed.
To Hell with you if I feel pity for your plight, as I
listen to the distress of your children, lamenting the company
which was in the battlefield, the wailing of the women
of Argyll.

Rothesay, Isle of Bute

N 55°50'17.6" W 5°03'25.5" Grid Ref: NS087648 Map Ref: 8 K9

The Isle of Bute town of Rothesay, handily placed a short steamer-ride down the Clyde from Glasgow, became the Glaswegians' favourite seaside resort. It got pretty crowded each July when the whole city went on its annual holidays around the time of Glasgow Fair:

'In search of lodgings we did slide,
Tae find a place where we could bide;
There was eighty-twa o' us inside
In a single room in Rothesay, O.
We a' lay doon tae tak' our ease,
When somebody happened for tae sneeze,
And he wakened half a million fleas
In a single room in Rothesay, O'.
- 'The Day We Went To Rothesay, O'

Oban, Argyll and Bute *N 56°24'53.1" W 5°28'27.2" Grid Ref: NM858301 Map Ref: 8 I4*

Looking from Oban across the Lynn of Lorn to the tumbled hills of Morvern. Like Mallaig and Kyle of Lochalsh, the name of Oban is associated with one image above all other: that of a Caledonian MacBrayne ferry setting out for the Isles. One of the great Scottish west coast triumvirate of ferry ports, Oban vessels serve the big neighbouring Isle of Mull and the further-flung islands of Coll and Tiree, as well as Barra and South Uist in the Western Isles.

Dunstaffnage Castle, Argyll and Bute *N 56°27'15.5" W 5°26'17.7" Grid Ref: NM882344 Map Ref: 8 I4*

The narrow mouth of Loch Etive, a few miles up the coast from Oban, was always a strategic trump card. The grim grey 13th-century stronghold of Dunstaffnage Castle, built by the Macdougalls, commands the straits here from the rocky islet of Eilean Mor. In 1746 Flora MacDonald, the Western Isles girl who had helped the fugitive Bonnie Prince Charlie, was held at Dunstaffnage for questioning over her part in his escape after the Battle of Culloden.

:ilean Musdile, Lismore, Argyll and Bute *N 56°27'19.3" W 5°36'28.2" Grid Ref: NM778351 Map Ref: 8 I4*

:ilean Musdile lies off the south-west tip of Lismore island where Loch Linnhe meets the Sound of Mull. The lighthouse on the islet was built in 1833 ɔ a design by the great lighthouse architect Robert Stevenson. Its first Principal Keeper, Robert Selkirk, must have had an attraction for small islands ı his blood – his direct ancestor was the Fife-born buccaneer Alexander Selkirk, who deserted his ship in 1704 and was marooned for nearly five years n an island in the uninhabited South Seas archipelago of Juan Fernandez. Selkirk's remarkable tale was reckoned to be the basis for Daniel Defoe's nmortal novel *Robinson Crusoe*.

Ballachulish Bridge, Highland

N 56°41'16.0" W 5°10'58.1"
Grid Ref: NN052596 Map Ref: 8 J2

Loch Linnhe stretches some forty miles inland to Fort William, with the easterly spur of Loch Leven branching off near its upper end. The narrows at the mouth of Loch Leven, a gap less than 200 yards wide, was bridged for hundreds of years by a small ferry until the opening of Ballachulish Bridge in 1974 did away with the notorious traffic queues on both sides of the gap.

Ballachulish, Highland

N 56°40'39.0" W 5°08'14.2"
Grid Ref: NN080584 Map Ref: 8 J2

Looking west down Loch Leven towards Ballachulish Bridge, with the wide waters of Loch Linnhe beyond. In the fairway lies the round green button of Eilean Choinneach, Kenneth's Isle. Some call it MacKenzie's Isle, and say it is named to commemorate the death of an expert swordsman of the MacKenzie clan who met his death there fighting a duel with an opponent that wee bit better than himself.

River Lochy at Fort William, Highland (right)

N 56°49'20.2" W 5°06'32.7"
Grid Ref: NN104744 Map Ref: 8 K1

On 2 February 1645, after a punishing march across snow-bound mountains, a Royalist force under the Earl of Montrose attacked the Marquis of Argyll's army of Covenanters or religious dissenters in the marshy meadows around the mouth of the River Lochy. Behind the political and religious stances, ancient clan hatreds seethed: Montrose's men were mostly Macdonalds, Argyll's their sworn Campbell foes. The Covenanters outnumbered their enemies two to one, but they fell like scythed corn to the Highland charge of the Royalists. Perhaps as many as 1,500 Campbells were slaughtered. It was to put an end to such actions – as much a Highland clan tradition as the wearing of tartan – that the garrison town of Fort William was founded next to the river mouth half a century later.

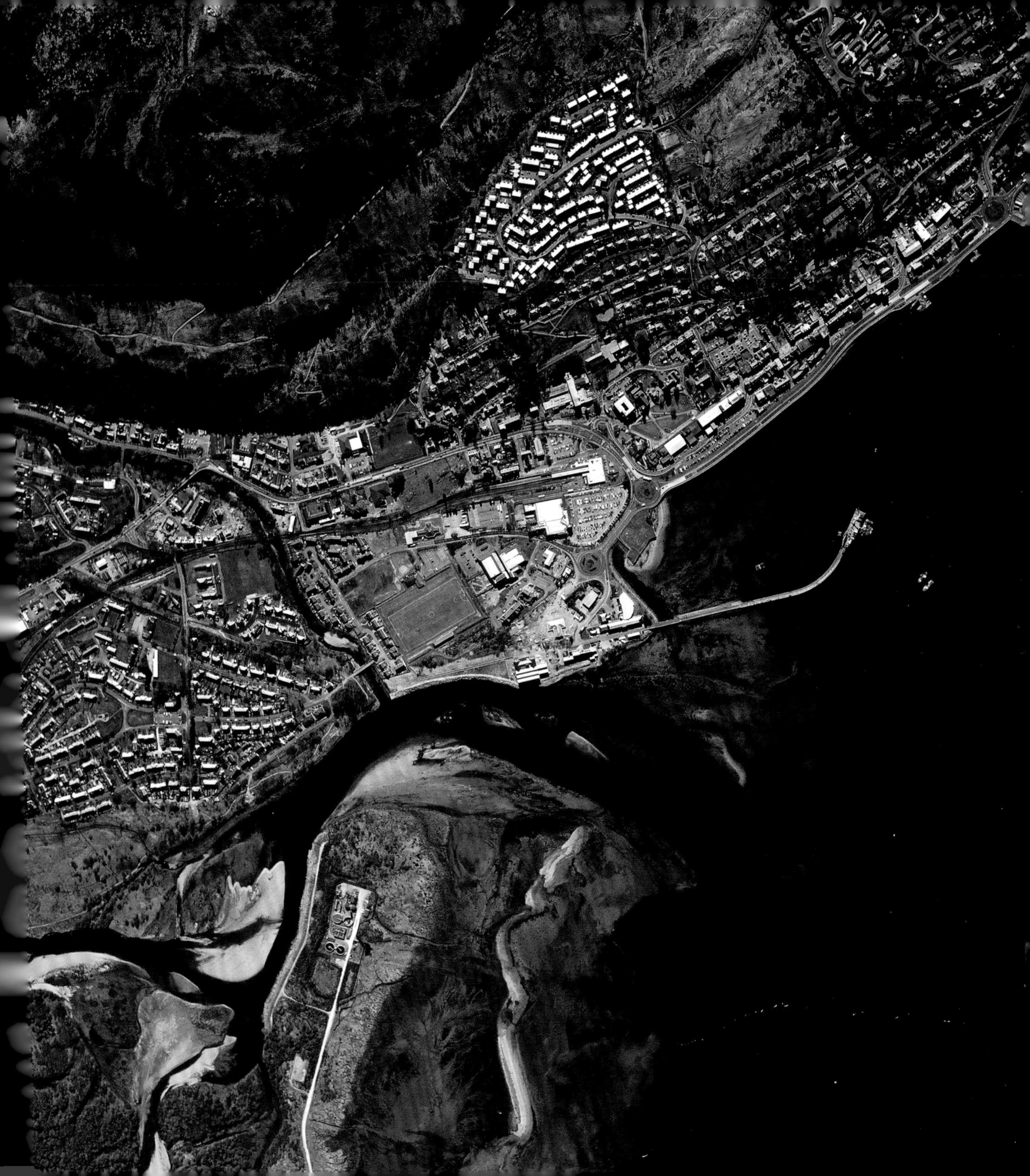

Duart Castle, Isle of Mull, Inner Hebrides

N 56°27'18.6" W 5°39'23.4"
Grid Ref: NM748352 Map Ref: 8 H4

The ancient seat of Clan Maclean guards the entrance to the Sound of Mull from its rocky knoll on the bleak headland of Duart - Dubh Ard, the black point, in Gaelic. The keep of Castle Duart dates from the mid 14th century. It was built by Lachlan Lubanach Maclean, by all accounts a gentleman of strong passions as well as canny hard-headedness. Tales say that he fell in love with beautiful Mary MacDonald, the daughter of John MacDonald, the first Lord of the Isles. The girl accepted him, but the father refused to allow the marriage. Maclean was not about to give up his beloved, nor his prospects. He kidnapped the all-powerful Lord of the Isles, and 'persuaded' him to sanction the match.

Iona, Inner Hebrides

N 56°19'52.9" W 6°23'30.9"
Grid Ref: NM286241 Map Ref: 8 E5

Pristine white-sand beaches, the rocky basalt hump of the hill of Dun-I, and the grey bulk of the restored Abbey in the middle distance – characteristic images of the Isle of Iona, burial place of fifty Scottish kings, foundation-stone of St Columba's great Celtic Church that lasted a thousand years, still today a spiritual centre and pilgrimage goal. Beyond in the sea, the low dark line of the Isle of Staffa, and out to the west the submarine profile of the Dutchman's Cap, one of the remote and magical Treshnish Isles.

Fingal's Cave, Isle of Staffa, Inner Hebrides *N 56°26'08.0" W 6°20'28.0" Grid Ref: NM325355 Map Ref: 8 E4*

Basalt's masterpiece in the Inner Hebrides, the Isle of Staffa lies alone in a wide stretch of sea. Millions of visitors have boated out there to marvel at the cathedral-like structure and size of Fingal's Cave, whose dark mouth opens between buttresses of columnar basalt. The young Felix Mendelssohn visited on a Sunday in 1829, horribly seasick, yet stirred to ecstasy by the music of the sea in the cave. When he picked out the tunes in his head on the piano at his lodgings that evening the budding composer was roundly admonished for making music on the Sabbath. But the haunting cave had sown the seeds for his immortal *Hebridean Overture.*

Achnaha volcanic ring, Ardnamurchan, Highland *N 56°44'13.8" W 6°08'01.2" Grid Ref: NM473682 Map Ref: 8 F1*

This stunning image is of a rare geological formation, a ring of eucrite or basalt spreading out from what was, 60 million years ago, an active volcano. This ring, known as the Great Eucrite, outlines the roots of what must have been a most impressive volcano on the north-east coast of the Ardnamurchan Peninsula, now eroded almost entirely away.

Castle Tioram, Loch Moidart, Highland *N 56°46'59.1" W 5°49'38.2" Grid Ref: NM663723 Map Ref: 8 H1*

The absolute archetype of a romantically sited castle ruin, the 14th-century Macdonald fortress of Castle Tioram, seat of Clan Ranald, stands in Loch Moidart in a location that is militarily canny – its island is only accessible at low tide – and politically astute, guarding the sea approaches to the long inland waterway of Loch Shiel. It was Clan Ranald's chief, Allan of Clanranald, who finally destroyed his own family stronghold – a whole-hearted Jacobite, he recaptured Tioram Castle during the 1715 Rebellion from the Crown garrison that had held it for over 20 years, and had it burned so that they could not use it again.

Ardnambuth, Highland *N 56°53'20.3" W 5°44'18.6" Grid Ref: NM724837 Map Ref: 10 M14*

A peninsula of ancient granite indented with bays of peerless white sand, Ardnambuth protrudes from the head of Loch nan Uamh, the 'loch of the cave'. It was on these shores that Charles Edward Stuart, Pretender-in-exile to the throne of England and Scotland, landed in such high hopes on 25 July 1745, to set the Highlands ablaze with clan fervour for his cause. And it was from here that he sailed away fourteen months later into exile once more, his dreams crushed, his future barren and his supporters facing persecution that would wring the last life from the old Highland clan system.

Mallaig, Highland *N 57°00'22.9" W 5°49'39.4" Grid Ref: NM677971 Map Ref: 10 L13*

The chunky ferries of Caledonian MacBrayne – 'Calmac' to everyone in these parts – load up at the quays of Mallaig, one of the Big Three west coast ferry ports. Sturdy breakwaters protect the north-facing port from the worst of winter weather, but the sea journey to the exposed Small Isles – Rhum, Eigg, Muck and Canna - can still be a sickener.

Loch Nevis, Highland *N 56°59'37.4" W 5°32'19.0" Grid Ref: NM852947 Map Ref: 11 A14*

In spite of its name, Loch Nevis is a very long way from Ben Nevis. The sea loch cuts in between the thin peninsula of North Morar and the broad and mountainous one of Knoydart. There's a lively debate about what's signified by 'Nevis', in Gaelic *nibheis*. It could be interpreted as poisonous or ill-omened; it might mean cloudy, as in this photograph, or it might express something much lighter – 'heavenly'.

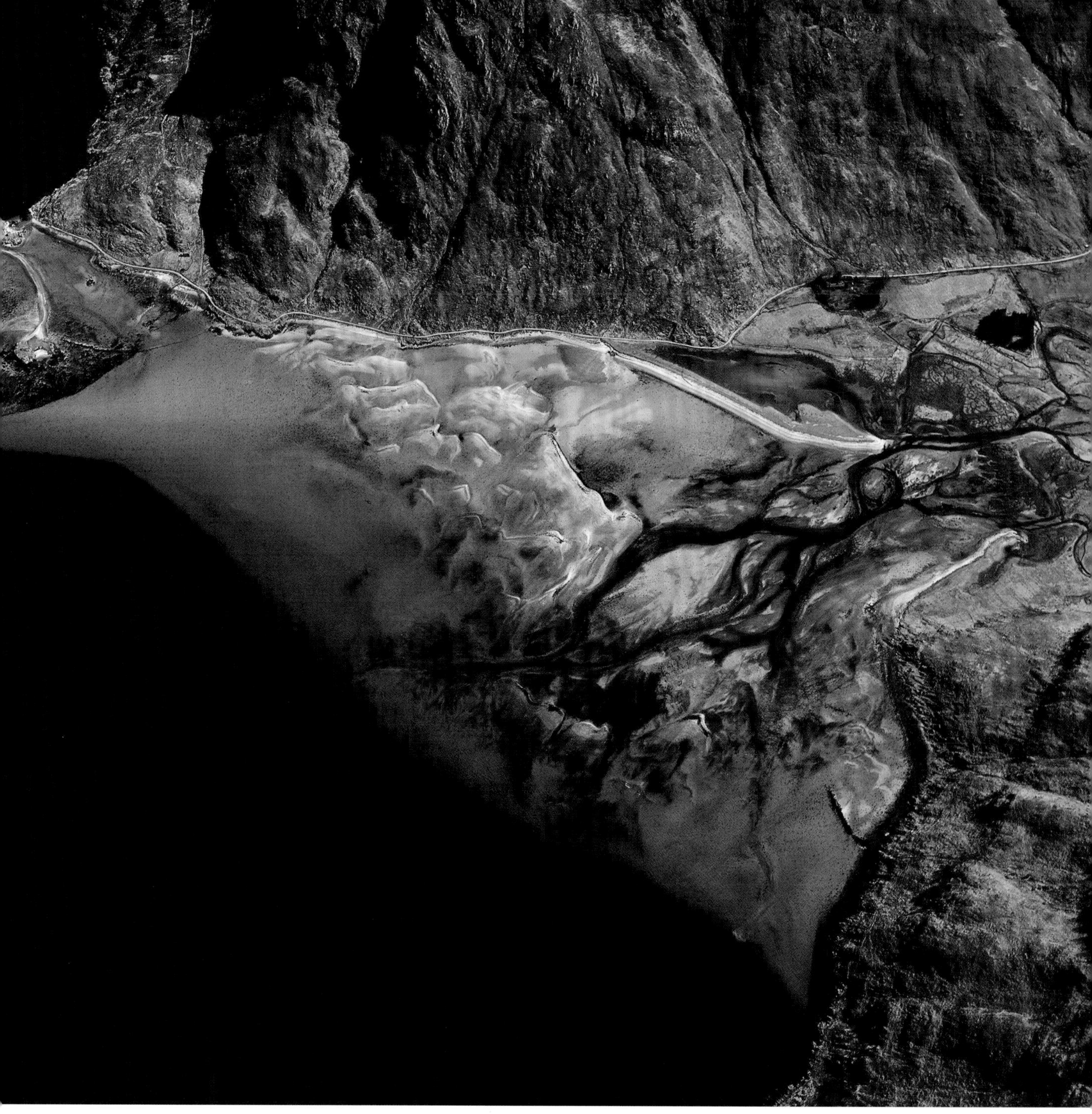

Barrisdale Bay, Highland *N 57°05'10.4" W 5°31'17.2" Grid Ref: NG867050 Map Ref: 11 A13*

Barrisdale Bay, a very isolated inlet on the north coast of the remote Knoydart Peninsula, is caught in a breathtaking image. The soft, wave-moulded sands could be subcutaneous fat, the flanking hills sinews of skinless muscle, and the blue-green shelving water an outpouring of organic juices. This is geology as landscape musculature.

Eilean Donan Castle, Highland *N 57°16'30.8" W 5°31'30.8" Grid Ref: NG876260 Map Ref: 11 A12*

In 1230, the year that Eilean Donan Castle was built, Viking raids still posed a deadly threat along the coasts of Scotland. To deter them, and to provide a place of refuge, the castle was built on its islet at the confluence of the three lochs of Aish, Duich and Long. It met a curious fate in 1719, captured by Spanish Jacobites, then bombarded by three Crown frigates and retaken before being blown up spectacularly, using the 343 barrels of gunpowder the Jacobites had been hoarding there. The castle lay in ruins for two centuries before being painstakingly restored by Colonel John Macrae-Gilstrap, who bought the island in 1911.

Skye Bridge, Inner Hebrides *N 57°16'42.6" W 5°44'28.9" Grid Ref: NG746271 Map Ref: 10 M11*

There was bitter controversy when the Skye Bridge was opened in 1995 at a cost of about £25 million. It put an end to a ferry service that had crossed the narrows between Kyle of Lochalsh and the island since 1600; it destroyed the island magic of Skye for romantics; and it infuriated travellers who found themselves paying expensive tolls. Activist 'Robbie the Pict' ran for election as a Member of the Scottish Parliament on a joint Pictish Independence and no-toll platform (he wasn't successful). In 2004 the bridge was bought by the Scottish Executive for around £27 million, and tolls were abolished.

The Storr, Trotternish, Isle of Skye, Inner Hebrides *N 57°26′53.2″ W 6°09′49.9″ Grid Ref: NG503474 Map Ref: 10 K*

Vast volcanic outpourings some 60 million years ago resulted in layer upon layer of molten rock building up to form what is now the Trotternish Peninsu of Skye – up to 24 consecutive flows and solidifications in places. This hugely heavy topping has slipped and fallen in many places, and its great steps ha smoothed out into huge cliff faces such as the one that drops from the hill called The Storr. Free-standing pinnacles of basalt rise from The Sanctuary, t rough scree slope at the foot of the cliff. The tallest is the Old Man of Storr; at 160 feet high, it is dwarfed by the mighty basalt wall behind.

Lazybeds, Bearreraig Bay, Isle of Skye, Inner Hebrides *N 57°30'15.0" W 6°08'43.0" Grid Ref: NG518536 Map Ref: 10 K9*

Was there ever a more inappropriate term than 'lazybeds'? The raised beds in which Highland people of vanished generations grew their life-sustaining potatoes were mounded with hard, back-breaking labour, sown and harvested by hand, and manured with sooty thatch, seaweed, sand and excrement. The poverty and over-population of the 19th-century Isle of Skye is well demonstrated here on the Trotternish Peninsula, where the corduroy stripes of the ridges, as close-packed as possible so as to use every foot of available land, run right to the lip of 300-ft cliffs.

Loch Mealt and Kilt Rock Waterfall, Isle of Skye, Inner Hebrides *N 57°36'40.7" W 6°10'20.1" Grid Ref: NG509656 Map Ref: 10 K9*

Just south of the village of Staffin, the outflowing waters of Loch Mealt tumble over the lip of a 350-ft cliff. The fierce winds along the cliffs often prevent the waterfall reaching the shore, snatching the stream half-way down and blowing it into mist. Loch Mealt is deep, dark and cold, ideal conditions for Arctic char to breed there. These salmon-like fish of the far north have maintained their population in Loch Mealt since becoming isolated there after the last Ice Age some 10,000 years ago.

Basalt cliffs at Kilt Rock, Trotternish, Isle of Skye, Inner Hebrides *N 57°36'52.1" W 6°10'26.9" Grid Ref: NG508659 Map Ref: 10 K9*

As on the Isle of Staffa, in many places the flanks of the Isle of Skye show immense walls of columnar basalt to the sea. Slow cooling of molten lava from volcanic eruptions 60 million years ago produced huge columns, as in these cliffs at Kilt Rock next to Loch Mealt, their basically hexagonal cross-section produced by horizontal contraction of the lava sheet with consequent cracking into tall, even sided columns.

Little Loch Broom, Highland *N 57°50'51.9" W 5°13'32.0" Grid Ref: NH087888 Map Ref: 11 C8*

Between harsh slopes of ancient sandstone lies Little Loch Broom, foregrounded in a panoramic view only accessible to golden eagles and humans in light aeroplanes. In the south rises the tumbled massif of Strathnasheallag Forest, dominated and dignified by the high crown of An Teallach. Ten tops over 3,000 feet beckon serious walkers who are prepared for a tough 3-mile hike before they even begin their climb. The reward? Strong air, heady elation, and transcendent views.

Ullapool, Highland *N 57°53'45.4" W 5°09'48.6" Grid Ref: NH126940 Map Ref: 11 C7*

Presided over by the tent-like silhouette of Beinn Ghobhlach, the planned town of Ullapool lies on Loch Broom. The British Fisheries Society engaged Thomas Telford, the most celebrated practical architect of his day, to design the fishing port in the 1780s to exploit the vast shoals of herring that were visiting Scottish waters each spring. The herring were over-fished and are long gone. But Ullapool reinvented itself in the late 20th century as a supply base for Iron Curtain 'klondykers', huge factory ships that processed fish caught by their trawler fleets.

Lochinver, Highland

N 58°08'49.1" W 5°14'43.2"
Grid Ref: NC091221 Map Ref: 11 C5

Up north of Ullapool, Lochinver sits in a sheltered niche of Loch Inver's west-facing inlet. This was another of the planned fishing towns that came into being during the 18th and 19th century herring boom. But Lochinver, unlike many similar settlements, kept its fishing trade – albeit through the boats and nets of French and Spanish fishermen, for whose trade the harbour was rebuilt bigger and stronger in the 1990s.

Soyea Island, Highland (right)

N 58°08'33.3" W 5°19'16.2"
Grid Ref: NC046219 Map Ref: 11 B5

Soyea, the Isle of Sheep, lies out at the mouth of Loch Inver at the fringe of the remote Assynt region. This low-lying isle with its tight grass sward has always been used by mainlanders for the grazing of sheep. Composed of Lewisian gneiss - the oldest rock in Britain, formed some two thousand million years ago - the Isle of Sheep looks out across the Minch sea channel towards Lewis itself and the ancient Western Isles, the next step in our journey round the Living Coast of Britain.

Achmelvich, Highland

N 58°10'11.1" W 5°18'21.3"
Grid Ref: NC057249 Map Ref: 11 B5

A little way north of Lochinver, and in a position far more remote, the peerless beach of Achmelvich faces north-west over blue-green shallows. Swimming is wonderful if you don't mind the cold or the companionship of dolphins; seals and sea going otters are everyday visitors. Behind the beach lie the dunes and *machair*, flowery sward, that gave the place its Gaelic name, Achadh Mhealbhaich, the meadow of sand dunes.

The Western Isles
Outer Hebrides

Some 50 miles west of the Inner Hebrides lies the remote archipelago of the Outer Hebrides, more commonly known as the Western Isles. Where the Inner Hebrides resemble a tumble of landforms scattered at random in the sea by a giant hand, the Western Isles possess a symmetry of arrangement. The long progression of islands forms a smooth north-easterly arc, the smallest at the southern foot and the largest, the 'capital island' of Lewis, at the northerly apex of the chain. They are remnants of a weather-eroded chain of volcanic mountains composed of Lewisian gneiss, the oldest rock in Britain, formed as much as 3,000,000,000 years ago. This ancient gneiss is acid rock that forbids the rotting down of dead vegetation: hence the building up across the islands of a thick carpet of peat, forming endless swathes of boggy moorland dotted with innumerable lochs and lochans, running out to ragged coasts savaged into fantastic shapes by the constantly gnawing North Atlantic.

Poor soil nutrients, treelessness and the consequent exposure to salt-laden sea winds, difficult, mountainous terrain and dangerous coasts spiked with reefs add up to a harsh living environment. Worldly prospects are limited, livelihoods hard earned. The Western Isles people, 26,000 strong, display a characteristic mixture of stoicism, dark humour and instant hospitality to the stranger. There is a lot of Norse in the place names and the blood-lines. Isolated island communities are adept at making the best of things, so that although most of the smaller isles lie deserted, thirteen still boast some sort of population. The way that people used to live is seen in the countless stripes of cultivation ridges on every available piece of half-decent land, in the narrow croft strips behind the houses, the squat Catholic churches of the archipelago's southern half and the looming chapels of the Free Presbyterian north, as well as in the reconstituted and re-thatched traditional blackhouses of holiday villages alongside the shells of those long abandoned by their inhabitants through poverty, emigration or forced clearance.

Life became a lot easier at the turn of the 21st century with the advent of broadband internet, sophisticated telecommunications and the linking-up of the main islands by a chain of causeways and bridges. On smaller islands unconnected to this umbilical cord, life continues to be hard, with rewards that remain intangible. 'Blow-ins', incomers with a dream of an island paradise or

The Western Isles
Outer Hebrides

a hard-headed realism, many in search of a cleaner environment and a simpler way of life, have been settling in increasing numbers, both diluting and enhancing traditional island ways and attitudes. The remoter groups of islets – the Flannan Isles, the Monach Isles, the Shiant Isles – are populated only by the seals and seabirds. Loneliest of all, St Kilda keeps station forty miles further into the Atlantic, its native people evacuated in 1930 when it became impossible to live so remotely, the roofless village houses eerily complete, the whole island soaked in poignancy.

This is a harsh landscape, the interior a progression of bog and loch, the coasts jagged, with carpets of brilliantly coloured wild flowers across the lime-rich *machair* grass swards. Strange to relate of a place so remote from urban cares, it is also a landscape under constant threat of development – ugly housing schemes, overkill roads funded to unnecessarily high standards, bridges that bring too much traffic to slow-paced places, and of course – in Britain's windiest corner - the omnipresent shadow of the 450-ft wind turbine mast. Planning permission for five hundred of these across the bleak interior of Lewis has been sought by outside developers in recent years, with local opposition placated by offers of that most precious commodity in the islands, jobs for locals. Vigorous representation about the dangers to birds, the building of roads and digging of quarries that would accompany such development, and the destruction of that intangible asset, the Lewis landscape, saw the most highly publicised application turned down by the Scottish Executive in January 2008. But there will be others.

One sure source of outside revenue in the past century has been tourism. It's often been said that if the sea were ten degrees warmer (and perhaps it will be, if climate change continues to accelerate), the Western Isles would be a holiday destination as popular – and as ruined – as the Costa del Sol. Bucket-and-spade holidaymakers of the tougher sort, lovers of wildlife, walkers and climbers, photographers and artists are all attracted by the magnetic beauty and loneliness of the Western Isles, the proximity of otters and seals. Above all, this is the land of romance, of the mystery of Flannan Isle, the poignancy of St Kilda, and the bright reflection of Tir na nOg, the Land of Youth, glimmering for ever just beyond the western horizon.

North Uist landscape: Loch Obasaraigh (main picture), Eigneig Bheag (top left), Flodaigh Mòr (top right), Ronay (below left) and Grimsay (below right)

N 57°32'23.9" W 7°11'18.5" Grid Ref: NF897618 Map Ref: 10 G9

These remarkable views of the Isle of North Uist, halfway up the long chain of the Western Isles, encapsulate the harsh volcanic look of the archipelago, founded on the oldest rocks in Britain. Lewisian gneiss three thousand million years old scabs a landscape of dark indigo lochs, dun bogs and ragged shores with scanty grazing.

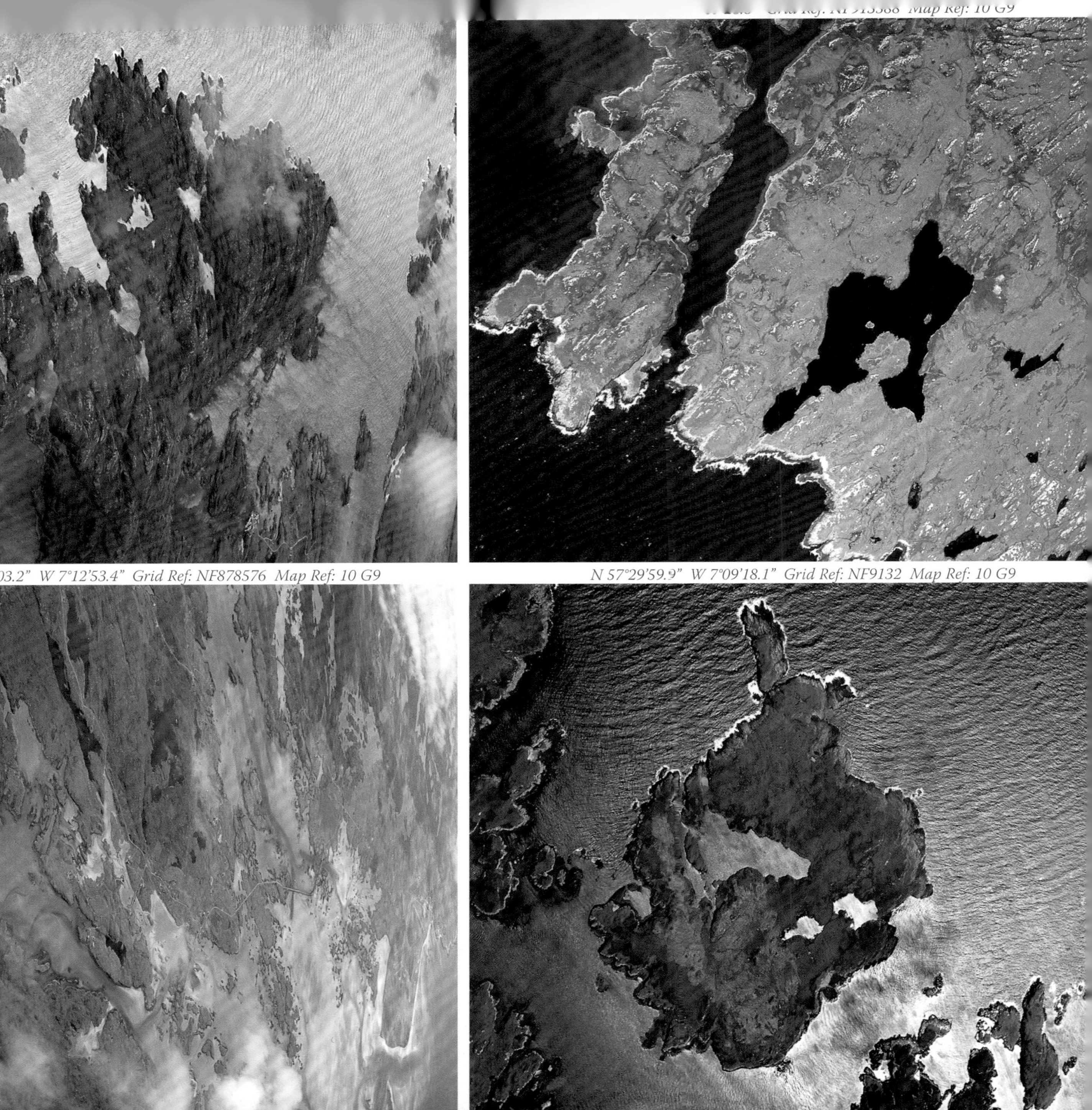

N 57°30'03.2" W 7°12'53.4" Grid Ref: NF878576 Map Ref: 10 G9

N 57°29'59.9" W 7°09'18.1" Grid Ref: NF9132 Map Ref: 10 G9

Vallay Strand (Tràigh Bhalaigh), North Uist *N 57°39'27.4" W 7°22'59.9" Grid Ref: NF791758 Map Ref: 10 F8*

The peerless white sand beach and turquoise shallows of Tràigh Bhalaigh, Vallay Strand, turn the other face of the Western Isles to the light. This beautiful Mediterranean aspect of the isles, mainly along the archipelago's west coasts, lasts just as long as it takes to shed the clothes and dip a toe in the freezing cold sea.

Berneray bridge *N 57°42'00.7" W 7°11'10.8" Grid Ref: NF912796 Map Ref: 10 F8*

The road bridge connecting the Isle of Berneray with the northern tip of North Uist was opened in 1999, putting the former ferry out of business but causing no real upheaval to the lives of the 136 islanders. There's much greater unease over the planned continuation of the causeways from Berneray to Harris, which would complete a 140-mile road link from Eriskay northwards to Lewis. Many Berneray islanders fear the coming of heavy lorries, pollution and road-related development.

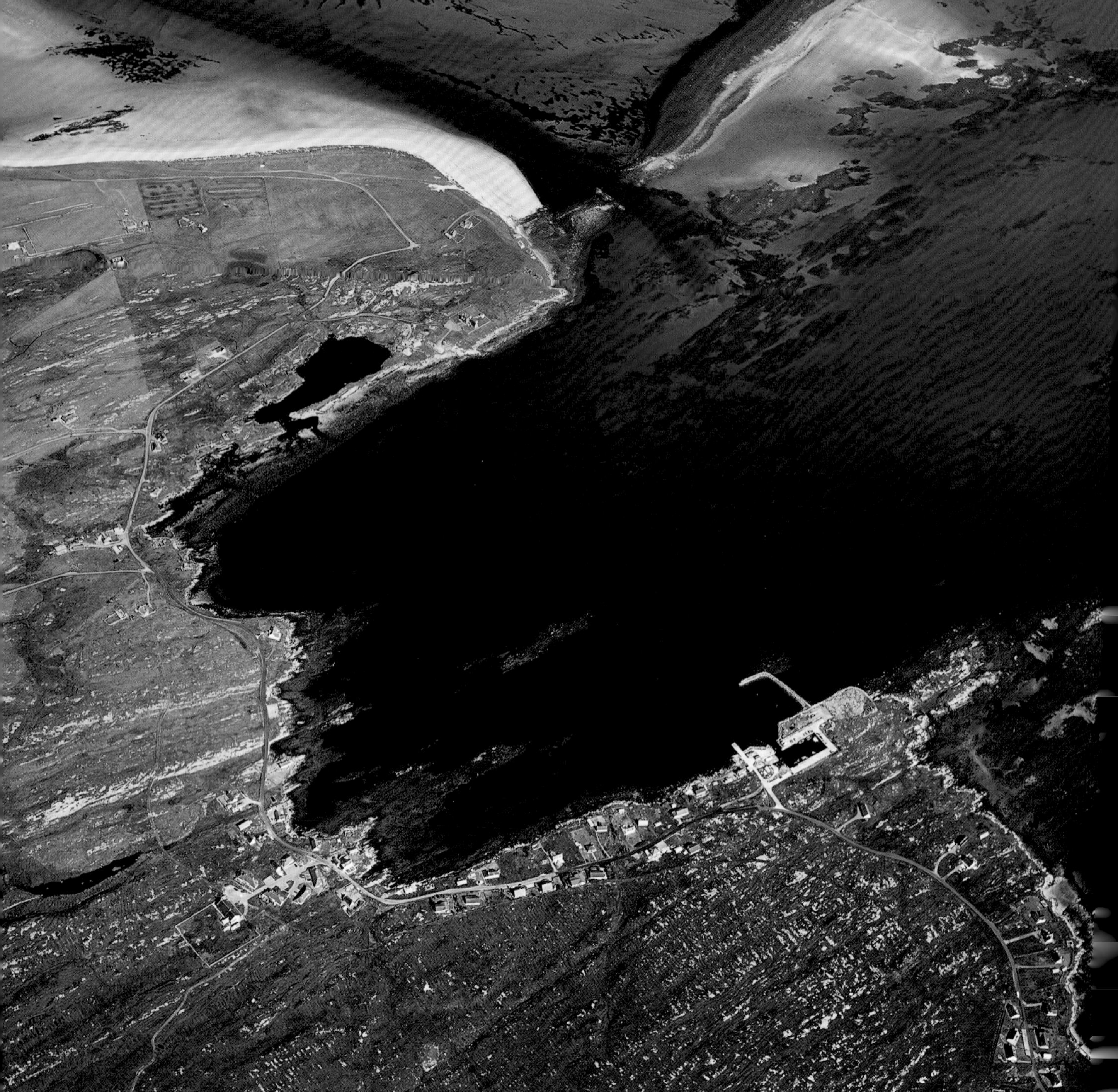

Loch a Bhàigh, Berneray *N 57°43'03.1" W 7°09'51.4" Grid Ref: NF926815 Map Ref: 10 G8*

Both facets of the Western Isles are shown in this view of Loch a Bhàigh, Bays Loch, on the south-east coast of Berneray: the hardness of the gneiss rock, its grain all running in parallel with the south-easterly set of the bay, and the soft beauty of the sands beyond as they lie sheltered by the out-thrust skerry of Bhaiteam.

Boreray *N 57°42'40.9" W 7°17'18.3" Grid Ref: NF852814 Map Ref: 10 G7*

Sited a couple of miles west of Berneray, the uninhabited Isle of Boreray lies shaped like a miniature Autralia, with the big water sheet of Loch Mòr at its heart. The small but perfectly formed white shell-sand beach of Tràigh na Lùibe, 'strand of the herbs', faces east towards the bigger island in a wonderful sheltered location.

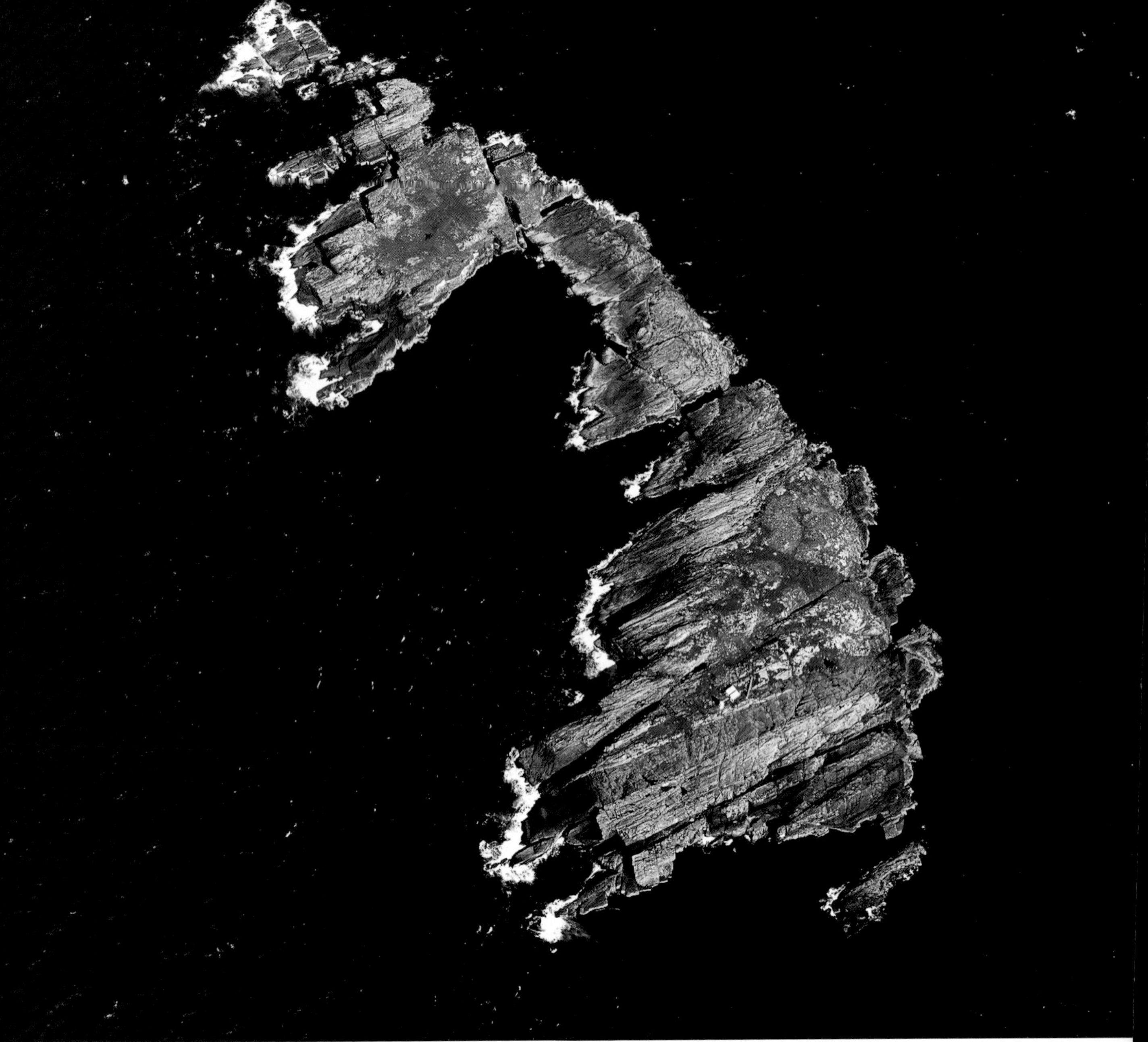

Haskeir *N 57°42'00.0" W 7°40'51.0" Grid Ref: NF617820 Map Ref: 10 D7*

The craggy islet of Haskeir – 'deep sea skerry' to the Norsemen who named it and may have used it as a seasonal fishing station – lies 8 miles out from the north-west corner of North Uist. Bare of most vegetation but sea plantain and sea pinks, the cliffs of ancient gneiss, hollowed with wave-worn arches, rise sharply to over 120 feet. There's an ancient burial site, and a shabby fishermen's bothy – what a remarkable night's resting place that would make.

Haskeir Eagach *N 57°41'00.9" W 7°42'57.0" Grid Ref: NF595803 Map Ref: 10 D7*

The 'notched skerry of the deep seas', a miniature archipelago standing a long mile south-west of Haskeir, is well named. It was once a coherent block of gneiss, but the wave and weather erosion of aeons has cut it apart into five great rock stacks around which the sea booms and hisses, pursuing its unceasing task of smoothing them away.

Hirta, St Kilda *N 57°48'53.1" W 8°34'48.6" Grid Ref: NF095996 Map Ref: 10 A6*

The compact and soaring archipelago of St Kilda, out in the Atlantic forty miles west of the Western Isles, is the great romantic outpost. Green and hilly Hirta, the chief island, can sometimes be glimpsed in fine weather from mountain tops in the Western Isles. There is a heroic human history to this lonely western bastion in the sea (see right). Deserted by its native population in 1930, it is now administered as a nature reserve and a UNESCO World Heritage Site jointly by the National Trust for Scotland, Scottish Natural Heritage and the MoD, who maintain a radar site here.

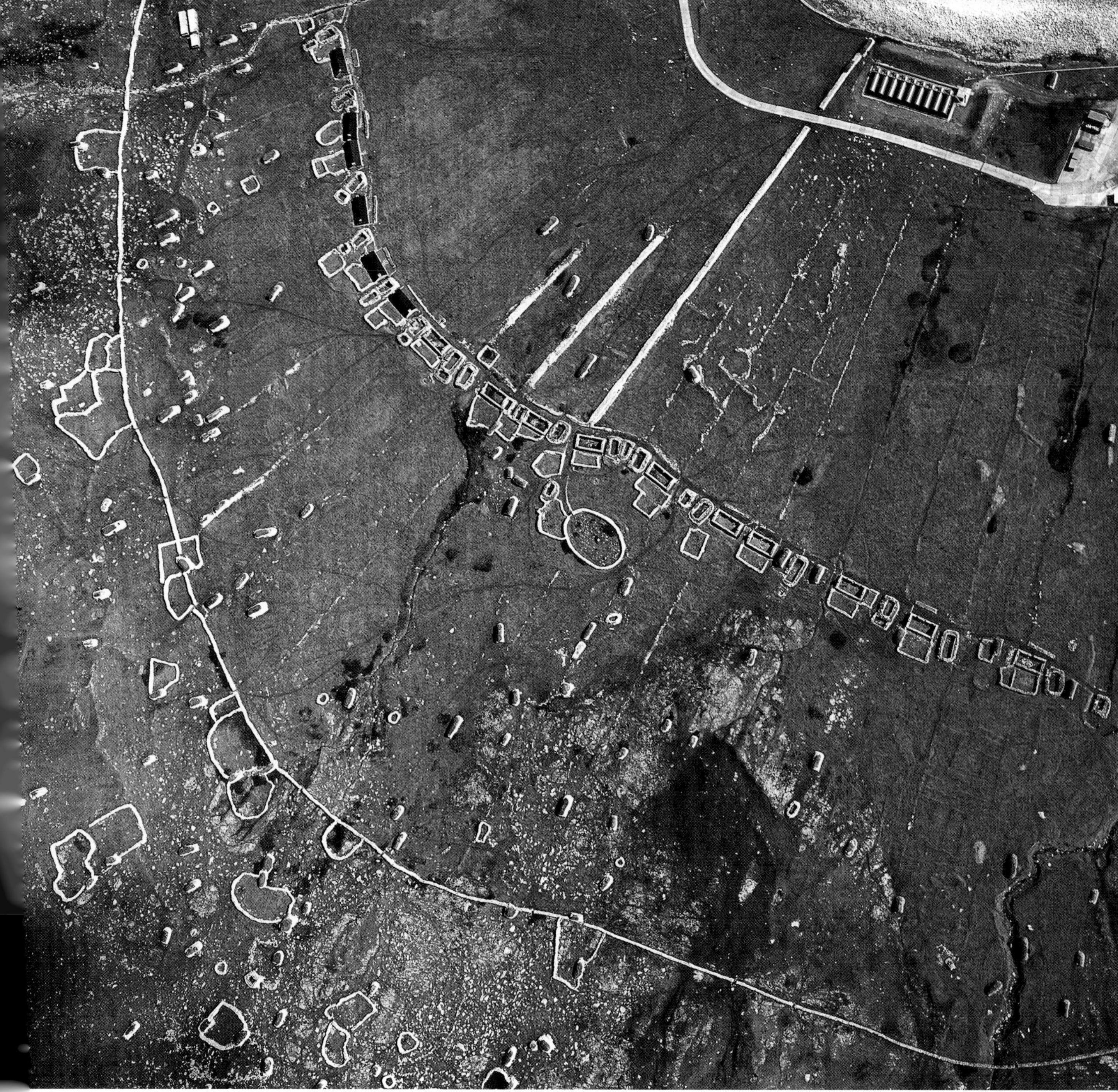

St Kilda village, Hirta *N 57°48'42.2" W 8°34'06.8" Grid Ref: NF102992 Map Ref: 10 A6*

The village houses of St Kilda, straggling out in a long ragged line behind the curve of the bay, were abandoned in 1930 by the St Kildans – some willingly, looking forward to a life 'ashore' in the Western Isles with fewer hardships than the tough, isolated existence they had clung onto, others with sorrow and heartache. Their evacuation had been necessitated by the withdrawal of the government grant that paid for their resident nurse and post office services. The roofless shells of their houses, maintained by the NTS and volunteers, bear poignant testimony to their vanished presences.

Boreray, St Kilda (left)

N 57°52'07.0" W 8°29'33.1"
Grid Ref: NA153051 Map Ref: 10 B6

Northern gannets swirl in a dense cloud about the pointed head of Stac Lee, a tremendous 564-ft rock stack that rises 4 miles north-east of Hirta. Behind Stac Lee slants the big green bulk of Boreray. Harvesting gannets here was one of the hazardous tasks of the St Kildans. Today, at over 120,000 birds, this northern gannet colony is the largest in the world. But climate change is forcing the cold-water fish on which the gannets feed further and further north, necessitating longer flights for the Boreray birds and longer periods away from their vulnerable nestlings. The future of the colony looks in the balance.

Rodel, South Harris

N 57°44'19.0" W 6°57'44.1"
Grid Ref: NG048829 Map Ref: 10 H7

The tiny hamlet of Rodel lies only a mile from Renish Point, the southernmost tip of the Isle of Harris. Sheltered by the rocky jaws of a very narrow inlet, the natural harbour makes a calm, safe anchorage for yachts these days. All is serene, quiet and timeless. Only the impressive bulk of St Clement's Church with its beautiful black granite knight-effigy tombs hints at Rodel's past glories as capital of the island.

Leverburgh, South Harris

N 57°46'13.0" W 7°01'32.7"
Grid Ref: NG013867 Map Ref: 10 H7

After Lord Leverhulme of Sunlight Soap fame bought the estate of South Harris in 1919, the tiny fishing town of The Obbe (in Gaelic, An t-Ob) underwent a transformation. Rechristened Leverburgh in honour of its benefactor, it was to become a thriving and prosperous centre for landing and processing fish. But when Lord Leverhulme died in 1925, the scheme fell apart. The remnants of the great sturdy piers, the docks and quays this practical philanthropist laid out still lie along the coast, poignant reminders of a dream that cost half a million pounds to put into practice and still came to nothing.

Stockinish Island

N 57°48'27.6" W 6°49'12.7"
Grid Ref: NG138900 Map Ref: 10 I7

On the edge of the Minch in south-east Harris, the uninhabited island of Stockinish fills the mouth of Loch Stockinish. Threaded by the famed Golden Road (some say because the roadside lochs shine gold, others because the looping track was so expensive to build), this part of Harris is tremendously rugged. At the heart of Stockinish island lies Loch an t-Saile, the Briny Loch, dammed in times past as a fish trap, used these days for rearing young lobsters.

Losgaintir and Sheileboist, South Harris (right)

N 57°52'29.9" W 6°56'52.6"
Grid Ref: NG068980 Map Ref: 10 H6

A stunning view of contrasting landforms – the glistening, ancient granite of the hills, knobbed and polished by weather; hard-won cultivated grazing around their feet; white sands of shell and quartz grains, ribboned through by freshwater streamlets reaching the sea between the dunes of Sheileboist and Losgaintir (Luskentyre).

Tarbert, Harris

N 57°53'55.9" W 6°48'20.6"
Grid Ref: NB154001 Map Ref: 10 I6

The Gaelic word *tearbeart* signifies an isthmus or crossing place. At Tarbert, the diminutive 'capital city' of the Isle of Harris, only the few hundred yards of low-lying ground that connect the two halves of the island prevent South Harris from being an island in its own right. All north-south land traffic goes through Tarbert, and in former times cargo would be transferred the short distance overland to cut out a 50-mile journey round the foot of Harris.

Scalpay *N 57°52'27.2" W 6°42'00.5" Grid Ref: NG214969 Map Ref: 10 I6*

Clustered around the pier of North Harbour are the houses where most of the 400 inhabitants of Scalpay live. It would be hard to find a more sheltered anchorage than North Harbour, tucked tightly into East Loch Tarbert and facing directly away from the open sea of the Minch. Early in the 20th century herring boats in their hundreds would take refuge from wild weather here.

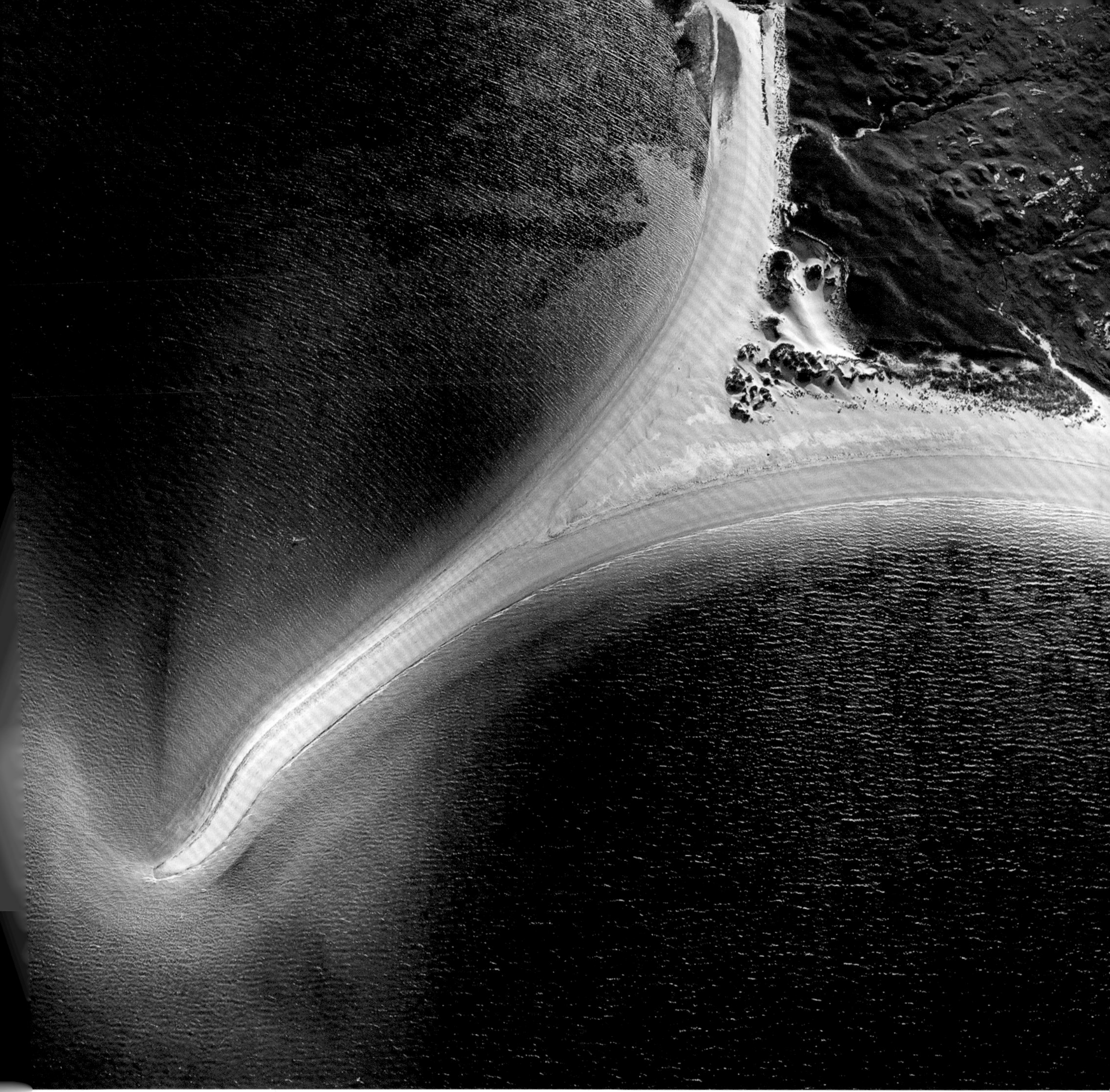

Corran Rà, Taransay *N 57°53'40.6" W 6°59'24.4" Grid Ref: NB044004 Map Ref: 10 H6*

Lying north-west of the South Harris coast, the uninhabited island of Taransay pokes its bird's-beak sandspit of Corran Rà out east into the Sound of Taransay. In 2000 the island became the temporary home of 36 men, women and children, 'stranded' here by BBC TV to be the subjects of the reality TV documentary Castaway 2000. Could they manufacture a new, utopian society for the new millennium? In the event, experiences varied: some adored the hard work and freedom, others crumpled and had to be repatriated.

Mangersta Sands, Lewis *N 58°09'53.4" W 7°05'24.5" Grid Ref: NB008308 Map Ref: 10 H4*

Everybody's dream of a pristine seaside is satisfied by Mangersta Sands, facing into the Atlantic on the westernmost coast of the Isle of Lewis. Mangersta catches tremendous surfing rollers, but its tide rips are strong and the sea can be ferociously unpredictable. It's exceedingly cold for most of the year, too. But with a good wetsuit and an eye on the tides, you can enjoy a heavenly swim with the seals here.

Great Bernera, Lewis *N 58°13'22.2" W 6°47'55.1" Grid Ref: NB184360 Map Ref: 10 I4*

The harsh environment in which the 230 islanders of Great Bernera live and make a livelihood is well demonstrated in this shot of the working jetty on Dubh Thòb, the Black Bay, with the sour granite land rising behind, striped with old abandoned cultivation ridges and indented with the dark waters of Loch Gobhlach.

Callanish Stone Circle, Lewis *N 58°11'51.5" W 6°44'41.5" Grid Ref: NB213330 Map Ref: 10 I3*

Whatever the truth about the origins of Callanish Stone Circle – were the Stones erected as an astronomical observatory, or a temple of sun worship, or for other unfathomable purposes? – their power and presence in the ancient landscape of western Lewis still resonate as clearly as when they were first set up in their complex, offset cross shape some 5,000 years ago.

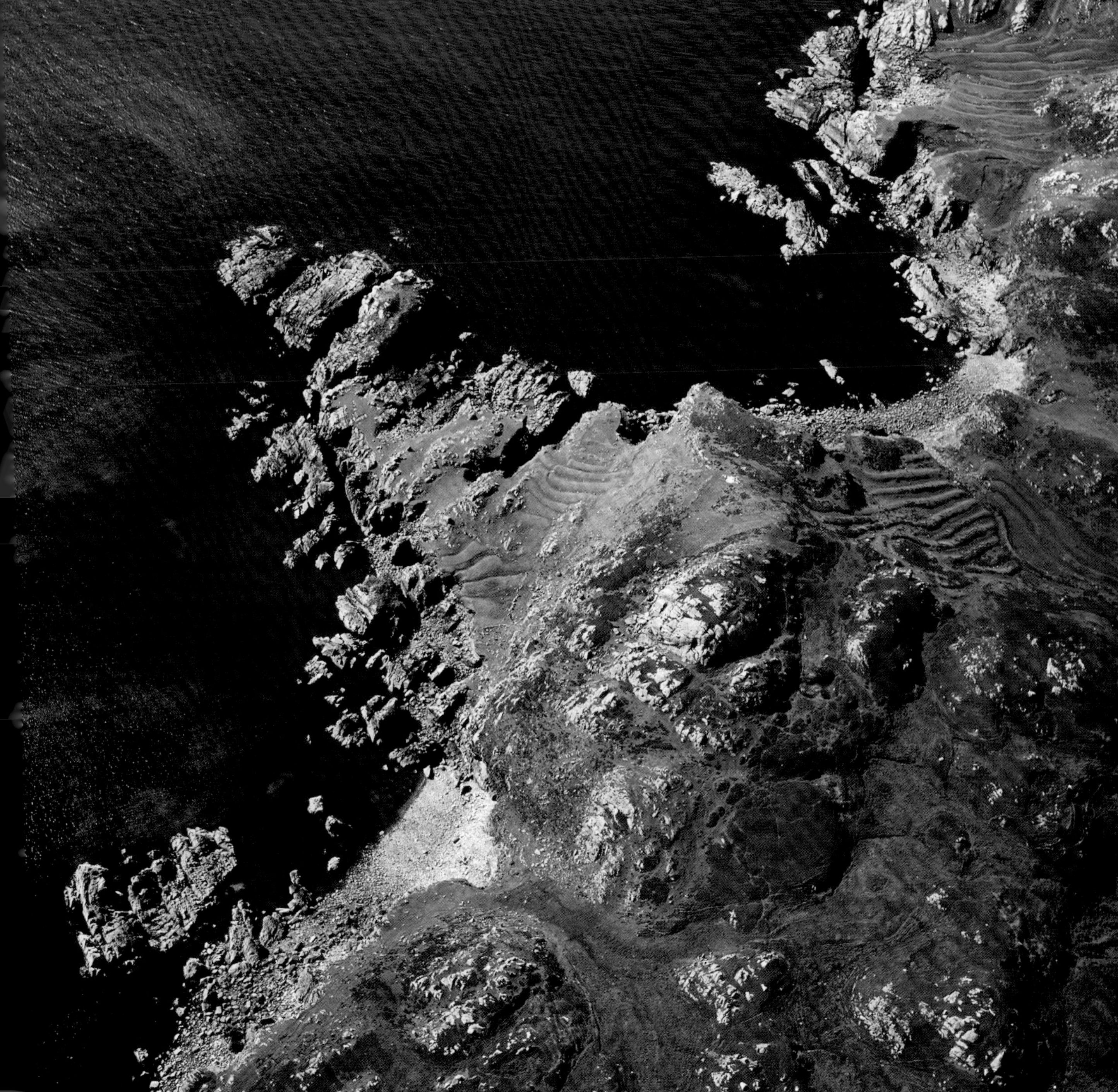

Spade cultivation ridges near Loch Chàrlabhaigh, Lewis *N 58°15'55.7" W 6°48'46.4" Grid Ref: NB179408 Map Ref: 10 I3*

South of Loch Chàrlabhaigh (Carloway), the ragged coast of west Lewis splits into a thousand tiny bays. Seamed into the ground here, like wrinkles in a worried brow, you'll find the cultivation ridges in which, in hungrier times, the people grew their oats and potatoes. Mounded by back-breaking spadework, fertilised with seaweed, shell-sand, soot-smoked thatch, animal dung and human excrement, these indelible marks on the face of the land represent hard times in a hard place.

Gearrannan Blackhouse Village, Lewis *N 58°17'47.0" W 6°47'33.6" Grid Ref: NB193442 Map Ref: 10 I3*

The old blackhouses in Garenin village near Carloway in west Lewis have been converted into holiday homes by Uras nan Gearrannan, the Garenin Trust. Painstakingly restored and refurbished, the dwellings of Garenin Blackhouse Village (Baile Tughaidh Gearrannan) give visitors an idea of the traditional old-fashioned Lewis house, built with double-thickness walls of untreated stone. When a mainland style of house – single-thickness walls, mortared with lime – was introduced to the Western Isles in the mid 19th century, it was referred to as *tigh geal*, 'white house'. By way of distinguishing between the two types, the old unmortared and smoke-darkened style of cottage was dubbed *tigh dubh* – 'black house'.

Stornoway, Lewis *N 58°12'09.3" W 6°22'54.0" Grid Ref: NB427321 Map Ref: 10 K4*

The name of Stornoway (Steòrnabhagh in Gaelic) derives from a Norse term meaning 'bay of good steering'. Stornoway's sheltered natural harbour is augmented these days with massive, hard-edged quays and breakwaters to accommodate the Lewis fishing fleet, some coasting and other commercial traffic, and the Caledonian MacBrayne ferry from Ullapool.

The Northern Isles
Orkney and Shetland

Like a pair of non-identical twins, the neighbouring archipelagos of Orkney and Shetland, while quite dissimilar in character and appearance, have more in common with each other than with either the Inner or Outer Hebridean island chains. Together Orkney and Shetland make up the Northern Isles, isolated in cold, stormy seas to the north of mainland Scotland. More Norse than Scottish by history and heritage, they are true North Sea islands.

Orkney is the younger of the twins, a roughly circular spatter of islands composed of Old Red sandstone perhaps 375 million years old, shot through with dykes of much older basalt. Shetland lies fifty miles further north, a ragged and elongated string of extremely ancient schist, serpentine and granite. The very different geological make-up of the two archipelagos has given them strongly contrasted characters. Orkney's sandstone has produced rounder and more elastic landforms, generating fruitful farming landscapes of small, productive arable fields and pastures, especially in the low-lying and sandy isles of Stronsay, Sanday and North Ronaldsay in the northern sector of the group. Orcadian sandstone splits readily and is easily worked; hence the abundance of remarkable Stone and Bronze Age tombs and monuments in these islands. Shetland's hard metamorphic volcanics and granites have inhibited production of soil; instead the islands lie jagged and lumpy, covered mostly in peat moorlands. The weather is always changeable, usually lively, and habitually stormy for the six winter months of the year. Nights are long, days short at the back end of the year. The arches and caves burrowed by waves in the hard granite of cliffs and rock stacks demonstrate the power of the winter sea up here. Farming in salt-scoured, almost treeless Shetland is difficult all year round, as is fishing. The ruins of abandoned settlements on smaller islands such as South Havra speak eloquently of the difficulties and hardships of everyday life in such circumstances.

The discovery of North Sea oil and its coming ashore at the Sullom Voe terminal from the 1970s onwards made a huge impact on what was a hard and threadbare economy, and on the insular, make-do-and-mend nature of Shetland society. Shrewd negotiations by the Shetland Islands Council secured royalties on the oil and rents on the terminal land for the benefit of the islands. Money rattled round the archipelago, building new hospitals and community halls,

The Northern Isles
Orkney and Shetland

and also fuelling a consumer boom that raised aspirations a long way from fishing and crofting. When the oil runs out, Shetlanders will have to look elsewhere for the means to support their new way of life.

There are notable similarities in the traditional characteristics of Orcadians and Shetlanders. These people are tough, hospitable, self-reliant and quick to sense and resent a patronising attitude on the part of outsiders. The Norse connection is strong. Picts and Vikings invaded and settled; the foundations of their houses are to be found at Jarlshof in southern Shetland and at the Broughs of Birsay and Broch of Gurness in Orkney, generally founded on yet older structures and themselves overlain with later buildings of Scottish influence. Shetland's native language, Norn, was closer to old Scandinavian tongues than anything Celtic or Scots. Many islanders have markedly Norse looks - short and dark-browed, or tall, fair and blue-eyed. Shetland's capital town of Lerwick, a huddle of low-built, grey stone houses, is only 200 miles from Bergen in Norway, the same distance as it is from Aberdeen.

The Northern Isles have never been insulated from the outside world. Situated so far north, they were always well placed to take part in whaling and fishing ventures, and in voyages of exploration. Whaler captains, fishing fleet owners and traders – notably the officials of the Hudson Bay Company in 19th-century Canada – looked to the Northern Isles for their work force, reckoning the islanders trustworthy and hard-working. The response of the islanders themselves to their harsh but magnificent native landscapes has been expressed in a remarkably lively and still vibrant culture of fiddle music, poetry and art.

It is in hearing the scurrying reels of Shetland or reading the poems of Orcadian George Mackay Brown that you get a sense of how these landscapes and people work together. Best of all is to visit Orkney in summer when the red sandstone glows and the white shell-sand beaches lie dazzlingly white under the northern sun. Keep Shetland for winter - a wind-battered walk along black cliffs in the island of Yell, a good-going session of tunes in the warmth of Lerwick's Lounge Bar, or the genial, fiery madness of the Up-Helly-Aa celebrations when a Viking longship is torched, and the Shetlanders use flame and whisky to put General Winter to flight once more.

Old Man of Hoy, Orkney

N 58°53'11.4"   W 3°25'52.5"
Grid Ref: HY176008 Map Ref: 12 B8

Rising off the west coast of the Isle of Hoy, the tremendous 450-ft rock stack of the Old Man of Hoy stands as guardian and sentinel of the Orkney Isles archipelago. Sea erosion has whittled the square-headed Old Man from his parent cliffs. Now he offers one of the most exhilarating rock-climbing challenges in the British Isles.

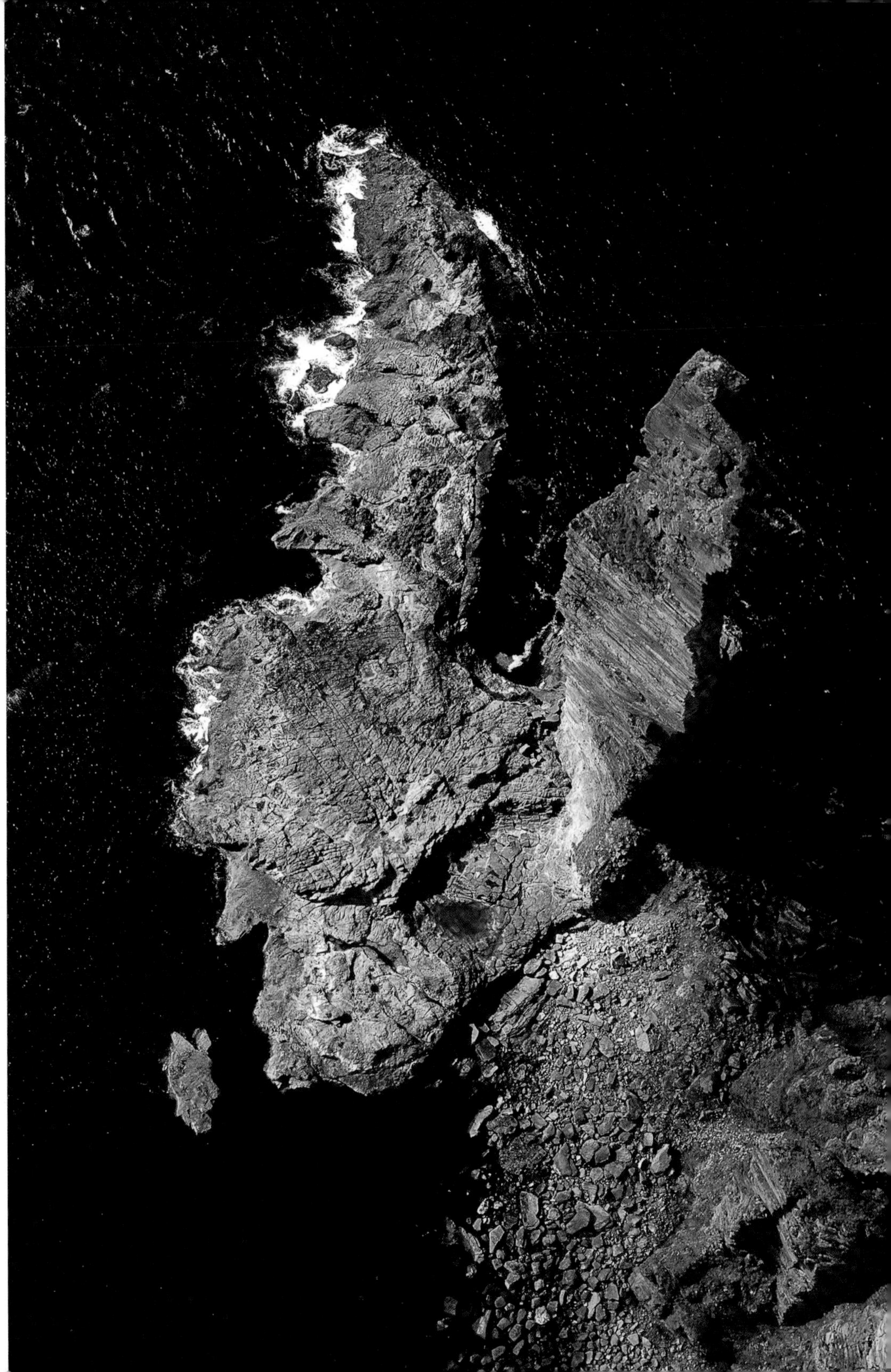

Churchill Barriers, Orkney *N 58°52'48.2" W 2°54'17.7" Grid Ref: ND479995 Map Ref: 12 D8*

Looking south along the line of islands that guards the eastern flank of Scapa Flow – Lamb Holm in the foreground, then leg-of-mutton Glims Holm, deeply-indented Burray and its big southerly neighbour South Ronaldsay. The causeways that connect them, dubbed the Churchill Barriers, were built to protect Scapa Flow, deep-water anchorage of the British Home Fleet, by Italian prisoners-of-war incarcerated in Camp 60 on Lamb Holm during the Second World War. The homesick PoWs built something else, too – a wonderful mock-Renaissance chapel, created from salvage and scrap, still beautifully maintained on its site near the northern causeway on Lamb Holm.

Brough of Deerness, Orkney *N 58°57'50.4" W 2°42'19.5" Grid Ref: HY595087 Map Ref: 12 E7*

Out at the eastern end of Orkney Mainland, the grassy-backed promontory of the Brough of Deerness was once joined by a rock bridge to the mainland. Long after the natural bridge collapsed, a Norse settlement was established on the headland, probably about a thousand years ago. Around the 10th-century chapel, lumps and bumps in the ground show the location of many former buildings and field walls. When two Norse houses were excavated in 2008, loom weights, spindle whorls and soapstone pots came to light. The motive for building a settlement in such a difficult and precarious location may have had more to do with the desire of a chief to show off his power and prestige than with any defensive reasons.

Kirkwall, Orkney

N 58°58'55.0" W 2°57'43.0"
Grid Ref: HY448109 Map Ref: 12 D7

On the north coast of Mainland, chief island of the Orkney archipelago, sits the 'capital' city of Kirkwall, its busy harbour defended by mighty breakwaters. Inland rises the magnificent red and yellow sandstone Cathedral of St Magnus, founded in 1137 by St Rognvald and his uncle Magnus. Oliver Cromwell's men, harrying the islands in 1651, used the cathedral's tall narrow nave as a stable and barracks. Neither they nor their versifiers cared for the islands:

'Henceforth, blue Orkney, bee thy poysnous name
Abhor'd, may none but witches use the same;
Hee that the nauseous name of Orkney heares
And spews not, sorrow fall his illbred eares.'

Stromness, Orkney

N 58°57'41.0" W 3°17'55.0"
Grid Ref: HY255090 Map Ref: 12 B7

South of the stout modern quays of Stromness, dozens of tiny jetties poke out into the sheltered waters of Hamna Voe from among the old stone houses along the waterfront. In the 18th and 19th centuries Stromness was an important base for Hudson Bay Company ships trading in North Canadian furs. Skippers of Hudson Bay vessels and of Davis Strait whalers preferred Stromness crews; they were reckoned cheaper than Englishmen and more sober than Irishmen. Stromness merchants grew fat on the profitable trade that came to their private jetties along Hamna Voe.

Ring of Brodgar, Orkney (right)

N 59°00'07.2" W 3°13'54.1"
Grid Ref: HY293134 Map Ref: 12 C7

A splendid view of the 4,500-year-old Ring of Brodgar on its narrow isthmus, with the waters of the Loch of Harray lapping along the adjacent road and the lead-grey sheet of the Loch of Stenness broadening beyond. The ring of 27 standing stones (originally there were 60) commands all eyes. Some call it the Circle of the Sun, but whether the thin blades of sharply-angled stone were erected as a solar calendar or in celebration of sun-worship remains pure conjecture.

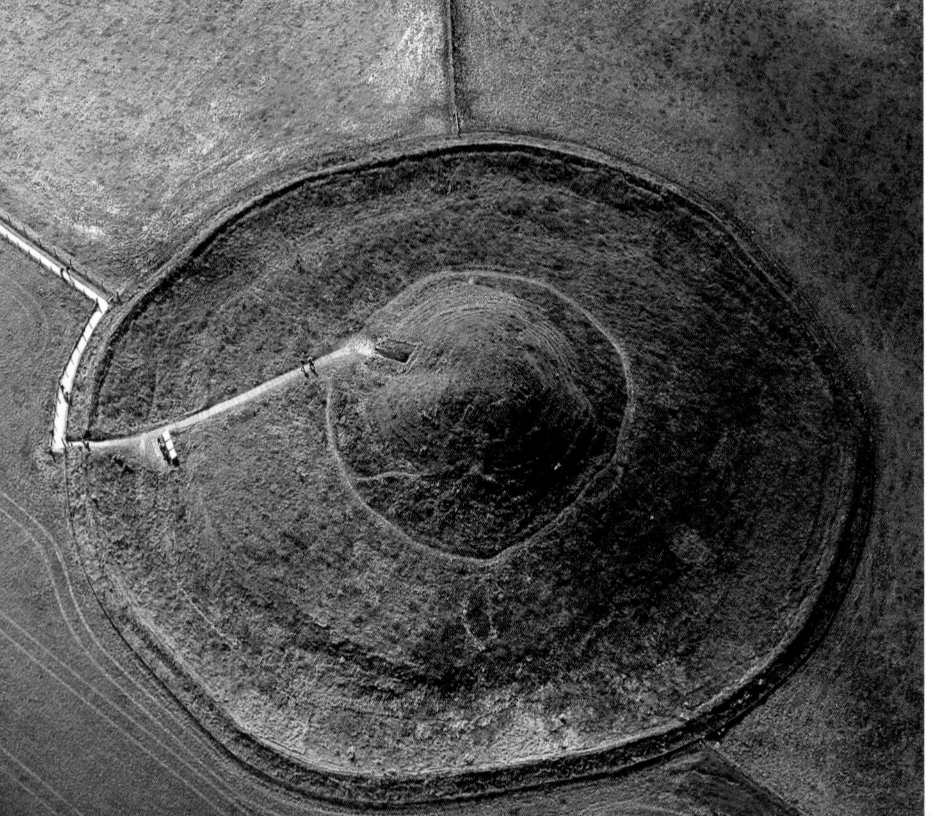

Barnhouse Neolithic Settlement, Orkney

N 58°59'38.8" W 3°11'57.3"
Grid Ref: HY312125 Map Ref: 12 C7

Sited on the shore of Loch Harray near Maes Howe (see below), Barnhouse Neolithic settlement was a primitive version of the later, more sophisticated development at Skara Brae (see below). Clearly seen at the centre of each circular house is a square-shaped hearth, outlined in thin kerb-stones. As the means of providing light and heat, and the centre of the family's story-telling and conversational circle, the central hearth was the focal point of Orcadian houses from Neolithic times onwards, right up until around 100 years ago when the fireplace within a chimney-breast replaced it.

Maes Howe, Orkney

N 58°59'48.4" W 3°11'23.9"
Grid Ref: HY317128 Map Ref: 12 C7

Humped in its field overlooking the Loch of Harray, the green hillock of Maes Howe guards its secret impassively. Once you have crouched down and wormed your way along the stone-lined passage into the heart of the mound, you find yourself in a tall chamber with compartments leading off it under a corbelled roof, all of cold, weighty, silent stone. This burial mound, the finest example of a passage grave in Europe, was already 4,000 years old when Viking warriors broke in during the Dark Ages, robbed what treasure had been left by previous raiders, and scratched the runic graffiti that we read on the stones today. – 'Thorni shagged while Helgi carved', 'Ingibiorh – she's hot!', and 'Tagged by Boss Rune-Scratcher.'

Skara Brae, Orkney (right)

N 59°02'56.4" W 3°20'35.4"
Grid Ref: HY230188 Map Ref: 12 B6

Sandstorms on the west coast of Mainland some 4,000 years ago made a miniature Pompeii out of the neolithic village at Skara Brae, burying it deep under sandhills. The little stone houses, their interiors complete with benches, cupboards and door frames, lay preserved until uncovered by fierce storms in 1850. Modern-day seekers after enlightenment and a sense of connection with the deep past erect stone circles on the beach below the site.

Brough of Birsay, Orkney *N 59°08'09.0" W 3°19'55.0" Grid Ref: HY239284 Map Ref: 12 B6*

This complicated and fascinating site lies on an islet out at Brough Head on the north-west shoulder of Mainland. The ruins of the settlement, occupied and developed from early Christian through Pictish to Norse times, face the main island across a tidal causeway. Here is a Norse-era church built in Romanesque style in the 11th century by Earl Thorfinn the Mighty, perched on the foundations of a much earlier Celtic church. Nearby lie the outlines of Norse longhouses, a sauna, and a large building that was probably the Earl's house. There's also a squared slab which carries very fine Pictish carvings of three noble warriors with spears and square shields, a splendid eagle and one of the long-snouted beasts peculiar to Pictish art.

Broch of Gurness, Orkney *N 59°07'18.8" W 3°05'13.7" Grid Ref: HY379266 Map Ref: 12 C6*

A delicate web of walls, remnant of a huddle of Pictish and Viking houses, hems in the round broch or defensive tower built in the 2nd century BC at the Broch of Gurness. Facing the Isle of Rousay over Eynhallow Sound, the settlement was well-placed for trade and communication by sea. The broch commanded the sea approaches, while three concentric arcs of ramparts looked landwards – a comprehensive system of defence against all comers.

Midhowe Broch, Rousay, Orkney

N 59°09'26.5" W 3°06'01.3"
Grid Ref: HY372306 Map Ref: 12 C5

Midhowe Broch rises on the western shore of the Isle of Rousay, a massive broch or cylindrical defensive tower some 2,000 years old whose drystone walls still stand up to 15 feet high. The walls are double-skinned, the outer and inner ones joined here and there by 'through' stones, with a stair ascending inside them to upper floors and the 'battlements'. The foundations of later buildings huddle round the broch – it must have been a reassuring presence on the bleak promontory, as well as a handy quarry for building stone.

Eynhallow monastery, Island of Eynhallow, Orkney

N 59°09'18.0" W 3°05'52.4"
Grid Ref: HY374303 Map Ref: 12 C6

The tiny island of Eynhallow (Eyin Helga, 'holy island', in the Norse), less than a mile long, lies off the south-east shore of the Isle of Rousay in narrow Eynhallow Sound. In 1851 the inhabitants were evacuated and the tightly clustered houses unroofed to combat a typhoid outbreak, and it was then that the peculiar shape of the largest building with its heavy buttresses was noticed. It turned out to be a 12th century church, which had been used as a dwelling for 300 years.

Westayre Loch and Beach, Sanday, Orkney (right)

N 59°17'10.0" W 2°29'04.0"
Grid Ref: HY725445 Map Ref: 12 F5

(see next page)

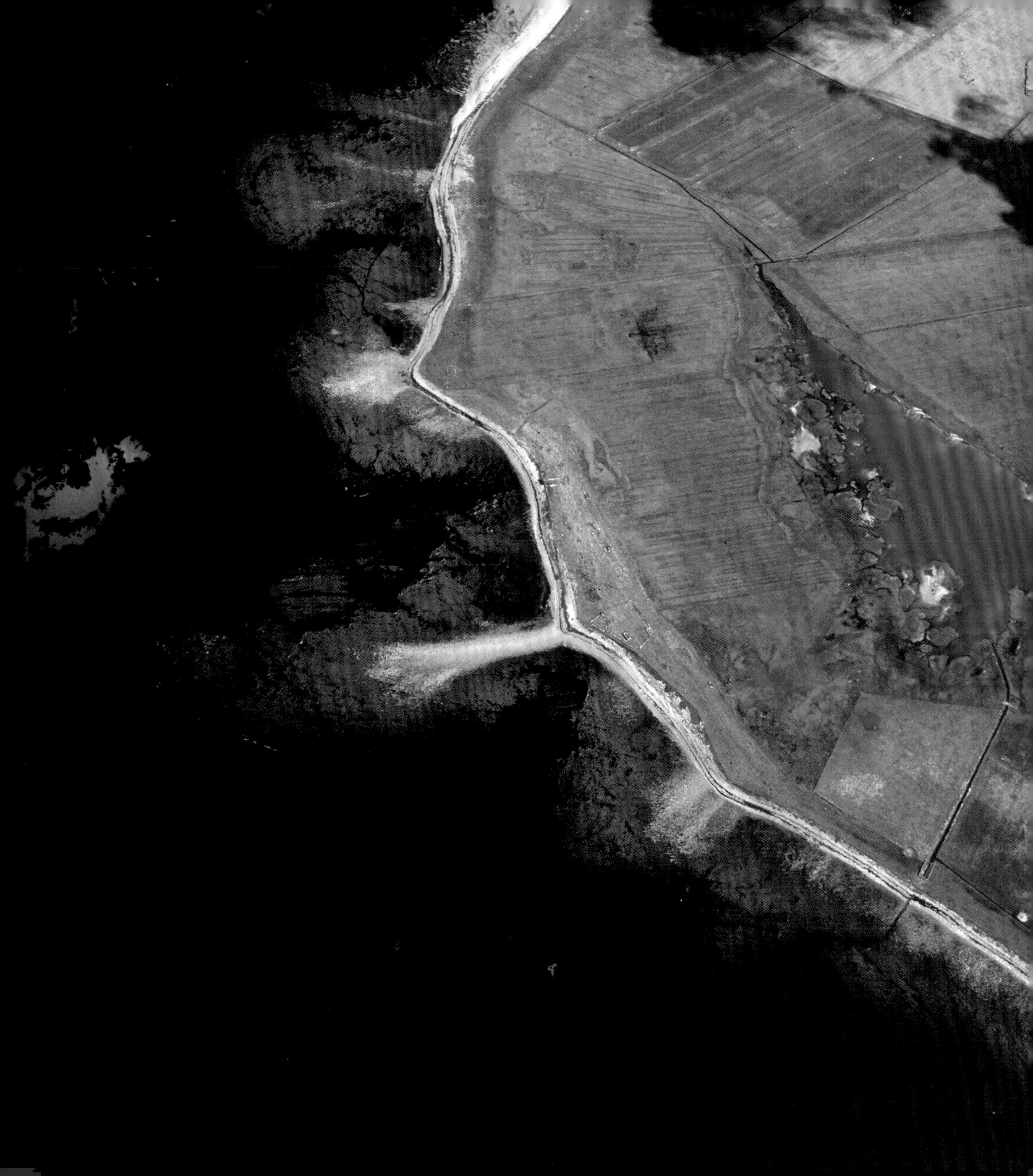

Sanday at Lama Ness (above), Tres Ness (right) and Westayre Loch (previous page), Orkney

N 59°14'18.0" W 2°31'22.0" Grid Ref: HY703392 Map Ref: 12 F5 (left) *N 59°16'34.0" W 2°33'19.0" Grid Ref: HY685434 Map Ref: 12 E5 (right)*

The Isle of Sanday lies sprawled between the North Sound and its own Sanday Sound in the northern arc of the Orkney archipelago. Flat, sandy, intensively farmed, the island is shaped like a joyfully cavorting sea dragon, a fish-tail splayed north-east, one spiky wing unfolded northwards, and the head with its half-open beak questing south-west. Sanday throws off slim peninsular legs to all quarters, each with its offshoot ness or headland – Lama Ness (**above**) and Tres Ness (**right**) are two especially striking examples. The interplay of turquoise sea, green land and white sand is mesmerising. The rocky tongues of Long Taing and the Taing of Tor Sker, near Westayre Loch on the lonely Bay of Sandquoy (**previous page**) are favourite hauling out and pupping sites for common seals. Altogether there is something marine, ethereal and strange about this ragged and beautiful island.

North Ronaldsay, Orkney *N 59°22'58.4" W 2°24'28.5" Grid Ref: HY769552 Map Ref: 12 F4*

On North Ronaldsay, the most northerly and remote of Orkney's inhabited isles, every square yard of good land is carefully farmed and husbanded within a protective dyke that keeps the sea out of the low-lying island. This view looks south over North Ronaldsay and on across Sanday into the heart of the archipelago.

Fair Isle, Shetland

N 59°31'54.9" W 1°37'49.9" Grid Ref: HZ210718 Map Ref: 12 H11

Fair Isle lies isolated in the sea some 25 miles north of Orkney, and the same distance south of its parent archipelago of the Shetland Isles. Three miles long, three miles broad, the island's high green interior runs in all directions to the edge of tremendously tall, rugged cliffs. The 70-odd human inhabitants are outnumbered at least 3000-1 by Fair Isle's resident seabirds and by passing birds that use the lonely island as a staging post on their epic migration flights.

Jarlshof, Shetland *N 59°52'08.7" W 1°17'26.5" Grid Ref: HU398095 Map Ref: 12 K11*

Near the southern tip of Shetland's chief island of Mainland lies Jarlshof - at first glance a hopelessly confused jumble of ruins, on better acquaintance one of Britain's most remarkable archaeological treasures. In this small site, occupied from the Stone Age up until the 17th century, lie piled in a rich chronological sandwich of human history the remnants of a Bronze Age blacksmith's workshop, an Iron Age broch or defensive tower and a cylindrical wheelhouse, round huts built by Picts, Norse longhouses, medieval farmhouses and a 17th-century manor house.

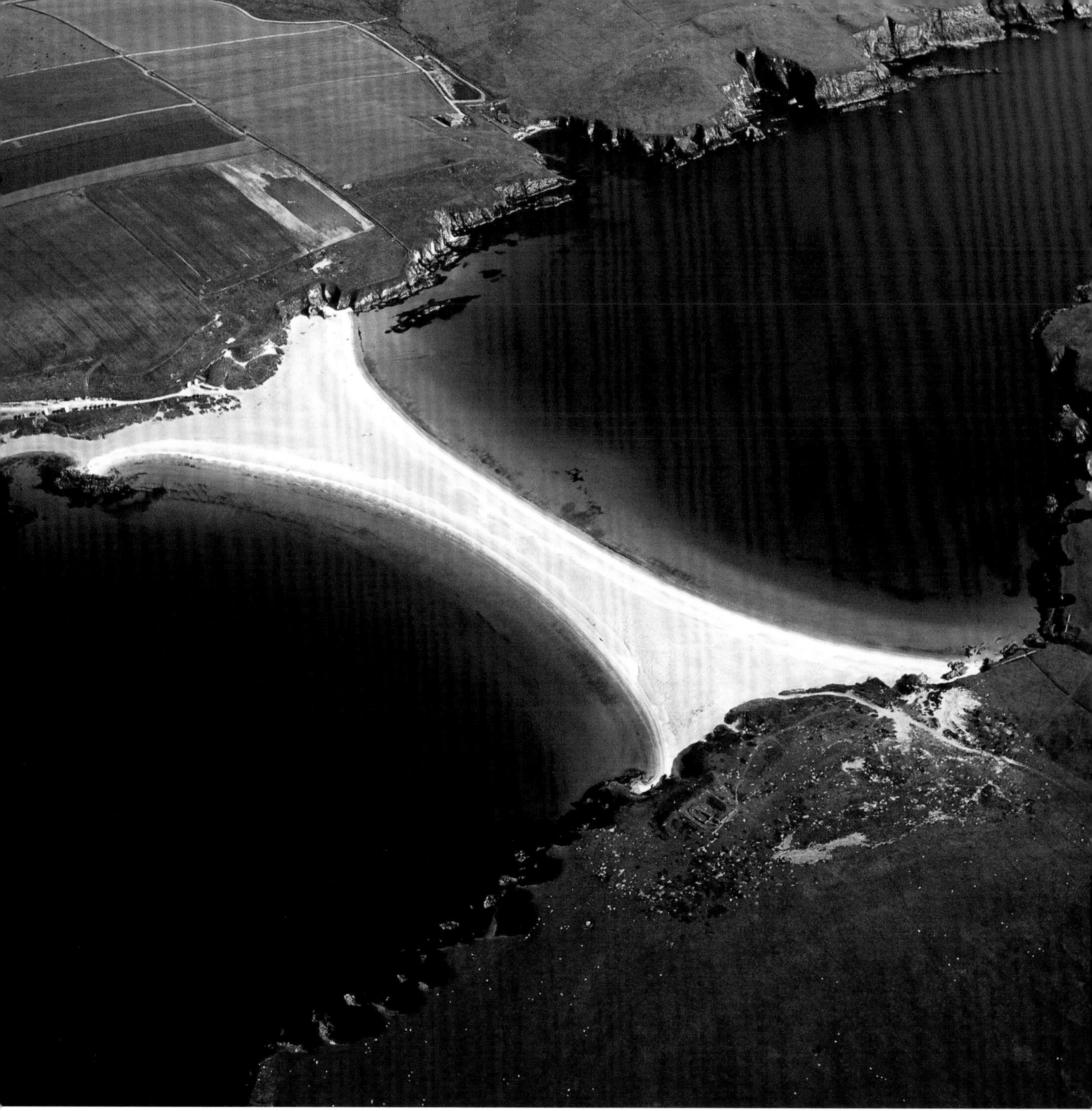

St Ninian's Isle tombolo, Shetland *N 59°58'13.5" W 1°20'14.1" Grid Ref: HU371208 Map Ref: 12 J10*

Shetlanders know a tombolo as an 'ayre' – but whatever the terminology, these scimitar-shaped isthmuses that bridge the gap between land masses are strange entities. The 550-yard-long tombolo of pure white shell sand linking the west coast of Shetland Mainland with the sacred site of St Ninian's Isle is the largest of its type in Britain, a dynamic creation of the waves that push onto both its shores simultaneously from opposite directions. Foundations of shingle keep the tombolo stable, though its shape changes according to the set of the tide and the force of the weather.

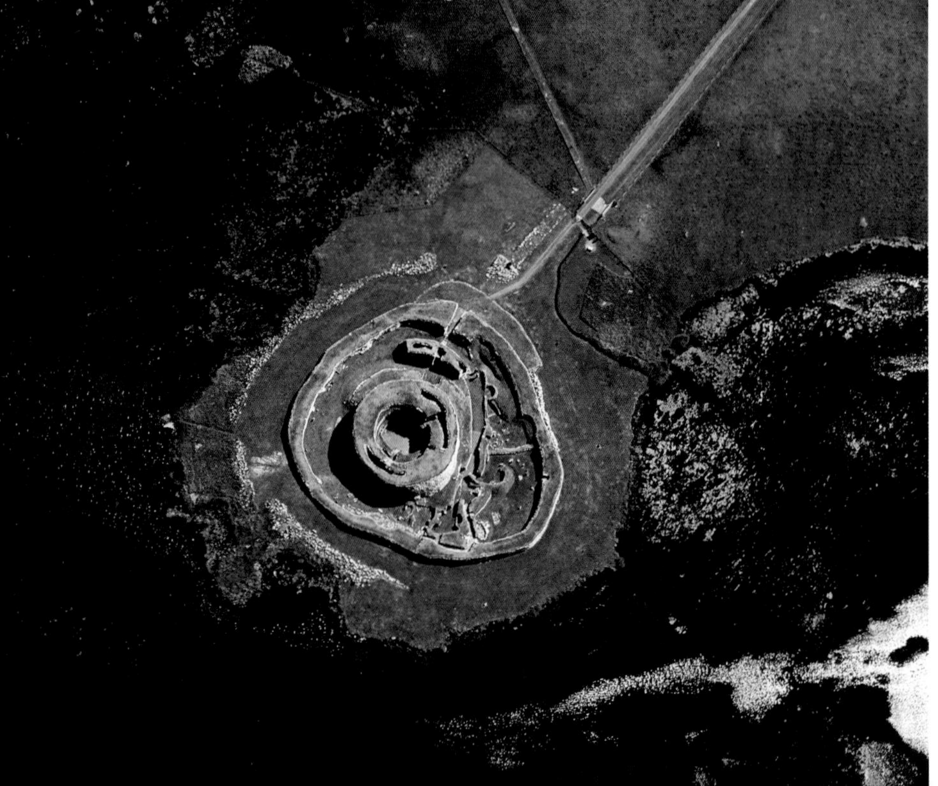

Broch of Mousa, Shetland

N 59°59'42.9" W 1°10'55.6"
Grid Ref: HU457236 Map Ref: 12 K10

How has Mousa Broch managed to remain virtually whole after 2,000 years of existence? Probably because this 45-ft-high, double-walled defensive tower stands in a remote location on the small, and now deserted, isle of Mousa off the east coast of Shetland Mainland. Visitors by boat can climb the ancient stairway and follow the walkway round the top, imagining the shipwreck which, the Norse sagas say, left the runaway lovers Bjørn Brynjulfsson and Thora Roaldsdottir to spend the winter here, snug in the broch and in each other's arms. Other tales tell of how Earl Erlend of Ungi abducted, or perhaps eloped with, beautiful Margaret, widow of the Earl of Atholl, and brought her to Mousa Broch. Margaret's son Harald Maddadarson, Earl of Orkney, tracked them down, but could not force his way inside the stout stone walls of the broch. Harald retreated, and the love-birds resumed their nesting.

South Havra, Shetland (right)

N 60°01'24.0" W 1°21'12.5"
Grid Ref: HU361267 Map Ref: 12 J9

The diminutive isle of South Havra lies at the southern end of Clift Sound, off the south-west coast of Shetland Mainland. Tiny though it is, the island supported a population for several centuries, until the remaining eight families finally abandoned it in 1923. It was a hard life on windy, cliff-encircled South Havra, an island with so little natural fuel in the form of peat that supplies had to be boated over from Mainland. On the highest point of South Havra stands a ruined tower, remnant of a windmill (unique in Shetland) which the islanders built themselves for lack of running water to drive a mill wheel.

Clickimin Broch, Shetland

N 60°08'56.7" W 1°09'55.8"
Grid Ref: HU464408 Map Ref: 12 K9

The Iron Age broch or stone-built defensive tower that occupies a promontory in the Loch of Clickimin on the south-west outskirts of Lerwick is a very fine specimen measuring 20 yard across, its circular walls 18 feet thick and still standing more than twice man height. The broch was founded around 100 BC on a site that had already been occupied by a farmstead for a thousand years, and continued to be used until its abandonment some time after AD 500.

Lerwick, Shetland *N 60°09'01.4" W 1°08'13.8" Grid Ref: HU480410 Map Ref: 12 K8*

Over on the east coast of Mainland, the grey stone houses of Shetland's 'capital' town of Lerwick huddle together in a tight mass as if seeking mutual shelter from the wild North Sea weather. Lerwick grew from a garrison settlement established during the Dutch wars of the 17th century into a prosperous fishing, whaling and trading centre. The town lies only 200 miles from Bergen in Norway, the same distance it does from Aberdeen, and the atmosphere is far more Scandinavian than Scottish.

Salmon farm, Shetland *N 60°13'08.3" W 1°11'22.0" Grid Ref: HU450486 Map Ref: 12 K8*

Salmon farming has been big business in Shetland since the 1980s, with overheads comparatively modest and generous grants available. Automated feeding and cleaning have replaced manual methods in the big operations, but problems of disease and of the quality of the fish on the table, allied to concerns about farmed salmon diseases being passed on to wild salmon, have rocked confidence in the industry.

Loch of Aithsness, Shetland *N 60°18'29.2" W 1°24'23.7" Grid Ref: HU329584 Map Ref: 12 J7*

The northern part of Shetland Mainland is a wilderness of dark bog and peaty loch, interspersed with the grazing fields of farms. This view looks west over the Loch of Aithsness and beyond it the Loch of Clousta, across a gleam of Brindister Voe to the far-off hump of Sandness Hill overlooking the coast. On the sea horizon some twenty miles away rises the crouched back of the Isle of Foula, home to Shetland's most isolated community.

Muckle Roe, Shetland *N 60°22'30.1" W 1°27'46.9" Grid Ref: HU298658 Map Ref: 12 J7*

The coastline of the west side of Muckle Roe island, facing the open Atlantic, shows very clearly the power of the sea to cut into solid granite. From bottom to top of the photograph: the curled promontory of Swabi Stack with its wave-hollowed arches, and the two-fingered headland of Fiska Ness cradling the narrow white beach of North Ham; the bulge of West Ness with the islet of Tame Holm off its nose, then the sheltered arc of South Ham; beyond these, the leaf-shaped islet of Qui Ness, the big lump of Strom Ness, and on its far side at the top of the picture the two supplementary 'leaves' of Kneefield Ness and Moo Ness.

Sullom Voe, Shetland *N 60°27'42.7" W 1°17'37.9" Grid Ref: HU389755 Map Ref: 12 J6*

Far from the heavily industrialised, urban surroundings associated with the oil industry, Shetland's Sullom Voe terminal lies in a beautiful voe or fjord in the remote district of north Mainland. The opening of the Brent oilfield in the 1970s brought a greedy scramble for land around the voe by outside speculators with an eye to future rents. But the governing body of Shetland, the Shetland Islands Council, stepped in quickly to buy up the land on behalf of the community. Revenues so far are estimated to amount to well over £500 million, bringing enormous benefit and profound social change to the archipelago.

The Neap and The Runk, Shetland *N 60°28'56.4" W 1°32'19.7" Grid Ref: HU254777 Map Ref: 12 I6*

Although some 200 miles of sea separate the mouth of the Great Glen at Inverness and the ragged archipelago of Shetland far to the north-east, the gigantic fault that produced the Great Glen runs this far and further under the North Atlantic. Upheavals along the line of the fault have contorted, torn, squeezed and jumbled the geology of Shetland – as evinced here at The Neap, a cliff looking south-west into the bay of Brae Wick whose old red sandstone, protruding among granite and volcanic rocks, has been sculpted by waves and weather into The Runk and other spectacular arches and sea stacks.

Dore Holm, Esha Ness, Shetland *N 60°28'10.1" W 1°36'09.2" Grid Ref: HU220762 Map Ref: 12 I6*

Standing south of the rugged Stenness headland of southern Esha Ness, the wave-cut arch of Dore Holm dramatically demonstrates how the force of big winter waves, allied to the sea's unceasing erosive action, can cut through basalt. The height and power of storm waves in Shetland waters have been steadily increasing for the past few decades, perhaps a consequence of general warming of the seas.

Esha Ness, Shetland *N 60°29'21.0" W 1°37'36.0" Grid Ref: HU206784 Map Ref: 12 I6*

Looking over the bleak landscape of westernmost Esha Ness, and on across St Magnus Bay towards the distant hills of Papa Stour and Sandness. Esha Ness, a bulbous promontory out at the north-west corner of Mainland, offers superb rough walking and fly fishing for brown trout – the Loch of Framgord, seen here close to the southern lip of the mighty crack of Calder's Geo, is a famous loch for 'da troots'.

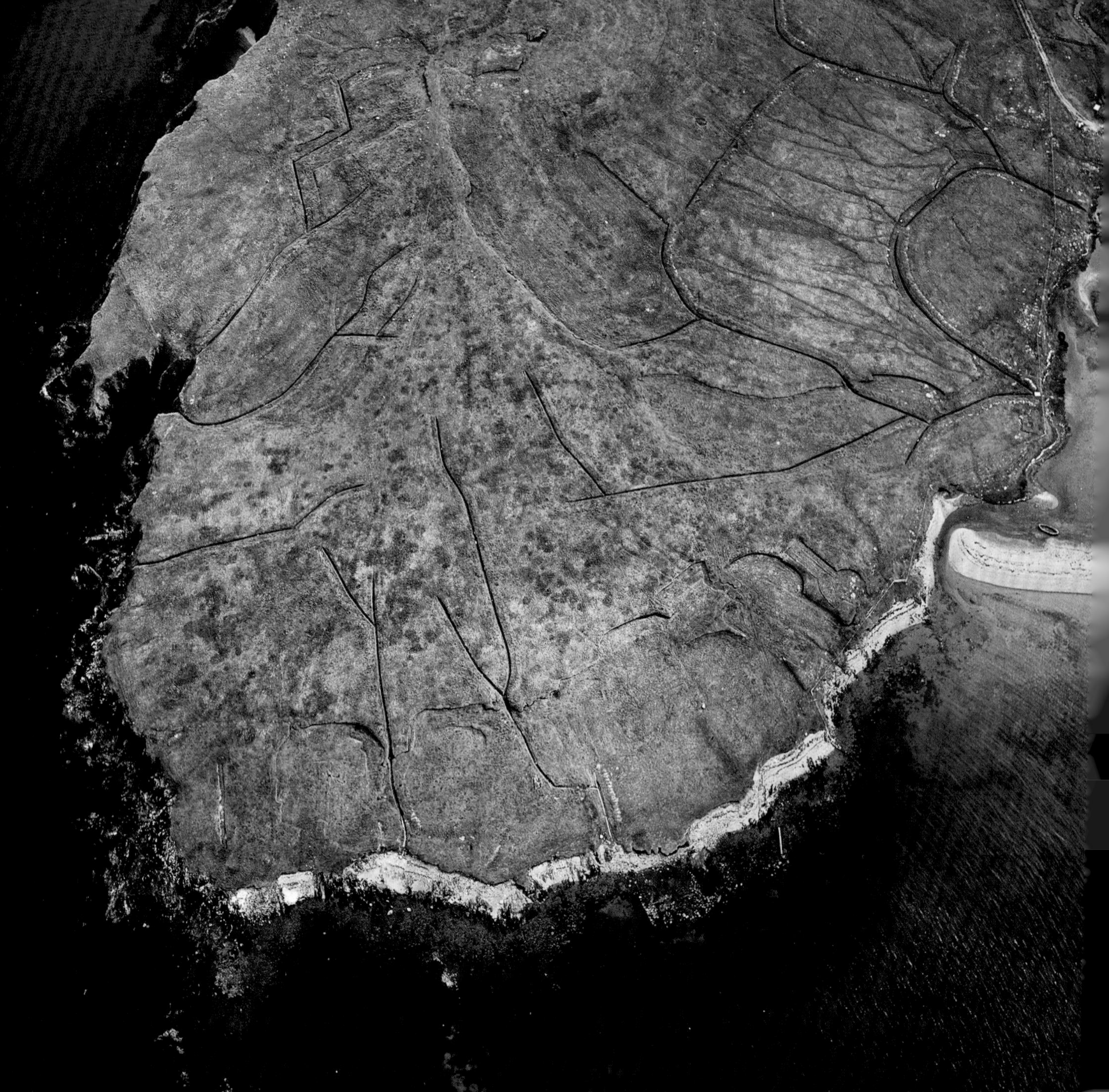

Peat banks at Ness of Houlland, North Roe, Shetland *N 60°34'36.9" W 1°19'27.9" Grid Ref: HU371883 Map Ref: 12 J5*

Shetland is pretty much treeless country, and possesses no coal. Before the advent of North Sea oil and gas, fuel for heating and cooking came courtesy of nature's other bounty, the peat that blankets the archipelago. The headlands and hills of Shetland are seamed with the dark lines of banks from which the peats are hand-cut with a tushkar or narrow-bladed spade, piled to dry and then transported home to burn long and slow on the domestic hearth.

North west coast of Yell at Eegittle, Shetland *N 60°42'53.5" W 1°07'40.5" Grid Ref: HP477038 Map Ref: 12 K4*

If you are looking for bleak, come to Yell. This large but almost entirely overlooked island, the penultimate in the northern march of the Shetland chain, is a place of rolling hills, deep peat bogs and wind-whipped, jagged cliffs. Storms, when they come (and they frequently do), march across Yell with battering force, then whirl away into the sea, leaving the green island soaked and glittering.

Vesta Skerry and Rumblings, Shetland *N 60°50′59.6″ W 0°53′37.0″ Grid Ref: HP602191 Map Ref: 12 L3*

The sea-polished schist of Vesta Skerry and Rumblings gleams under the 'whitewash' bestowed by tens of thousands of gannets who roost on this pair of heavily canted sea stacks. Two of a small fleet (their sister stacks are Tipta Skerry and Muckle Flugga, exotic names to an outsider's ear), they rise off the port bow of Hermaness, the most northerly point of Britain.

Muckle Flugga, Shetland *N 60°51'19.8" W 0°53'06.6" Grid Ref: HP607197 Map Ref: 12 L3*

This gannet's-eye view of Muckle Flugga brings home the full import of what it meant to be a lighthouse keeper. Even in the days when crew and supplies were landed on the sea stack by helicopter, the transfer was always vertiginous. In former times every cargo, whether of materials or humans, had to be transferred by small boat, usually in a pitching sea, often in high wind and driving rain. One can appreciate only too vividly the head-spinning hazards of this exceptionally precarious lighthouse station off the northern tip of Britain.

Braw and Bleak

Scotland's North Coast to Scottish Border

Of the entire circuit of the British coastline, the north and east of Scotland is the bleakest section of all. There is something truly forbidding to the first-time visitor about the bastion-like cliffs of flagstone, basalt and sandstone, the huddled grey stone fishing towns that hide in clefts of the cliffs like hermit crabs in sea-worn shells. Caithness, the bare region that forms the north-east tip of Scotland, is Old Red Sandstone, thinly layered into flagstone. The Aberdeenshire coast offers hard ancient granites, declining southwards to magnificent cliffs of sandstone, seamed with faults which the sea has worked on to carve out coves for fishing villages, as well as the countless sea stacks, caves and arches of the Moray and Angus coasts. Gritstone, limestone and sandstone of the promontory of Fife are similarly burrowed and hollowed; while the presence far inland of huge deposits of ironstone has seen ironworks and quarries scar the land around the inner end of the Firth of Forth. Basalt rears its volcanic head again as the coast swings east and south beyond the Forth, blobbing bare islet rocks such as the Bass into the sea and corresponding hillocks – Berwick Law and Largo Law – on the shores.

The Forth is the most southerly of the three great firths or estuaries that bite into this easterly face of Scotland – the others are the Firth of Tay, just north of the Forth, and further north the enormous acute angle of the Moray Firth that forms the entire upper 'jaw' of the coast with its foot pointing inland at Inverness, all the way down the Great Glen. Up in the far north the fishing towns are dour grey places. Viking foundations such as Thurso, Wick and Helmsdale, they are fascinating to the aficionado in their hard Scandinavian character, but scarcely cosy or easy. Inland they are backed by the endless mosses or peat bogs of the Flow Country, a million acres of empty bogland whose rivers run turbid and dark into the sea over pristine white sands. Castles with grimly murderous histories stand sentinel on the cliffs, refuges for warriors, as uncompromising as the scattered fishing towns that offer safe haven to storm-bound seafarers.

Kyle of Tongue *N 58°30'27.5" W 4°24'42.7" Grid Ref: NC596602 Map Ref: 11 F3*

The Kinloch River reaches the sea on the bleak north coast of Scotland through the long and narrow estuary of the Kyle of Tongue, flanked by beaches and banks of white sand. By means of a bridge across the narrows and a long approach causeway, the road was carried across the estuary in 1971, cutting out a long detour round the foot of the Kyle.

Torrisdale Bay, Highland *N 58°31'37.0" W 4°15'22.3" Grid Ref: NC687621 Map Ref: 11 G3*

A little east of the Kyle of Tongue, the famous surfing beach of Torrisdale Bay is shaped by the mouths of two rivers – the Borgie (bottom left), stained with peat from its moorland journey to the sea, and the Naver (top right). The sand dunes between the two rivers have built up on top of a ridge of rock, and rise some 300 feet above the sea.

Braw and Bleak
Scotland's North Coast to the Scottish Border

North Sea weather is boisterous in summer, though the Moray Firth is one of the sunniest places in Britain. In winter it howls along the coast, fiercely enough on occasion to blow down a bridge – as happened on 28 December 1879, when the Tay railway bridge collapsed in a storm, plunging a passing train and the 75 souls on board to destruction in the estuary. Everything tells you that this is a land of hard living and tough conditions. Folk have historically had to be pretty hard and tough, too. But the last thing they are is unfriendly. In fact holidaymakers and other strangers, being rarer birds here than on the romantically mountainous west coast, find themselves welcomed and offered some of the most unstinting hospitality in these islands.

In the southern sector lie harbours developed to take advantage of the great herring boom of the 19th century, when enormous shoals would make annual migratory runs clockwise around the coast. Over-fishing put paid to them, as it did to a whitefish glut in the 1960s and 70s. Times are really tough in the fishing towns of the Moray Firth, of Angus and Fife at present. The East Neuk or east end of Fife, in particular, carries a succession of towns cheek by jowl whose names were once synonymous with fishing: Leven and Largo, Elie and St Monan's, Pittenweem, Anstruther, Crail. Of these only Pittenweem retains a working fleet and fish market.

People up and down the east of Scotland are looking to attract visitors to what is an overlooked, under-visited coast, amazingly beautiful, wonderfully empty of tourist crowds. The Firth of Forth is crowded with tiny islands you can reach by boat; anyone who pays a visit to the jam-packed puffins of the Isle of May or the gannets of the Bass Rock is guaranteed an experience never to be forgotten. The Firth of Tay is edged with nature reserves of sand dunes, marsh and forest. Dolphins, porpoises and basking sharks, minke whales and killer whales abound in the Moray Firth. This is a coast of bleak severity, of scenic grandeur and of stunning natural beauty.

Thurso, Highland

N 58°35'49.6" W 3°30'57.9"
Grid Ref: ND120687 Map Ref: 11 J2

Windy, north-facing Thurso, built of cold grey stone, is the most northerly town in mainland Britain. The 'town on Thor's river' was a Viking fishing and trading port more than a thousand years ago, and enjoyed 19th-century boom times through herring fishing and the profitable business of shipping out locally quarried and dressed flagstones. Nowadays it is the big ferries to the Orkney Isles that leave from the sharp-pointed mouth of Thor's river.

John O'Groats, Highland

N 58°38'41.6" W 3°04'06.7"
Grid Ref: ND381735 Map Ref: 11 L2

Although the most northerly place in mainland Britain is Dunnet Head to the west of John O'Groats, and the outermost north-easterly corner is Duncansby Head to the east, the village of John O'Groats lies at the point where the coast road turns from north to east along the crown of Scotland. So this is where the visitors fetch up, to have a cup of tea, buy a souvenir and have their photo taken under the giant signpost that measures the miles to their home city anywhere in the world. And this is the point at which those intending to walk, run, bicycle, push a pram or hop barefoot the 1,000 miles to Land's End start their brave journeys.

Duncansby Head, Highland (right)

N 58°38'41.4" W 3°01'41.5"
Grid Ref: ND404734 Map Ref: 11 L2

Tide rips off Duncansby Head, the outermost point of the north-east mainland of Britain, are ferocious, and fogs frequently sweep in off the sea with no warning. The castellated tower of the 'lighthouse at the end of the world' was built in 1924 on a headland riven with deep, abrupt 'geos' or square-cut miniature fjords. Come here in harsh weather and you will hear the waves thumping in the depths and see spouts of water flung high from the lips of the geos.

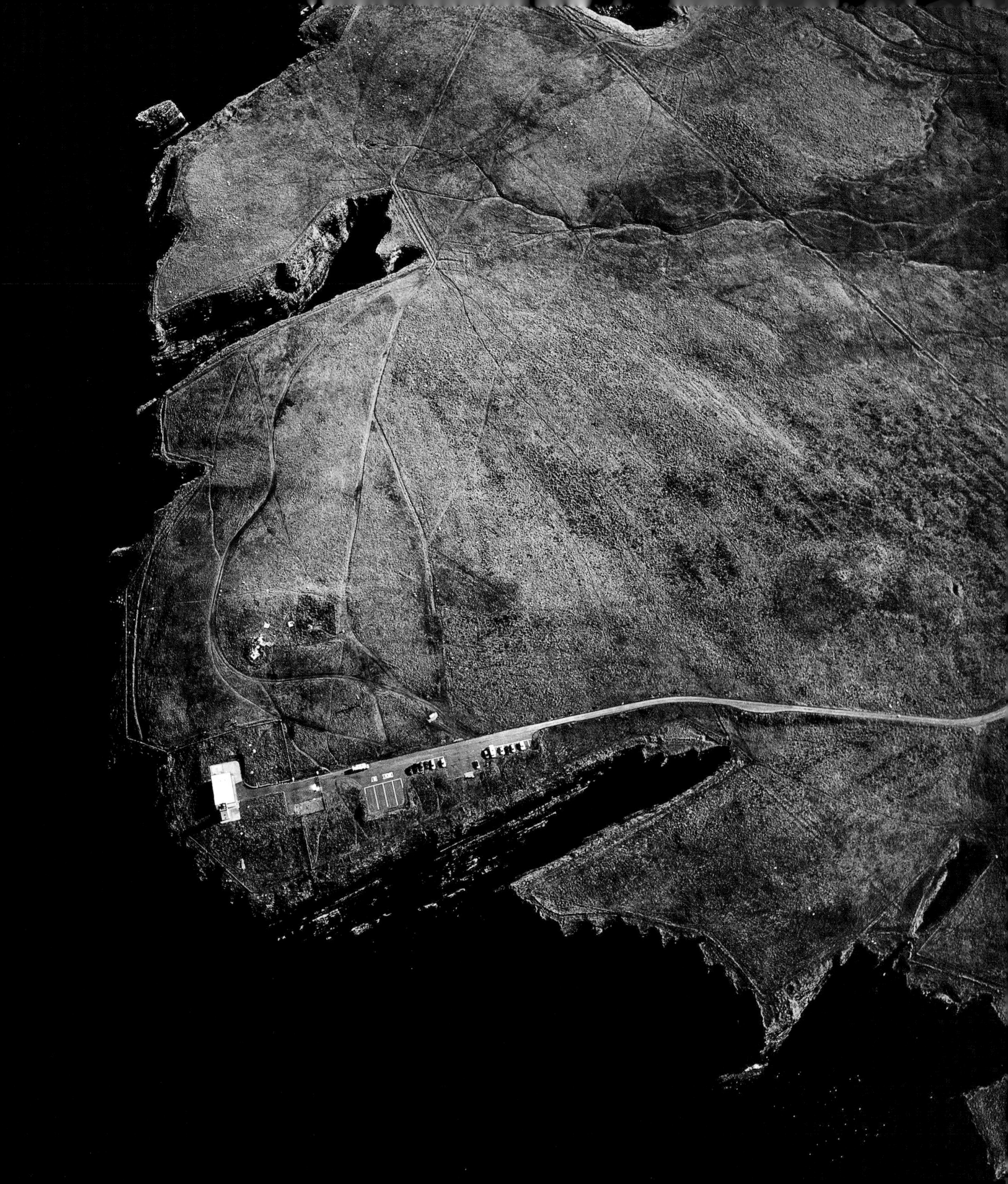

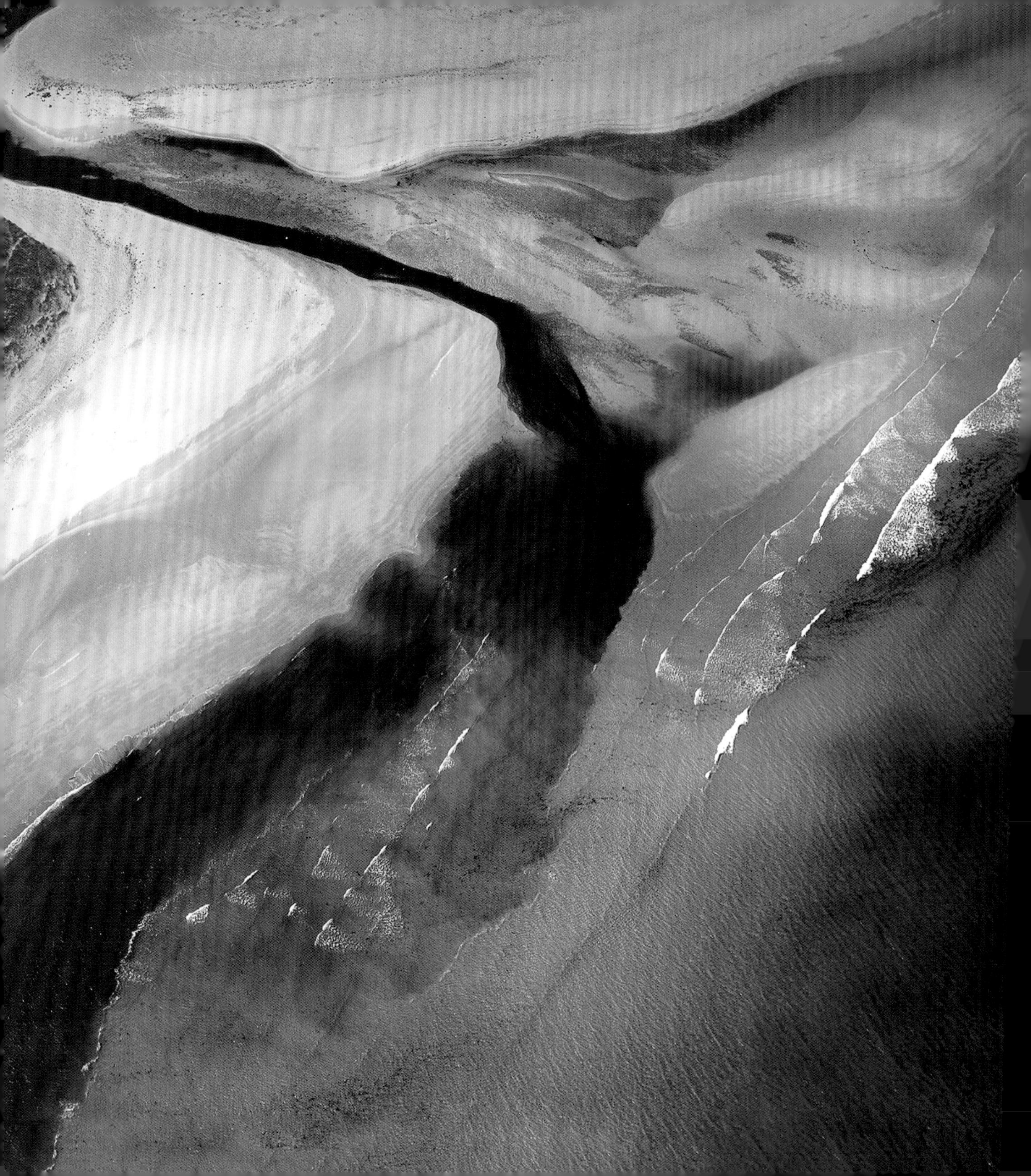

Water of Wester, Highland (left)

N 58°31'14.2" W 3°07'46.2"
Grid Ref: ND344597 Map Ref: 11 K3

Just south of Keiss on the coast of north-east Caithness, the Water of Wester meanders to the sea by way of the Loch of Wester and the vast, sodden peat bog that is the Moss of Wester. Charged with diluted peat from the moss, the Water of Wester resembles a flow of blood more than of water as it spreads across the white sand to meet the North Sea.

Castle Sinclair & Girnigoe, Highland

N 58°28'41.0" W 3°04'01.0"
Grid Ref: ND379549 Map Ref: 11 L3

Rising among the rock stacks of Noss Head just north of Wick as if part of the cliffs themselves, Castle Sinclair & Girnigoe makes a formidable spectacle. Built in the late 15th century by William Sinclair, 2nd Earl of Caithness, the castle was added to over the centuries. Its grim history contains one outstandingly macabre episode from the 1570s - the murder of John Sinclair, Master of Caithness, by his own father George, 4th Earl of Caithness, who felt threatened by John's popularity with the locals. George kept John in the dungeons for 7 years, then brought about his death through thirst by allowing him a diet of nothing but salt beef, and not a drop to drink.

Wick Harbour, Highland

N 58°26'30.0" W 3°05'26.8"
Grid Ref: ND364509 Map Ref: 11 L3

The creation in 1786 of the resplendently-titled 'British Society for Extending the Fisheries and Improving the Sea Coast of this Kingdom' (eventually to be shortened to 'The British Fisheries Society') was the making of many lonely Scottish fishing communities desperate for markets for the huge glut of herring they were catching. The north-east Caithness town of Wick, its harbour modernised in 1810 by the great engineer Thomas Telford, boomed all through the Victorian era until by the turn of the 20th century there were a thousand herring boats working out of the town, and 10,000 men and women employed in catching, sorting, gutting, salting and barrelling the 'silver darlings'. Then, within three decades, it all turned upside down. The herring were grossly overfished, catches nose-dived, business dwindled. By 1930 there were just 30 boats left – roughly the same number as today.

Fort George, Highland *N 57°35'02.7" W 4°03'49.0" Grid Ref: NH767568 Map Ref: 11 G10*

Between 1748 and 1769, Fort George was constructed on a spit of land dominating the narrows of the Moray Firth just north-east of Inverness. A bastion halfway down each side and at each of the four corners gave the fort an impregnable look. It was built more as a symbol to cow the natives than because serious trouble was expected from the clans, demoralised, broken and plundered as they were after their disastrous defeat at the Battle of Culloden, fought in 1746 on nearby Drummossie Muir. Fort George is still partly in use as a barracks, but some sections are open to the public. Military museums and live costume shows recreate the life of the 18th-century soldier with its ferocious discipline and hard living.

Stonehaven, Aberdeenshire *N 56°57'37.6" W 2°12'17.2" Grid Ref: NO876855 Map Ref: 9 I7*

Tucked into a sheltered bay in the cliffs south of Aberdeen, Stonehaven is the only safe port of refuge along this coast when one of the region's frequent north-easterly gales blows up. The Auld Toon around the harbour grew up on the foundations of a fishing village at least 2,000 years old. Early in the herring boom of the 19th century, massive new harbour walls were built. The fishing has declined, but Stonehaven proudly trumpets another splendid claim to fame – it was here in the 1990s that the now famous batter-coated, deep-fried Mars Bar was first unveiled.

Dunnottar Castle, Aberdeenshire *N 56°56'46.0" W 2°11'46.4" Grid Ref: NO882839 Map Ref: 9 I7*

Dunnottar commands a most dramatic site, a great puddingstone promontory that sticks out between guardian bays, separated from the shore by a chasm as effective for defence as any man-made moat. The headland, a superb defensive position and lookout, has been fortified and occupied since Pictish times. Dunnottar Castle was built from the late 14th century onwards. In 1685 a group of 122 men and 45 women, all Covenanters – people persecuted for their non-conformist religious beliefs – were locked up in the Whig's Vault dungeon. Nine died of disease and neglect. Tortured when they tried to escape, half-starved and brutally treated, the survivors were finally transported across the Atlantic, true martyrs for their faith.

Todhead Point, Aberdeenshire *N 56°53'04.6" W 2°12'52.6" Grid Ref: NO870770 Map Ref: 9 I8*

South of Stonehaven lies a belt of Old Red Sandstone conglomerate, a rough and coarse-textured rock whose slanting strata form the promontory of Todhead Point. The stumpy light tower was erected in 1897 by David A. Stevenson of the famous family of lighthouse-builders. A review of UK and Irish aids to navigation concluded in 2005 that Todhead Point lighthouse was of more use to seafarers as a coastal feature by which to check their location than as a warning of any specific hazard. So the light was switched off on 11 July 2007, leaving Stevenson's tower as a lonely landmark on the cliffs.

Montrose Basin, Angus

N 56°42'42.4" W 2°30'08.7" Grid Ref: NO693579 Map Ref: 9 H9

The ancient town of Montrose sits along the Angus coast, with the wide tidal inlet of Montrose Basin forming an inland sea just behind the shore. There are over 1,600 acres of mudflats exposed in the basin at low tide, a rich store of invertebrate food for dunlin, shelduck, curlew and other birds of the estuaries. In winter huge numbers of wildfowl arrive from the north to spend the cold months here; big crowds of pink-footed geese several thousand strong make a remarkable show.

Arbroath, Angus

N 56°33'26.4" W 2°34'30.6"
Grid Ref: NO647407 Map Ref: 9 G10

Arbroath is built of handsome red sandstone, the same material that forms the adjacent cliffs that are so spectacularly shaped and burrowed by the sea. 'Fit o' th' toon' (Foot of the town), the old part of Arbroath around the harbour, is famous among lovers of fishy delicacies for its smokies – herrings that are salted and then hung over a fire of beech and oak chips to develop the smoky taste and coppery sheen of a proper Arbroath smokie.

Dundee and the Tay Road Bridge

N 56°27'28.8" W 2°57'36.3"
Grid Ref: NO409299 Map Ref: 9 F11

Looking north-west across the Tay road bridge towards Dundee. The Tay Bridge Disaster took place just upriver on 28 December 1879, when the recently opened railway bridge collapsed in a storm, hurling a train into the Firth of Tay with the loss of 75 lives - as recorded in the strangely moving doggerel of William Topaz McGonagall, 'poet and tragedian' of Dundee:

It must have been an awful sight,
To witness in the dusky moonlight,
While the Storm Fiend did laugh, and angry did bray,
Along the Railway Bridge of the Silv'ry Tay.
Oh! ill-fated Bridge of the Silv'ry Tay,
I must now conclude my lay
By telling the world fearlessly without the least dismay,
That your central girders would not have given way,
At least many sensible men do say,
Had they been supported on each side with buttresses,
At least many sensible men confesses,
For the stronger we our houses do build,
The less chance we have of being killed.

- 'The Tay Bridge Disaster'

Ballinbreich Castle, Fife *N 56°22'07.8" W 3°10'32.4" Grid Ref: NO275202 Map Ref: 9 E12*

The 'castle of the town of trout' stands ten miles upriver of Dundee on the south bank of the Firth of Tay, a stronghold of the powerful Leslie clan since it was built early in the 14th century. The original stark tower was soon supplemented by a courtyard in an enclosing wall, followed by a range of other more or less domestic buildings and apartments, including a chapel. Nowadays a poignant ruin invaded by trees, Ballinbreich Castle crouches modestly, half-forgotten at the edge of a cornfield.

St Andrews, Fife *N 56°20'23.4" W 2°47'14.7" Grid Ref: NO514167 Map Ref: 9 F12*

St Andrews, a charming small town set amid broad sand dunes, is notable for the impressive ruins of the Cathedral of St Andrew, sacked in the mid-16th century during the Scottish Reformation. Nowadays the town is known as the place where Prince William went to university (its University, founded in 1413, is the oldest in Scotland), and also as the Home of Golf. In 1567 Mary, Queen of Scots played golf here, but her compatriots had been chasing the wee white ball around the dunes for at least a century before that. Golfers from all over the world come to St Andrews these days to play a ceremonial round on the famous Old Course, seen here stretching seaward behind the town.

Anstruther, Fife *N 56°13'16.5" W 2°41'50.5" Grid Ref: NO569034 Map Ref: 9 G13*

The fishing town of Anstruther – 'Ainster' in the broad Doric of the local dialect – lies in the East Neuk of Fife, its harbour sheltered by the praying mantis arms of elongated breakwaters. Anstruther was once the principal fishing port of the Fife coast, so busy during the 19th-century herring boom that a fisherman could walk across the decks of the packed herring boats from one side of the harbour to the other. These days the harbourside's most lucrative connections with fish are its excellent Scottish Fisheries Museum, and the Anstruther Fish Bar, home of some of the best fish and chips in Scotland.

Pittenweem, Fife *N 56°12'44.9" W 2°43'43.9" Grid Ref: NO549024 Map Ref: 9 G13*

Tightly knit Pittenweem, just west of Anstruther on the East Neuk coast of Fife, has little time for the pleasure boating that has replaced serious fishing in the other local coast towns. Times are tough for Scottish fishing communities as they contend with EU quotas and other regulations, rocketing costs and the consequences of over-fishing. But Pittenweem's fleet continues in business, and the town's early morning fish market on the quay is still a noisy, salty, bustling place.

Forth Railway Bridge (left)

N 56°00'04.9" W 3°23'19.8"
Grid Ref: NT135796 Map Ref: 9 D15

Like the disarticulated segments of a dinosaur's backbone, the three huge cantilever sections of the Forth Railway Bridge march across the Queensferry narrows of the Firth of Forth. The central cantilever is footed on the rocky islet of Inchgarvie whose heavy concrete fortifications stand as mementoes of the world wars of the 20th century, when the bridge, and Rosyth naval dockyard just upriver of its northern end, needed to be defended against attack by German bombers.

Grangemouth, Falkirk

N 56°01'07.1" W 3°41'04.8"
Grid Ref: NS951819 Map Ref: 9 B14

Not exactly where you'd pick for a nice holiday on the beach, but Grangemouth oil refinery, fifteen miles upstream of the Forth Railway Bridge, is a vital local centre of employment and economic activity. The refinery, which processes nearly a quarter of a million barrels of North Sea crude oil every day, is just one of a number of heavy industries - iron foundries, coal mines, salt pans, lime kilns, lead works - that have settled over the years on the shores of the inner Firth.

Leith Docks, Edinburgh

N 55°58'53.1" W 3°10'21.7"
Grid Ref: NT269771 Map Ref: 9 E15

What would Edinburgh have been without its port of Leith? Just another inland town on a hill, probably. Leith Docks were the gateway through which prosperity reached the Scottish capital. The 20th century saw a big slump in Leith's fortunes; Irving Welsh's grim-and-gritty vernacular novel *Trainspotting* memorably portrayed the town's druggy end-of-century violence and despair. But early 21st-century gentrification has given Leith a wholly unexpected boost, and it's now a very trendy place to live and work.

North Berwick, East Lothian *N 56°03'35.8" W 2°43'01.2" Grid Ref: NT554855 Map Ref: 9 G14*

This view perfectly catches two contrasting aspects of the East Lothian golfing resort of North Berwick. Behind the beautiful sandy swimming beaches, the well-ordered neat little Scottish seaside town; out front, the rugged volcanic headland with its simple harbour, safe behind the breakwater's mighty arm, from which adventurers, travellers and pilgrims on their way to St Andrews and the shrine of Scotland's national saint have made their way across the storm-prone Firth of Forth for the past thousand years.

antallon Castle, East Lothian *N 56°03'22.5" W 2°39'03.3" Grid Ref: NT596850 Map Ref: 9 G14*

his 14th-century stronghold of Clan Douglas looks out from its clifftop across the Firth of Forth to the gannet-haunted basalt plug of the Bass Rock rising ore than a mile offshore. Tall curtain walls of red sandstone, the ruin of two towers and the Great Hall still stand. The back of the castle falls 100 feet eer into the sea. 'As lief ding doon Tantallon as bigg a brig tae th' Bass,' men said: 'As easily knock down Tantallon as build a bridge to the Bass.' But in 551, when General Monk and his Ironsides besieged Tantallon, a 12-day bombardment did succeed in knocking down the wall, which collapsed across e moat, filling it with rubble. The castle garrison of a hundred men, seeing their enemies provided with this fortuitous bridge, decided to surrender.

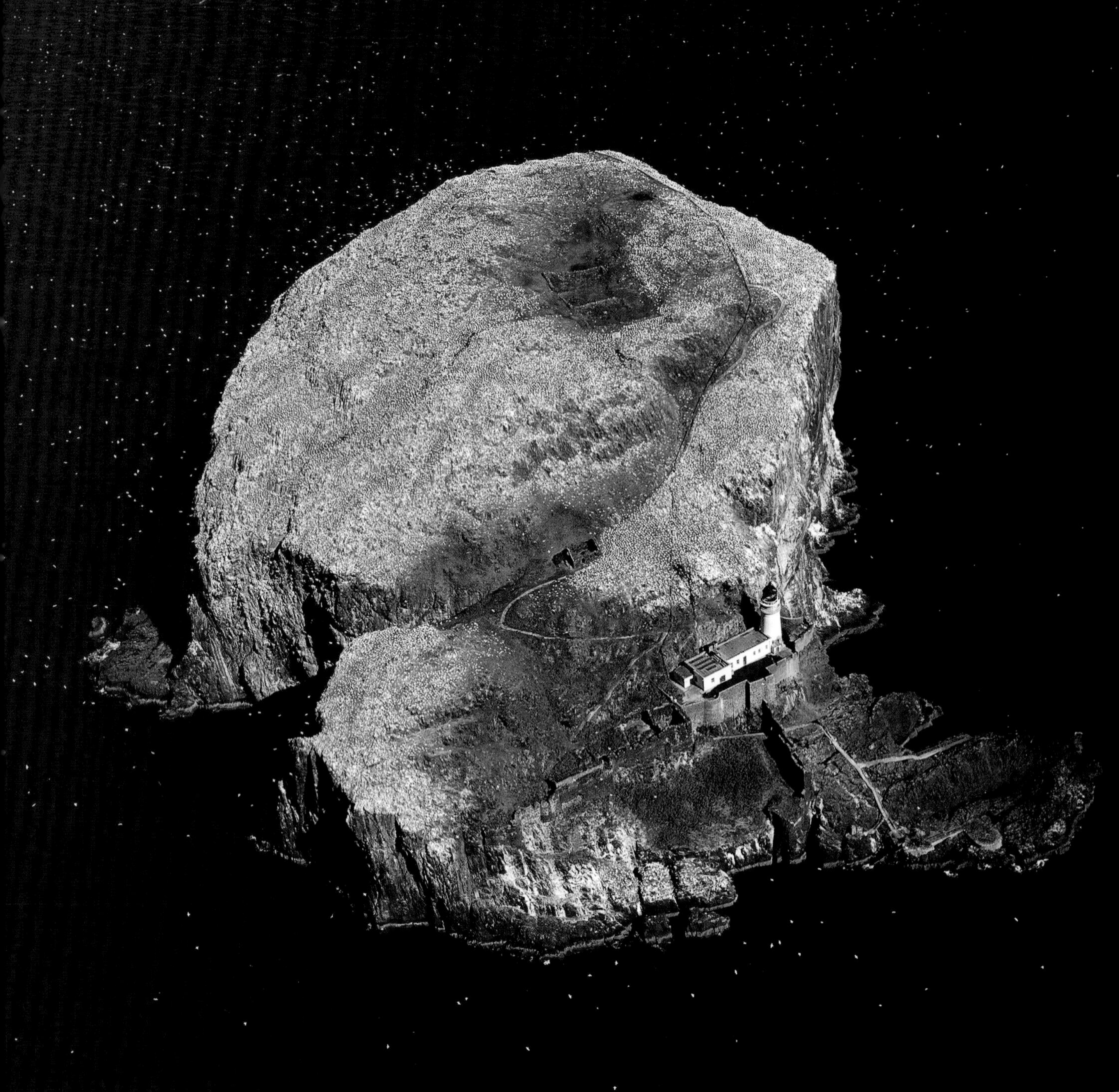

Bass Rock, East Lothian *N 56°04'39.4" W 2°38'25.0" Grid Ref: NT602874 Map Ref: 9 G14*

Clouds of gannets swirl above the Bass Rock, a volcanic plug 350 feet tall that stands white-topped and massive in the Firth of Forth off the East Lothian coast. In times past the Bass played host to the 7th-century hermit St Baldred, pirate gangs, Covenanter ministers and Jacobite plotters (as prisoners), garrisons of soldiers and lonely groups of lighthouse keepers. The present-day incumbents are 100,000 gannets, packed wing-to-wing across the upper slopes, their fishy stench and gabbling roar dominating all.

Dunbar, East Lothian *N 56°00'16.3" W 2°31'00.9" Grid Ref: NT679792 Map Ref: 7 A1*

Dunbar's Old Harbour lies towards the top of this gull's-eye view. The larger Victoria Harbour, seen on the left, was constructed in the 1840s, with a new entrance being blasted through the rock on which stand the ruins of Dunbar Castle (bottom left). This ancient stronghold changed hands between Scots and English many times over centuries of strife. Towards the top of the photograph the D-shaped shell of Dunbar's cannon battery lies across the basalt islet of Lamer, where it was built in 1781 to warn off pirates.

Defiance and Defence

Berwick-upon-Tweed to River Humber

Cold water, cold wind, bloody heritage, pollutant industry, uncertain future – such are the snapshots by which most outsiders judge the north-east coast of England. Such images fail to acknowledge the grand remoteness of the region's more northerly sector, its astonishing archaeological and paleontological richness, its dynamism in interaction with waves and weather, and – perhaps understandably – its wonderful beauty. For an area so blighted (in parts) by the grossest consequences of heavy industry, this coast is nothing short of a revelation.

Low cliffs, small islands and long sandy beaches are the keynotes of the coast of Northumberland and Durham, a stretch of glorious country and sea only saved from having been ruthlessly developed as a Riviera of the North by the coldness of the sea and the windswept openness of the beaches. People have always been inclined to settle around the mouths of the principal rivers - Aln, Coquet, Tyne, Wear, Tees – fishing, farming and later establishing early Christian monasteries, rich in silver and gold, on sketchily defended promontories. It was the perfect coast for invasion by any Scandinavian determined (or desperate) enough to cross the North Sea and come ashore with sword swinging. Monks and Vikings came bloodily into each others' orbit at Lindisfarne, Tynemouth and Wearmouth, the monks to die or flee, the sea wolves to burn, steal, rape and kill.

The Vikings had faded out of the picture by the 12th century, to be replaced by local warlords and by the incursive Scots. Hard basalt outcrops (some in the furthest north were part of the famous Whin Sill feature) made excellent upstanding foundations for the building of impressive castles for Border defence – Lindisfarne, Bamburgh, Dunstanburgh, Warkworth, Tynemouth. Terrible, history-searing incidents took place all along this coast, such as the sack of Berwick-upon-Tweed on 30 March 1296 in which several thousand townspeople were butchered by the victorious English. Representative of that era's swaggering, swashbuckling Border landowners was young Henry Percy, son of the Earl of Northumberland, dubbed 'Harry Hotspur' for his impetuosity, immortalised by William Shakespeare in *King Henry the Fourth, Part I.*

It was not only bloodshed and plunder that formed this coast. The skill of exploiting whatever the land and sea could offer bulked large, too. Fishing villages and towns from Berwick to Hull show long defensive harbour breakwaters to the North Sea. In the low cliffs of Northumberland and Durham lay hard basalt whinstone, ideal for quarrying for building and road-making, and of course the black diamonds of King Coal, the fuel that drove the Industrial Revolution. Coal staithes or loading platforms sprang up at Amble and Blyth, Tynemouth and Seaham. Shipyards spread along the banks of the Rivers Tyne and Wear. Collieries proliferated along the cliffs; so did bottle-works and iron foundries, gasworks and chemical plants, and the serried ranks of cheap, uniform workers' housing to accommodate those who laboured there. Further south it was jet and alum mines, ironstone and chalk quarries that disfigured the cliffs. The 18th, 19th and 20th centuries saw this coast so fouled and blighted by industrial waste and brutal ugliness that it seemed it could never recover.

Berwick-upon-Tweed, Northumberland *N 55°46'14.0" W 1°59'43.3" Grid Ref: NU004530 Map Ref: 7 D2*

Hunched together inside the tight embrace of their Elizabethan town walls, the householders of Berwick-upon-Tweed face no greater danger these days than rising damp. It was different during the long centuries of struggle between England and Scotland when Berwick was a border town on the front line of a vicious war. Between 1147 and 1482, when the English finally repelled their enemies, Berwick changed hands no fewer than thirteen times, and the townsfolk suffered plunder, rape and murder on many of those bloody occasions.

Lindisfarne Castle, Northumberland *N 55°40'08.2" W 1°47'05.0" Grid Ref: NU136417 Map Ref: 7 E3*

The Tudor fortress of Lindisfarne Castle sits atop Beblowe Crag, an outcrop of the dolerite rock sheet called the Whin Sill as it reaches the Northumbrian coast just south of Berwick-upon-Tweed. Built as a border fort to guard Lindisfarne – better known as Holy Island - against the irruptive Scots, the castle was improbably captured in 1715 by a Jacobite ship's captain who was being shaved by the garrison's Master Gunner. Realising that the rest of the garrison had gone ashore and left the amateur barber as sole incumbent, the captain and his nephew took over with a crisp 'Damn you! The castle is ours!' Next day, uncle and nephew were thrown into Berwick Gaol for their cheek; a day or two after that, they burrowed their way to freedom.

Defiance and Defence

Berwick-upon-Tweed to River Humber

Yet what a transformation there has been along the Durham coast in the few short years since the coal mines closed. The notorious 'minestone' or miniature cliffs of clotted, solidified industrial waste that scabbed the beaches is steadily being eroded by the sea. Sewage is properly treated. The 'denes' or curving valleys that lead down to the beaches are now nature reserves. New coastal footpaths have been opened. There are tentative steps to establish a green, eco-friendly tourist industry. Such a notion would have been laughed out of court only twenty years ago.

Teesmouth with its still active industries - chemicals, oil, gas, a nuclear power station, ironworks at the mouth of the River Tees – will not be following suit any time soon, especially since the establishment there of the Teesside Environmental Reclamation and Recycling Centre, a centre for ship-breaking, rubbish storing and the housing of industrial plant. Yet the grey and common seals that have returned to breed on Seal Sands, the godwit and dunlin that come to spend the winter in this most unlikely National Nature Reserve seem indifferent to the flaring and hulking and humming monstrosities that form the backdrop to their activities.

The Industrial Revolution hit Yorkshire hardest well inland, where the bulk of the coal and minerals lay. The Yorkshire coast became dotted during Victorian times with not-too-expensive holiday resorts catering for hard-pressed working families on their one or two weeks' annual holiday - Whitby, Scarborough, Reighton Sands, Filey, Bridlington, Hornsea, Withernsea. Under the feet of these local holidaymakers, unappreciated by all but a select few, lay the fossil-stuffed rocks of what is now called the 'Dinosaur Coast'. The voracious sea has been exposing the plesiosaur bones and teeth, the crinoids and ammonites, the delicate fern heads since time out of mind as it gnaws blindly at the cliffs.

This North Sea has turned out to be a foe more insatiable, more unstoppable than any Viking horde. It has been destroying villages, demolishing sandspits, dragging clifftop farms to their doom and threatening the lives and livelihoods of locals ever since history was first recorded here; and it looks like doing so with increasing power as the rising sea levels and worsening storms of climate change continue to draw their upward curve. Parts of the River Humber will be defended, say the Environment Agency's plans – those portions of the river banks that secure human life and prosperity in the shape of dwellings and businesses. Other parts will be 'let go' like unsatisfactory employees, as part of the process euphemistically known as 'managed realignment'. This has already started at Alkborough Flats and at Paull on the Humber, where sections of sea wall have been deliberately breached to let the sea reclaim some land and start its natural construction of mudflats and salt marsh – nature's own buffers against the sea, which we have been busily ignoring and building on over several decades. Maybe we have actually turned the corner, and are listening to what Mother Nature has been trying to tell us about our *folie de grandeur* and its unsustainability.

Bamburgh Castle, Northumberland (left)

N 55°36'33.8" W 1°42'39.7"
Grid Ref: NU183351 Map Ref: 7 E4

Magnificent upon its perch of dark dolerite rock, Bamburgh Castle is without question the most superbly posed castle in Northumberland. The curtain walls hug the edges of the crag, another of the extrusions of the Whin Sill volcanic cliff that outcrops all across the north. Bamburgh's tall, forbidding keep is Norman, but the crag with its commanding outlook along the coast and out to sea has been fortified and occupied for at least 2,000 years.

Inner Farne, Northumberland

N 55°36'58.0" W 1°39'18.6"
Grid Ref: NU218359 Map Ref: 7 E4

A remarkable view of the Farne Islands – yet more outcrops, the final ones, of the dolerite Whin Sill rock sheet before it slips out of sight beneath the waters of the North Sea. We see in the foreground the rugged shape of Inner Farne, where the shepherd bishop St Cuthbert lived from AD 676 to 684 as a hermit while he wrestled demons on goat-back. Beyond Inner Farne lie the twin green islets of East and West Wideopen, joined in butterfly shape to barren Knoxes Reef; beyond them, the submarine profile of Staple Island; in the far distance, the lighthouse tower on Longstone from which 23-year-old Grace Darling rowed in a storm on 7 September 1838 to rescue seafarers from shipwreck.

Dunstanburgh Castle, Northumberland

N 55°29'26.0" W 1°35'39.2"
Grid Ref: NU257219 Map Ref: 7 E5

The 14th-century sea fortress of Dunstanburgh Castle was built on its cliff in 1313-16 by Thomas, Earl of Lancaster. The massive drum towers of the gatehouse were later converted to serve as the castle's keep. Legend tells how Sir Guy the Seeker sought refuge from a storm in the keep, and was awoken in the night by a fearsome ogre who commanded him to choose between a horn and a sword, with a beautiful princess as the prize. Unlucky Sir Guy chose to blow the horn, and was condemned to pace the castle bounds as a ghost for ever more.

Craster, Northumberland

N 55°28'22.2" W 1°35'33.1"
Grid Ref: NU259200 Map Ref: 7 E5

The Craster family have lived for the best part of a thousand years around the village from which they took their name. They built the harbour and its defensive breakwaters in the early 20th century to export whinstone – hard dolerite rock quarried from the cliffs of the Whin Sill behind the village – for road-building. These days Craster ('Crawchester', the Place of Crows) is celebrated for the delectable kippers produced at Robson's smokehouse in the village.

Alnmouth, Northumberland

N 55°23'06.1" W 1°36'37.3"
Grid Ref: NU248102 Map Ref: 7 E5

At the heart of a magnificent stretch of Northumbrian coast lies Alnmouth, a red-roofed village snug on a headland on the north bank of the River Aln's curving, bird-thronged estuary. Terns plunge after fish, and oystercatchers and sandpipers probe the sandbanks and mudflats. A mile or so through the grazing meadows south of the estuary mouth and you reach the tall sand dunes of Buston Links, lime-rich mini-mountains of sand with damp slacks and hollows sheltering bloody cranesbill, cowslips and delicately trembling, sky-blue harebells.

Warkworth Castle, Northumberland (right)

N 55°20'52.8" W 1°36'38.9"
Grid Ref: NU248061 Map Ref: 7 E6

The ruin of Warkworth Castle, guarded by a mighty loop of the River Coquet, was a stronghold of the Percy family, Earls of Northumberland, so memorably portrayed by William Shakespeare in the person of Henry Percy, or Harry Hotspur. In *King Henry the Fourth, Part 1* it is at Warkworth that the doomed, fiery-tempered Hotspur takes distracted leave of his exasperated wife Kate:

> *Lady Percy*: What is it carries you away?
> *Hotspur*: Why, my horse,
> My love, - my horse.
> *Lady Percy*: Out, you mad-headed ape!

And in *King Henry the Fourth, Part II* Shakespeare has the Earl of Northumberland maddened with grief upon receiving the news of the death of his son Hotspur at the castle gate:

> 'Now bind my brows with iron; and approach
> The ragged'st hour that time and spite dare bring
> To frown upon the enraged Northumberland!
> Let heaven kiss earth! now let not Nature's hand
> Keep the wild flood confined! let order die!'

Blyth, Northumberland *N 55°07'03.0" W 1°29'23.5" Grid Ref: NZ326805 Map Ref: 7 F7*

Mighty breakwater arms, cradling the outflow of the River Blyth, reach a long way into the North Sea. Blyth has been a ship-building town and a harbour since early medieval times, first exporting salt from its monastic salt pans, then coal, loaded into the collier boats from tall wooden staithes or loading platforms – five and a half million tons of the 'black diamond' in the port's 1930s heyday. Salt, ship-building and coal exports are all long gone, but Blyth docks are still active. They deal with paper, timber, fertiliser, machinery – even coal once more, though that is strictly an import trade these days.

St Mary's Island, Tyne and Wear *N 55°04'18.8" W 1°26'58.5" Grid Ref: NZ352754 Map Ref: 7 F8*

Lying less than half a mile offshore from the seaside town of Whitley Bay, St Mary's Island with its tidal causeway has always been a magnet for holidaymakers in the Tynesiders' favourite resort. The tall finger of the lighthouse beckons folk to race the tide. The white tower was built in 1898, but there has been a light of some sort on St Mary's, a notorious reef on a busy coast, since monks maintained a beacon in the tower of their chapel on the island in early Norman times.

Tynemouth Priory and Castle, Tyne and Wear (left)

N 55°01'03.8" W 1°25'01.7"
Grid Ref: NZ374694 Map Ref: 7 F8

If Tynemouth Priory was a fortress of God, it was also one of man's – and it needed to be. Founded in the 7th century on the headland of Pen Bal Crag, the original priory was sacked and plundered at least three times between AD 800 and 870 by the Danes, before being destroyed in 875. Refounded in 1090 after the sea wolves' menace had receded, the priory became a fortified stronghold against the Scots. It was garrisoned against Napoleon, and again in both World Wars of the 20th century. What stands today are the moated towers and gatehouse of the castle, the shell of the Norman church, and a tiny, miraculously preserved and beautifully carved 15th-century chantry chapel of the Percy family.

Sunderland, Tyne and Wear

N 54°54'28.0" W 1°21'22.5"
Grid Ref: NZ414572 Map Ref: 7 F9

This view of the mouth of the River Wear looks over the North-East Pier and the dock it shelters to the green of Sunderland's Town Moor or common behind it. The town sprawls beyond along the Wear, whose naked river banks bear witness to the collapse of the ship-building industry that once roared, clanged and smoked here. There were dozens of shipyards, great and small, in Sunderland a hundred years ago, but competition and financial squeezes had starved them all.

Seaham, County Durham

N 54°50'13.0" W 1°19'26.7"
Grid Ref: NZ435493 Map Ref: 7 G9

The skinny arms of the North and South Piers enclose the outer harbour at Seaham, a former coal port just down the coast from Sunderland. Seaham was planned as an upmarket little resort by local coal-owner Lord Londonderry in the 1830s, but lack of money and a rise in the industrial fortunes of the North-East shelved that notion in favour of a hastily run-up workers' town where coal staithes, chemical and gas works, bottleworks, coal mines and blast furnaces lined the cliffs and shore. All are now gone, and Seaham is finally looking to the future as an upmarket resort.

Hartlepool *N 54°41'32.4" W 1°10'27.7" Grid Ref: NZ533333 Map Ref: 7 G11*

Grouped together on their crab's claw of a headland, the houses of Old Hartlepool cluster round the 12th-century parish church of St Hilda. Opposite lie the docks which brought prosperity to the town. Hartlepool was always a place rather apart, the Hartlepudlians too – it was they who tried and hanged a monkey as a spy when they discovered it cast up from the wreck of a French ship in Napoleonic times.

Seal Sands, Tees Estuary *N 54°37'42.2" W 1°10'34.4" Grid Ref: NZ533262 Map Ref: 7 G11*

Tanker jetties and oil silos flank the wide estuarine shelf of Seal Sands, where Atlantic grey seals and their cousins the common or harbour seals have taken up breeding again after a long absence because of industrial pollution and human disturbance. Conservationists wait to discover how the seals will react to the planned operations of the Teesside Environmental Reclamation and Recycling Centre at Graythorp (just out of shot on the right), where plans are afoot to establish a huge ship-breaking yard, a waste storage centre, a wind turbine construction factory, a concrete production plant and vast industrial storage units.

Tees Estuary *N 54°38'39.3" W 1°08'56.4" Grid Ref: NZ550280 Map Ref: 7 G11*

Looking over South Gare Breakwater and its shingle spit at the mouth of the River Tees, with the long run of Coatham Sands stretching away eastwards and the rather murkier and more inland bay of Bran Sands beyond. Behind Bran Sands looms the giant complex of Redcar steelworks. Oil terminals and chemical plants line the far bank of the Tees in the middle distance, while just seaward of them stands the tall block of Hartlepool nuclear power station. Amidst all this pollutant industry lies Teesmouth National Nature Reserve. Seal Sands (page 233), seen just to the right of the oil terminal, is a wintering haven for thousands of seabirds; North Gare Sands, seaward of the power station, is a pupping ground for both grey and harbour seals.

Whitby, North Yorkshire *N 54°29'27.5" W 0°36'43.4" Grid Ref: NZ900115 Map Ref: 7 J12*

The East and West Pier at Whitby reach out into the North Sea like two narrow insect jaws. Or should that be 'like two sharp vampire teeth'? Whitby was where Bram Stoker set three chilling chapters of his classic 1897 Gothic horror tale *Dracula*, and much of the most spine-tingling action took place on the East Cliff. In the graveyard of St Mary's Church (centre of picture) the suave but deadly Transylvanian Count sucked the jugular blood of pale but interesting heroine Lucy Westenra, before flitting in spectral shape around the 13th-century ruins of Whitby Abbey, seen rising just beyond.

Scarborough, North Yorkshire *N 54°16'45.4" W 0°23'48.5" Grid Ref: TA045883 Map Ref: 7 K14*

Scarborough grew quickly in the 19th century from a genteel spa to a rumbustious resort for Yorkshire mill and factory workers and their families. Sheltered from north and north-east winds by the great promontory nose of the Castle Headland, the famous South Bay is still the town beach *par excellence*, with every facility from fish and chip shops to beach emporia catering for the tens of thousands that continue to flock here on sunny Bank Holidays.

Reighton Sands, North Yorkshire

N 54°09'30.8" W 0°13'17.5" Grid Ref: TA162751 Map Ref: 7 J14

Greensand, gault and clay – three of the slipperiest geological entities. Put them together, and you get cliffs that are ready at the drop of a hat to slip and slide into the sea. Instability is the name of the game here towards the southern end of the North Yorkshire coast, looking towards the sloping, tottery cliffs that hem in Reighton Sands. Notwithstanding the uncertain ground, Reighton Sands have long been a favourite resort for East Yorkshire families. As the old music-hall song says:

'Me and wife and family of three
Went to Reighton by the sea,
We watched 't clog dancers and we listened to 't bands,
And then we went on Reighton Sands.
And we kept eating parkin,
We kept eating parkin,
We kept eating parkin –
That's why we are so brown.'

Bempton Cliffs, North Yorkshire *N 54°08'42.7" W 0°09'27.6" Grid Ref: TA204737 Map Ref: 5 B1*

Somewhere around a quarter of a million seabirds – gannets, guillemots, razorbills, puffins, kittiwakes, fulmars – nest in the ledges of Bempton Cliffs each spring and summer, a truly staggering sight, sound and smell when experienced from the viewing platforms of the RSPB's reserve. Travel writer and heroic enthusiast H.V. Morton got even closer to the action in 1927, when he had himself lowered over the cliffs in an egg-collector's harness. Trembling with fear at the sight of a chunk of chalk he had dislodged falling, seemingly for ever, towards the sea many hundreds of feet below, Morton had himself ignominiously hauled up again 'in an agony of self-contempt.'

Flamborough Head, East Riding of Yorkshire *N 54°07'03.6" W 0°04'59.0" Grid Ref: TA254708 Map Ref: 5 B1*

The arrow-headed promontory of Flamborough Head (*Flaneburg*, 'arrowhead place', to the Danes) spears eastward into the sea from the southernmost sector of the North Yorkshire coast. The Head boasts two lighthouse towers. Beside the road to Selwicks Bay rises an octagonal 17th-century tower of chalk blocks, which may in fact have been used only as an observation post – archaeological investigation has failed to find any evidence of a fire having been maintained in it. The tower on the bay, still in use, was built in 1806 to warn off shipping from the very dangerous hazard of the out-thrust Head.

Cliffs south of Flamborough (left)

N 54°06'08.3" W 0°08'53.3"
Grid Ref: TA212690 Map Ref: 5 C1

Thickly plastered, a dark wedge of boulder clay overlies the pure white of the chalk cliffs to the south of Flamborough. The clay, dragged eastwards by melting glaciers at the end of the last Ice Age, is easily eaten away by the sea, an effect seen to sobering effect further south along the East Yorkshire coast where North Sea storm waves bite further inland each winter.

Bridlington, East Riding of Yorkshire

N 54°04'36.7" W 0°11'54.9"
Grid Ref: TA180660 Map Ref: 5 B1

Cradled in the armpit of Flamborough Head's peninsula, the seaside resort of Bridlington relies on its fine sandy beaches of North and South Sands, separated by the concrete and stone pincers of the harbour. South of Bridlington some forty miles of sand, backed by ever-diminishing cliffs, stretches with hardly a break to the ant-eater snout of the Spurn Head promontory at the mouth of the Humber Estuary.

Kingston-upon-Hull, East Riding of Yorkshire

N 53°44'23.5" W 0°15'47.9"
Grid Ref: TA146285 Map Ref: 5 B4

The Port of Hull lies 20 miles inland of the mouth of the River Humber, yet the river is still nearly two miles wide here. The Humber is a mighty waterway, and Hull Docks bustle with large-vessel activity. This view, looking across the Queen Elizabeth and King George Docks, illustrates a multifarious trade including sand and gravel, timber, fertiliser, and bananas carried to Hull from the Caribbean by the long-established Geest line.

Under Attack
Lincolnshire Coast to Thames Estuary

Between the River Humber and the River Thames curves a coast under constant attack by the sea. East Anglia possesses the moodiest coastline in England, a great double bulge of sand and mudflats, a salt marsh and shingle coast that runs from Lincolnshire into Norfolk around the square-mouthed estuary of The Wash, rises briefly in a line of crumbly chalk and clay cliffs along the coast of North Norfolk, then subsides to sea level in shingle, marsh and mud once more along the lonely shores of Suffolk, Essex and North Kent.

This is the youngest region, geologically speaking, in Britain, a mostly flat coastal tableland spread with rich arable clay and silt by the torrents of meltwater vomited by retreating glaciers at the end of the last Ice Age. Great extinct rivers flowed here, out across what was once a dry North Sea, to join what is now the River Rhine. Many estuaries, creeks, marshes and outfalls of water characterise the coast today. The big rivers that empty into The Wash – Witham, Welland, Nene, Great Ouse – flow in man-made watercourses to artificially shaped mouths, eloquent of the need to control their flow and prevent the flooding with which outrushing rainfall or incoming high tides have so often devastated this low-lying countryside in the past.

Despite its generally smoothly convex profile, there are enough promontories, sand and shingle spits, islands and nesses to provide shelter and food for the millions of birds that find landfall here on their spring and autumn migration flights. Gibraltar Point in Lincolnshire, Scolt Head Island and Blakeney Point on the North Norfolk coast, Orford Ness in Suffolk and the marsh islands of Essex and North Kent are cases in point. Then there are the huge stretches of mudflats in the estuaries of Humber, Wash, Deben, Stour, Blackwater, Thames and Medway, the extensive marshes of North Norfolk and Essex, to attract wintering ducks and geese in hundreds of thousands. Birds of prey follow the smaller birds: marsh harrier in summer, and in winter short-eared owls and hen harrier, in addition to fast-moving smaller species such as hobby, merlin and peregrine. A string of nature reserves all down this coast attests to these natural riches.

There are other riches here, too, aesthetic ones that draw painters, sculptors and musicians to the East Coast. The endlessly varied and ever-changing colours of the mudflats have a sombre beauty, especially when the sun draws out gleaming subtleties of colour, grading from shimmering green to a desert-like tan and a deep midnight blue. Their shapes shift under wind and tide, too, so that after gazing a while you begin to see them in the same way as photographic negatives, and to wonder which of the thread-like creeks and miniature spits of marsh is the land, and which the water. As for the melancholy, rhythmical sigh and hiss of waves on the pebbly shore, it so inspired Benjamin Britten that the Lowestoft-born composer moved to Aldeburgh where he could hear it night and day and weave it into *Billy Budd*, *Albert Herring*, *Peter Grimes*, *Curlew River* and many other works.

Grimsby, Lincolnshire *N 53°34′59.3″ W 0°04′05.5″ Grid Ref: TA280114 Map Ref: 5 C5*

The hoary old tale of a fisherman being able to walk from one end of Grimsby Docks to the other along the decks of moored fishing boats without getting his seaboots wet might actually have been true in Grimsby's 1950s heyday, when the Lincolnshire town was the busiest fishing port in the world. These days, with tumbling fish stocks in the North Sea, you can count the number of deep sea trawlers in Grimsby Docks on one hand. It's fish processing that rules the roost around these vast empty basins now – a million tonnes a year, with almost all the fish being caught elsewhere.

Ingoldmells caravans, Lincolnshire *N 53°11'28.5" E 0°21'18.1" Grid Ref: TF574686 Map Ref: 5 E8*

Why does the anagram 'old lemmings' spring to mind ...? Just north of Skegness on the outermost bulge of the Lincolnshire coast lies a gigantic conglomeration of caravan parks at Ingoldmells, clustered around the point where eternal showman Billy Butlin established the first of his holiday camps in 1936. In the midst of the serried waves of caravans rises Fantasy Island theme park, from whose white-knuckle rides the screaming can be heard for miles along the otherwise eerily silent shore.

Under Attack
Lincolnshire Coast to Thames Estuary

This coast is still dynamic, building and vanishing, throwing out a shingle spit here, absorbing a swathe of salt marsh there, a process that happens every day, yet can take a thousand years. The shingle spits of Blakeney Point, Scolt Head Island and Orford Ness have all grown by five miles or more since medieval times, while a wide apron of salt marsh has developed along the North Norfolk coast, stranding a line of former coastal ports a mile or more inland. Their former ways of life, based around fishing and coastal trading, have all but vanished.

These are not the only East Coast livelihoods under attack, as dwindling North Sea fish stocks and increasingly stringent conservation regulations reduce the once-vibrant fishing industry to a pale shadow of its former self. Shellfish trawlers and long-line specialists are still viable, but in reduced circumstances, their small boats tying up to bollards where deep-sea trawlers once moored. The huge, strong dock basins at Grimsby and Lowestoft, the busiest in the world during the 20th-century cod and herring booms, now lie all but empty. Their owners are considering how to market them into the leisure and holiday business - which has itself recently gone through hard times at the 'cheap'n'cheerful' end of the spectrum, as cut-price flights to inexpensive foreign destinations in the sun have siphoned away holidaymakers from the traditional East Coast resorts of Cleethorpes, Skegness, Great Yarmouth, Clacton-on-Sea and Southend-on-Sea. As with fishing, it is small-and-classy that is winning the day, with seaside towns such as Sheringham, Cromer, Southwold and Aldeburgh attracting middle-class custom with arts and music festivals, decent restaurants, tidy beaches and clean sea.

It is that sea, ever-hungry, ever rising, which is proving the most dramatic agent of change along the East Coast. Cliffs are falling to the attacks of storm waves at an ever-increasing rate, as seen at Hunstanton, Sheringham and Overstrand. Man's works are threatened, too, by the attacking sea: houses and gardens at Happisburgh in Norfolk, the unique quatrefoil Martello Tower at Aldeburgh in Suffolk, the splendid twin towers of St Mary's Church on the North Kent cliffs at Reculver, apt symbols of man's aspirations and his vulnerability.

In Hunstanton, in Overstrand, in Happisburgh there is fury at the failure of the Environment Agency, of local councils, of national government to guarantee protection of these places. Everyone wants his or her own particular, much-loved patch to be saved. Everyone has a very special case to urge, a uniquely worthy cause to plead. We love the place we love. But there is just not enough money to shore up everything along this crumbling, sliding, stealthily disappearing coast.

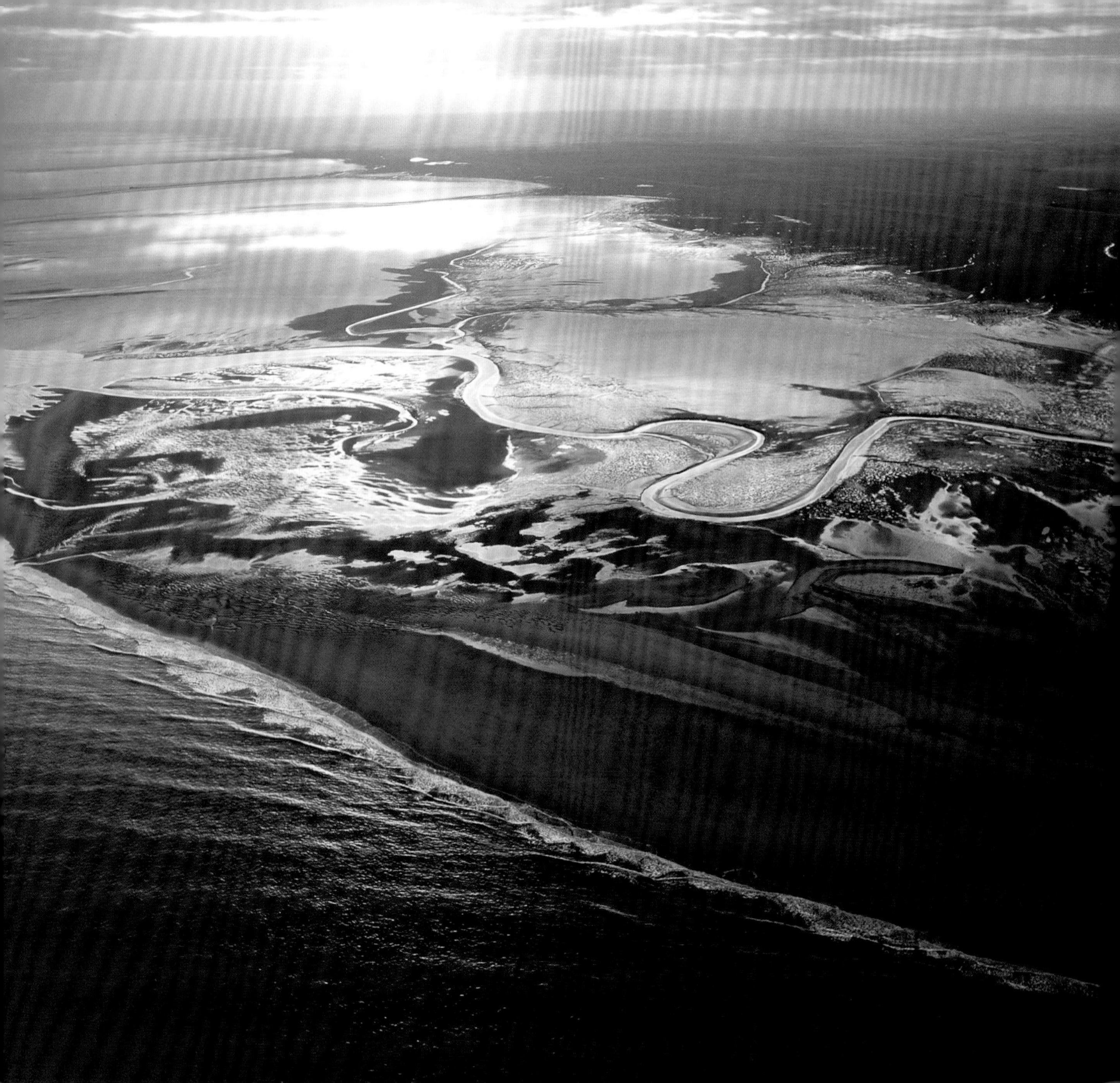

Gibraltar Point, Lincolnshire *N 53°06'21.5" E 0°20'49.4" Grid Ref: TF572591 Map Ref: 5 E9*

Like tendrils of mermaid hair, creeks lazily curl to the sea through the mud and sand flats of Gibraltar Point. This southward-pointing peninsula is surrounded by many miles of tidal muds, a well-stocked larder of invertebrate food for seabirds – in particular the dunlin, stout little wayfarers with pointed black bills and white scimitar-shaped wing flashes who twist and turn over the flats all together as if at a single command.

Frampton Marsh, The Wash, Lincolnshire *N 52°54'33.4" E 0°02'17.4" Grid Ref: TF372366 Map Ref: 5 C10*

On the left the Witham (known in this estuarine stretch as The Haven), on the right the Welland: the two Fenland rivers converge as they reach the broad tidal basin of The Wash. Artificially straightened and dredged to allow a permanent passage to the sea through ever-changing mud and sand banks, Witham and Welland carry a vast freight of Grade One silt, which they spread at their mouths to form the muddy salt marsh of Frampton Marsh. In winter this windy nature reserve is quartered by birds of prey – small deadly peregrine and merlin, and the larger hen harrier with its majestically slow wing beats.

Great Ouse, Norfolk *N 52°48'53.9" E 0°21'15.1" Grid Ref: TF588268 Map Ref: 5 E11*

All the sculptural beauty of the great salt marshes of The Wash is caught in this wonderful shot. Fringed by flat banks of mud and marsh as delicately fronded as a tropical leaf, a fishing boat alters course at the mouth of the River Great Ouse to enter the Lynn Channel which will guide her inland to the ancient port of King's Lynn.

Hunstanton Cliffs, Norfolk *N 52°56'25.6" E 0°29'10.9" Grid Ref: TF672410 Map Ref: 5 F10*

Facing the North Sea at the outer edge of the eastern Wash shore, the cliffs around the Norfolk resort of Hunstanton are a geological jam sandwich. Crimson Hunstanton red chalk forms the filling, with white chalk on top and brown sandstone below. Only a narrow grassy sward separates the rapidly eroding cliff edge from the houses behind. How long before the sea is at their feet?

Scott Head Island, Norfolk *N 52°58'55.0" E 0°41'39.6" Grid Ref: TF810461 Map Ref: 5 F10*

Scolt Head Island, a bird-haunted National Nature Reserve accessible only by boat in spring and summer, is a supreme example of a barrier island created by longshore drift. This steady, westward-moving process has seen the shingle spit grow four miles long over the past 1,000 years. What painter could catch the other-worldly scene around the westward tip of the island, where translucent blue divides the subtlest of salt marsh colours – cream, biscuit, ochre, tan and a hundred others yet to be named?

Wells-next-the-Sea, Norfolk *N 52°57'30.7" E 0°51'09.6" Grid Ref: TF917439 Map Ref: 5 G10*

The quays at Wells-next-the-Sea lie three miles from the open sea, isolated by coastal processes that have strangled the commercial life out of a whole string of former sea ports along the North Norfolk Coast. The local rivers are the villains of the piece, spreading their fertile silt along the shore. Saltmarsh develops and grows, sheltering the mud banks from erosion and forming a barrier between the coast towns and the sea.

Blakeney Point, Norfolk *N 52°58'23.4" E 0°57'35.0" Grid Ref: TF988459 Map Ref: 5 H10*

Though not yet an island, the 3.5 mile shingle spit of Blakeney Point continues to grow westward under the same tidal process of longshore drift as its near neighbour Scolt Head Island (see page 250). The hooked tip of the Point reaches into the shallow mouth of Blakeney Harbour, a connecting channel that now snakes for five miles through the mudflats before it reaches Blakeney, a town whose quays faced the open North Sea in Tudor times.

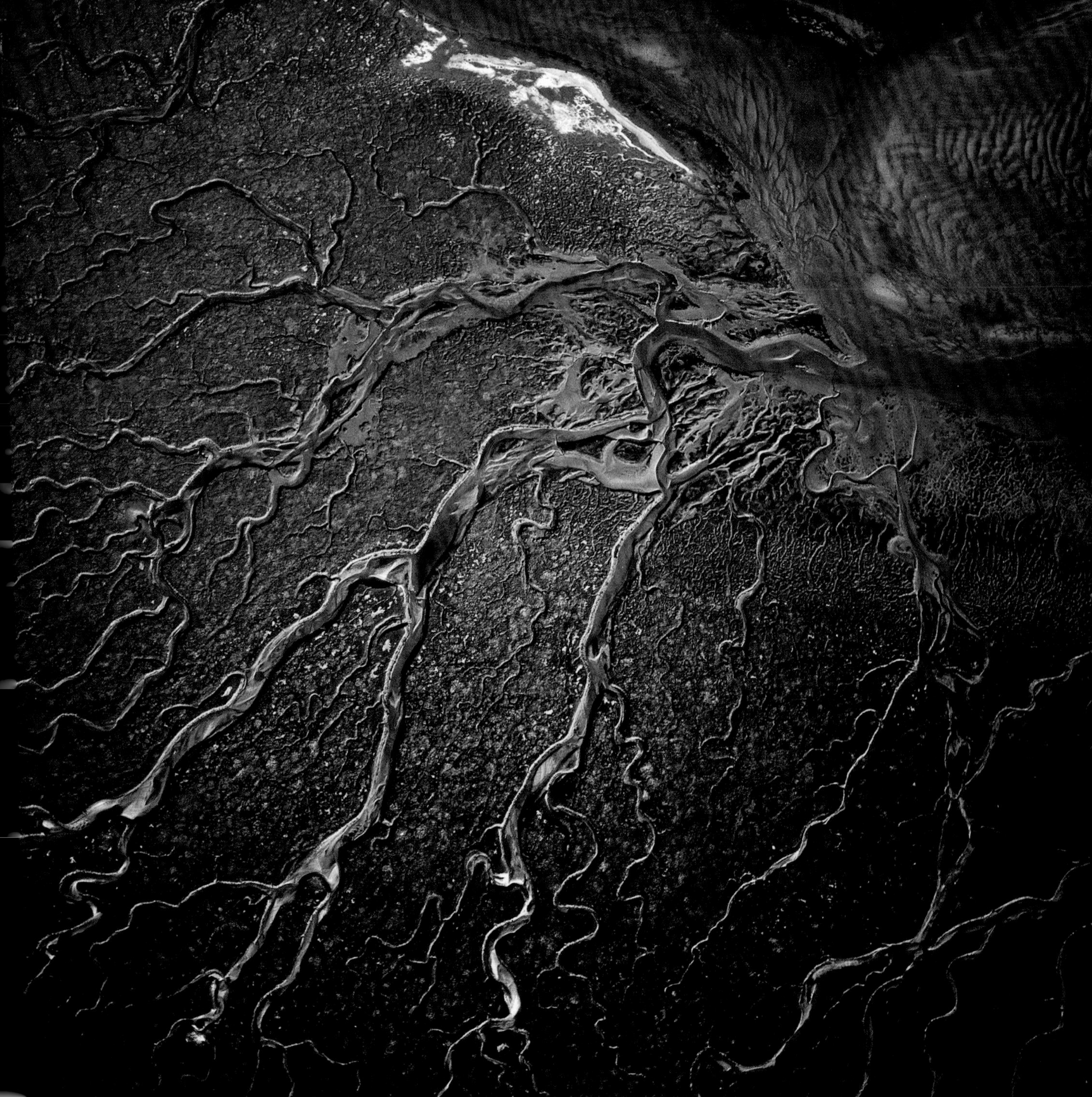

Mudflats at Blakeney Point, Norfolk *N 52°58'16.6" E 0°59'43.3" Grid Ref: TG012457 Map Ref: 5 H10*

A stunning view of salt marsh and mudflats just north of Tibby Head, the flat body of these vegetated silt deposits invaded by wriggling threads of creek. The impression of an enormously magnified sea creature, a shrimp or flea, extending a cluster of amorphous limbs, is very striking.

Cromer, Norfolk *N 52°55'57.9" E 1°18'03.1" Grid Ref: TG219424 Map Ref: 5 I10*

Huddled around the splendid tower of the church of St Peter and St Paul – at 160 ft the tallest in the county – the former fishing village of Cromer became North Norfolk's premier family seaside resort during the 19th century. There's a pleasingly old-fashioned air to Cromer, encapsulated in its enduring and still popular end-of-the-pier shows. The end of the pier is also the scene of deadly serious business: this part of the coast is a treacherous one, and the lifeboat is housed here. Henry Blogg, recipient of three Gold and four Silver Medals of the RNLI – the most famous and most-decorated lifeboatman in the history of the service – served the Cromer lifeboat for 53 years, 38 of them as Coxswain.

Overstrand cliffs, Norfolk *N 52°54'34.8" E 1°21'40.6" Grid Ref: TG261400 Map Ref: 5 J10*

Just along the coast from Cromer the cliffs of soft yellow clay are continually sliding into the sea, the frequent falls and slips lending them a backward-sloping profile. The cliff-edge path which London journalist Clement Scott followed in 1883 through poppy-strewn cornfields has long crumbled away. Scott fell romantically in love with this corner of the Norfolk coast, christened it 'Poppyland' in his writings, and sparked a craze for the area which grew into a huge tourist boom.

Happisburgh, Norfolk (left)

N 52°49'22.1" E 1°32'22.4"
Grid Ref: TG386309 Map Ref: 5 J11

A mess of stone blocks, timber baulks and metal guards the base of a sharp and rapidly diminishing promontory at Happisburgh. None of the many forms of beach defence installed in the past has succeeded in keeping the sea from these crumbling cliffs of soft crag and clay. There is bitterness among locals at the failure of the 'powers-that-be' to guarantee the safety of the village, a scenario set to become all too familiar along this fragile and steadily eroding coast.

Lowestoft, Suffolk

N 52°28'19.5" E 1°45'16.0"
Grid Ref: TM551926 Map Ref: 5 L13

Like its sister port of Grimsby up on the Lincolnshire coast, the north Suffolk fishing port of Lowestoft was tremendously busy and prosperous in the early to mid-20th century, when hundreds of herring drifters and cod trawlers packed the docks. Celebrated for their outlandish shape were the 'beamers' – beam trawlers with wide gantries like giant arms akimbo holding the nets out each side of the boat. Now Lowestoft's fishing trade is confined to a handful of gill netters, long-line and crab boats, and the famous docks lie all but empty.

Slaughden, Aldeburgh, Suffolk

N 52°08'23.0" E 1°35'55.5"
Grid Ref: TM463552 Map Ref: 3 L1

A crucial place in the sea defences of the Suffolk coast, Slaughden – just south of Aldeburgh - is the point where the River Alde would reach the sea, were it not for the 100-yard-wide neck of shingle that forms the northward end of Orford Ness shingle spit. Instead of meeting the sea directly here, as it did in medieval times before the Ness began to form, the Alde is forced round the tight bend of Westrow Reach before commencing a southward run inside the arm of the spit to its far-off mouth near Shingle Street, ten miles to the south. Coastal erosion and rising ocean levels will see Alde and sea reunited at Slaughden in the not too distant future.

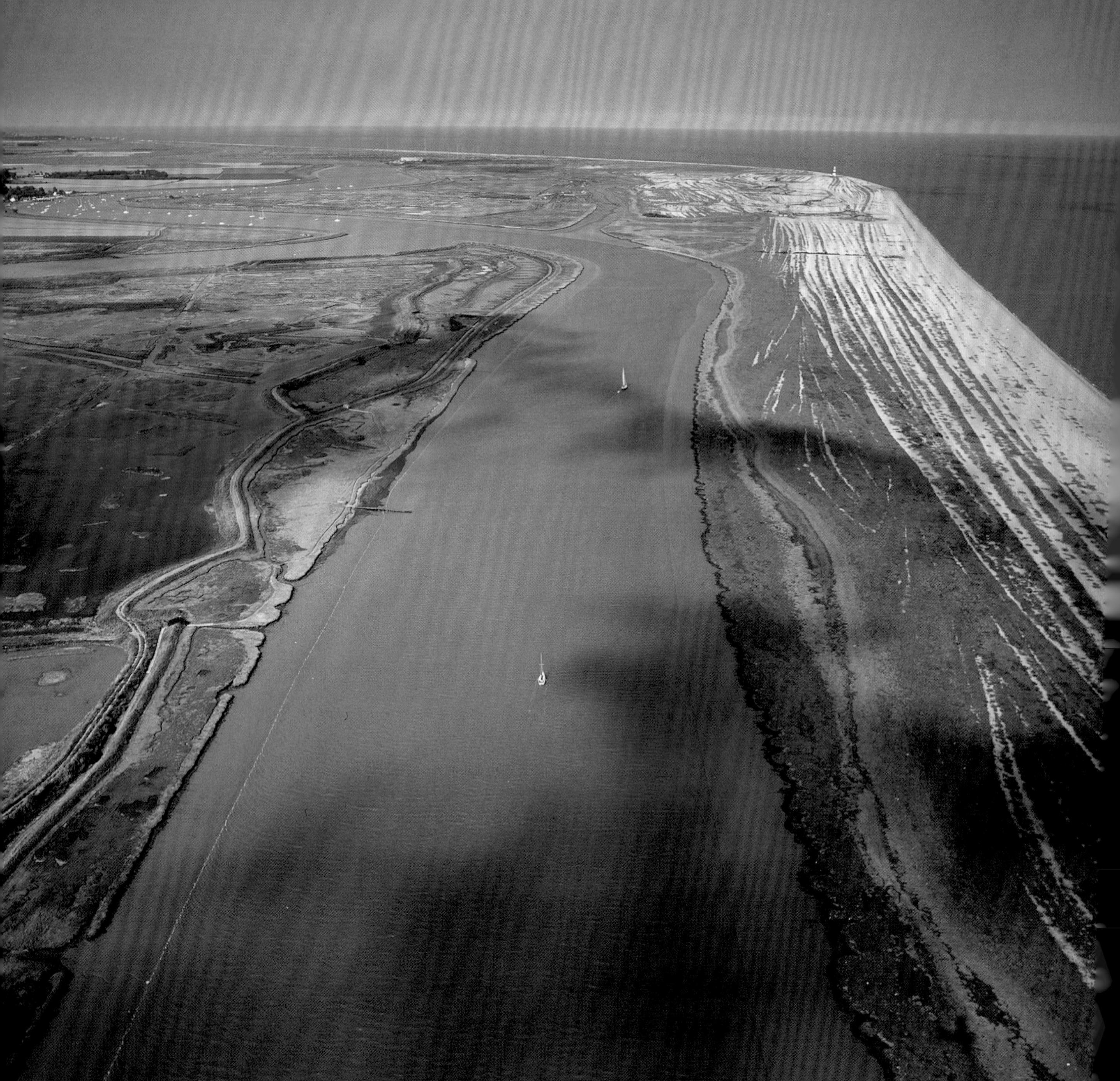

Orford Ness, Suffolk *N 52°04'14.1" E 1°31'44.4" Grid Ref: TM419472 Map Ref: 3 L2*

Orford Ness is one of the most mysterious and remote places in Britain, a lonely shingle spit off the Suffolk coast that was out of bounds as a MoD experimental establishment throughout the two World Wars and the ensuing Cold War of the 20th century. Now owned and run as a nature reserve by the National Trust, the Ness is revealed as Europe's finest vegetated shingle spit, a haven of wild flowers and seabirds, one of the truly wild places along the English coast.

Orford Ness mouth, Suffolk *N 52°02'28.4" E 1°27'47.9" Grid Ref: TM376438 Map Ref: 3 L2*

A remarkable panorama of the entire 10-mile course of the River Alde inside the protective arm of Orford Ness shingle spit. As it flows past the one-time port of Orford, now cut off from the sea by the Ness, the Alde changes its name to Ore, under which title it passes the club-shaped head of Orford Ness to reach the sea. Whether the spit will continue to exist once it is breached at Aldeburgh (see page 257) is a matter of conjecture.

Landguard Point, Felixstowe, Suffolk *N 51°56'04.5" E 1°19'11.8" Grid Ref: TM283314 Map Ref: 3 K3*

With the containers massed in Felixstowe Freightliner Terminal crowding at its back, the fort on Landguard Point looks a bit threatened from the north these days. But menace from that direction is something the old stronghold has survived before. In 1667, during Britain's now forgotten war with Holland, a force of one and a half thousand Dutch grenadiers and sailors wielding pikes and muskets attacked Landguard Fort from its landward side, and was repulsed. It was the only time the fort – built in 1543 to guard the joint entrance to the rivers Orwell and Stour, and many times altered and expanded – saw any action. Nowadays the spit of land at the southern tip of the Suffolk coast is a peaceful nature reserve, a noted landfall for migrating birds and a haven for rare shore plants.

Harwich Harbour, Essex *N 51°56'54.5" E 1°16'48.5" Grid Ref: TM255329 Map Ref: 3 K3*

Stena Line's HSS (High Speed Sea-service) catamaran ferry leaves Harwich for the Hook of Holland. The 40-knot crossing on board *Stena Discovery* took 3 hours 40 minutes, about half the time of conventional ferry crossings – a great advantage for passengers going on booze cruises to stock up on cheap drink in Hook of Holland hypermarkets. But *Stena Discovery* was withdrawn from the route in January 2007, owing mainly to rising fuel costs – she used more fuel than Stena Line's seven other conventional North Sea ferries put together.

Clacton Pier, Clacton-on-Sea, Essex

N 51°47'11.6" E 1°09'19.6"
Grid Ref: TM177145 Map Ref: 3 J4

It was the energetic and visionary Manager of the Eastern Union Railway, Peter Bruff, who oversaw the construction of the first wooden pier at Clacton-on-Sea in 1871. Bruff foresaw the holiday boom which would result if steam pleasure boats from London could be accommodated on this shallow coast. The pier was soon rebuilt in cast iron, and when a branch railway line reached Clacton-on-Sea in 1882 the town's future was assured. The former fishing village became a Londoners' resort, its pier a fairground above the sea.

Northey Island, Essex (right)

N 51°43'21.5" E 0°43'28.5"
Grid Ref: TL883062 Map Ref: 3 H5

As blotchily beautiful as a jaguar's skin, the numberless mazy curlicues of Northey Island's salt marshes fill with water on a rising tide. Northey Island, these days a nature reserve, lies in the Blackwater Estuary, an estuarine highway used by the Danes during their invasions of the British coast. The Battle of Maldon took place here on 10 August 991, a complete rout of the Saxons who had penned up a strong force of Danish marauders on the island and then – either through hubris or stupidity - unwisely allowed them to cross the causeway and fight on solid ground.

Maldon, Essex

N 51°43'40.7" E 0°41'39.8"
Grid Ref: TL862067 Map Ref: 3 H5

With the characterful old sailing-barge quays of the Hythe (seen on the left) facing the busy industrial area of Heybridge across the salt marshes of the River Blackwater, the Essex town of Maldon is a bustling place. One of its traditional industries, salt-making, is going stronger than ever. On high spring tides in dry periods of the year, when the salt is at its greatest concentration, water is extracted from the sea and evaporated in big pans, the hollow pyramidal crystals being collected by hand using long-handled paddles. Drained, dried, packed and sold, the sea-salt of the Maldon Crystal Salt Company is the connoisseur's choice.

Southend-on-Sea, Essex

N 51°30'54.1" E 0°43'18.8"
Grid Ref: TQ890831 Map Ref: 3 H6

Southend-on-Sea began as an obscure Thames Estuary fishing village, developed into a genteel Regency watering hole, and then became an all-out East Enders' Bank Holiday resort with the advent of the railway and the building of Southend Pier, first in wood, completed in 1830, then rebuilt in iron, opening in 1887. The longest in the world at 1.34 miles, the pier has endured and survived accidental fires, arson and ship collisions.

Coryton Oil Refinery, Essex

N 51°30'24.3" E 0°31'15.0"
Grid Ref: TQ750817 Map Ref: 3 H7

Downriver of London, the north or Essex shore of the River Thames is cluttered with industrial plant, ancient wharves, gargantuan rubbish tips and factories. Of these gritty purlieus, one of the most impressive is the oil refinery at Coryton, opened in the 1950s between Tilbury and Canvey Island. The last working refinery on the Thames, the Coryton plant accommodates crude oil tankers of up to a quarter of a million tonnes, and produces about 10 million tonnes of refined fuel each year.

cobelfret - ferries

Dartford Crossing *N 51°27'53.0" E 0°15'30.5" Grid Ref: TQ570764 Map Ref: 3 F7*

The graceful shape of the Queen Elizabeth II Bridge, another of those late 20th-century bridges so pleasingly fashioned like ethereal sails or white-strung harps, spans the River Thames at Dartford, downstream of Tower Bridge. Opened in 1991 to take some of the pressure off the Dartford road tunnels under the river, the bridge carries traffic in an exhilarating arc more than two hundred feet above the water.

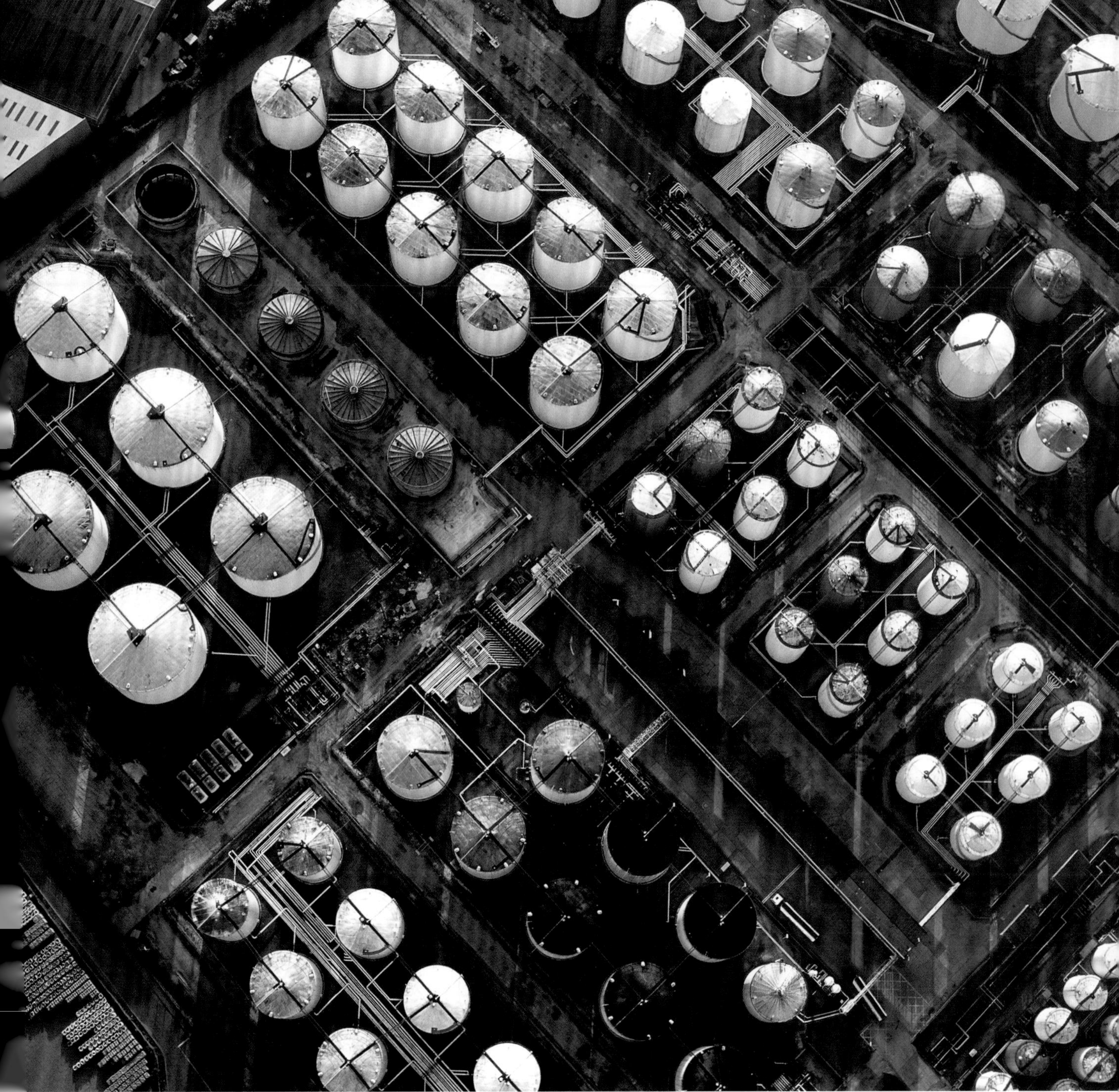

Silwood Oil Depot, West Thurrock, Essex *N 51°28′06.0″ E 0°16′05.7″ Grid Ref: TQ576768 Map Ref: 3 F7*

Like so many strange fungi, storage tanks cluster according to capacity in the Thames-side depot of Silwood Petroleum Ltd. The depot, one of many oil industry plants along the Essex shore of the Thames east of London, stands on West Thurrock Marshes in the shadow of the Queen Elizabeth II bridge (see left). Immediately to the east of the depot lie West Thurrock lagoons, site of a redundant power station. This wildlife haven, especially rich in flower and insect life, is considered a brownfield site by the local planning authority, and is under constant threat of development.

Colemouth Creek, River Medway, Kent

N 51°26'45.1" E 0°39'43.6"
Grid Ref: TQ851752 Map Ref: 3 H7

Looking east along the south or Kentish shore of the River Thames to where the eastern tip of the Isle of Grain rounds into the mud-stained waters of the River Medway. In the foreground lie Stoke Saltings, a range of salt marshes that has formed in the wide crook of tidal ground shaped by the outflow of Colemouth Creek. Plans are afoot to realign the southern edge of the saltings, in order to create more brackish and saline habitat against the predicted rise in sea levels.

Car Depository, Isle of Sheppey. Kent

N 51°26'01.0" E 0°44'26.5"
Grid Ref: TQ906741 Map Ref: 3 I7

The Isle of Sheppey lies just east of the Isle of Grain on the south shore of the River Thames. The former naval dockyard of Queenborough at the island's north-west tip has become a gathering ground for enormous numbers of cars imported through its docks. Seen from an aeroplane passing overhead, they form a bizarre pattern like colourful corduroy or multiple strings of beads.

Reculver, Kent (right)

N 51°22'47.3" E 1°11'58.4"
Grid Ref: TR227694 Map Ref: 3 K7

Caught within the square defences of the Roman shore fort of Regulbium, the towers of St Mary's Church at Reculver seem solid and four-square as they stand looking east over the tanks of a shellfish farm and on up the River Thames. The towers are ruins, though, and so is the Saxon monastic church they were grafted onto in the 12th century. The whole structure stands at the edge of soft clay cliffs, waiting for the inexorable effects of tide and time to break through the sea defences and topple it to the beach and final dissolution in the muddy Thames tides.

The Chalk Barrier
Thames Estuary to Selsey Bill

The coast of the great white cliffs is all about chalk. This iconic substance, so white and clean, so strong when coherent and upstanding yet so brittle when broken, so fertile and full of uses, symbolises quite a lot about how the British view themselves. The coastline of Kent and Sussex was closest to the enemy during the two World Wars of the 20th century, only a matter of a few miles. German bombers pounded and fighters strafed targets along familiar promenades and High Streets. Armadas of small boats set out from Dover, from Folkestone, from Ramsgate and Hastings to ferry the men of the British Army home from Dunkirk in the summer of 1940. It was to the White Cliffs of Dover, the solid white chalk bulwarks of Britain, that people looked for reassurance, courage and a sense of identity.

The great deposits of chalk that form the south-east corner of England were laid down some 60 to 80 million years ago, and they are composed entirely of the bodies – the shells and hard body parts – of trillions upon trillions of tiny marine creatures, *Foraminifera*, which lived and died in the warm tropical seas that covered north-west Europe then. Within the matrix of the chalk lie nodules of flint composed of compacted crystals of silica from the skeletons of other sea creatures. This flint with its cutting edges, so useful to man in his early struggles to survive, is by far the most solid thing about the chalk. Those apparently strong cliff ramparts are actually weak, vulnerable to collapse owing to undermining by the sea or cracking through the actions of frost and rainwater. Water cuts them like cheese, scooping out deep valleys as it flows to the sea; and it spreads their flints in gigantic pebbly sheets such as that at the promontory spit of Dungeness.

The knolls and headlands along this coast have been utilised since time out of mind by human settlers and defenders, people with enemies on their mind and a need to stay up high with a clear view all round. Great castles such as that at Dover, lighthouses, lookout towers and Iron Age hill forts lie dotted along the coastal hills of Kent and Sussex, while

The Chalk Barrier
Thames Estuary to Selsey Bill

shore defences, Tudor castles and Martello towers fromNapoleonic times fill in the gaps. Hilltop towns like Rye and Winchelsea were sited with the same aims in mind.

When it came to pleasure rather than survival, the chalk cliff coast was perfectly placed, close to London but with its own strong non-urban character. The Georgian craze for drinking and bathing in seawater for the good of one's health saw many a small fishing village swollen with visitors and their money. Seaside resorts developed early and boomed with the coming of the cheap railway train: Margate and Brighton for a Bank Holiday knees-up, Broadstairs and Eastbourne for a genteel sojourn.

Today's coast dwellers feel the same urge to live as close as possible to the sea, behind man-made defences such as the immense breakwaters of the Black Rock marina near Brighton, or Sovereign Harbour along the coast at Eastbourne. The force and the power of the sea seem easily resistible with the application of modern technology like this. But one only has to look at the sad, skeletal wreck of Brighton's West Pier, eaten into collapse and dissolution within a matter of decades by the elements, to see what nature can do to our grandiose schemes and triumphant creations. This coast is set for profound change, if current predictions of rising sea levels and intensifying storms are borne out. Low-lying, traditionally tidal ground such as Pagham Harbour and Cuckmere Haven could be inundated. The chalk cliffs could be bitten into by the sea with unprecedented vigour. The seemingly static coast of chalk could prove to be as dynamic and changeable as that of East Anglia. Time will tell. One returns with fascination and foreboding to Dae Sasitorn's brilliant but disturbing photograph of Black Rock marina, the slender arm of its breakwater extended between the ordered, man-made calm of the lagoon and the random, untameable energy of the sea.

Margate, Kent

N 51°23'25.4" E 1°22'46.0" Grid Ref: TR353711 Map Ref: 3 L

Cradled by the broad arm of its jetty, Margate's wide sandy beach lies uncharacteristically empty. A Margate man, Benjamin Beale, is credited with inventing the bathing machine in about 1750 to safeguard the modesty of ladies. Margate was a genteel resort back then, reached after a journey of several hours by sailing hoy from London. Paddle steamers began to bring day passengers to the pier from 1815 onwards. When the railway arrived in 1863, the seaside town at the mouth of the Thames Estuary was suddenly under two hours' cheap train journey from the capital. Margate became feisty and fun.

Kingsgate Bay, Kent

N 51°22'57.0" E 1°26'38.6"
Grid Ref: TR397705 Map Ref: 3 L7

Around Kingsgate Bay the chalk begins to rise into the first recognisable examples of the famous White Cliffs of England's south-east coast. Here stands the white-painted mansion of Holland House, and beyond it at the edge of the cliffs the massive bulk of Kingsgate Castle, originally built in the 1760s by Lord Holland as a set of splendidly extravagant stables, then extended at the end of the 19th century by Lord Avebury. Kingsgate Castle looks as if it could stand there till Doomsday; but, like a castle in a parable, its foundations are terminally shaky.

Broadstairs, Kent

N 51°21'30.0" E 1°26'36.9"
Grid Ref: TR398678 Map Ref: 3 L8

Wind and tide cut across each other to produce a vigorous swirling pattern in the east-facing bay of Broadstairs, the Isle of Thanet's traditionally genteel resort. Gentry dismayed by the advent of *hoi polloi* in Margate in the early 19th century removed to Broadstairs and made it a bastion of respectability. Charles Dickens loved the place, spending many holidays here in the 1830s and 40s and writing all or part of *David Copperfield, The Old Curiosity Shop, Barnaby Rudge* and *Nicholas Nickleby.*

Ramsgate, Kent

N 51°19'33.2" E 1°25'11.8"
Grid Ref: TR384641 Map Ref: 3 L8

Ramsgate's Royal Harbour, facing south from the underside of the Isle of Thanet, shelters a yacht marina in its inner basin and many kinds of motley craft in the outer section, all guarded by the protective arms of East and West Pier. It was an ill wind that blew the town some good in December 1748, when that era's rudimentary harbour proved equal to sheltering hundreds of vessels during a savage winter tempest. Ramsgate's reward was the construction of a fine new harbour with cross-walls, breakwaters, dry docks, a lighthouse, and sluices designed by the great engineer John Smeaton which are still in operation today.

Deal Castle, Kent (right)

N 51°13'10.2" E 1°24'13.1"
Grid Ref: TR378522 Map Ref: 3 L9

A few miles down the Kentish coast from the Isle of Thanet lies the old smuggling and fishing town of Deal. In 1539, fearful of an invasion after having provoked Catholic Europe by breaking with the Church of Rome, King Henry VIII ordered the construction of three 'Castles in the Downs' – Deal, Walmer and Sandown – to command the Channel coast overlooking the sheltered anchorage known as The Downs. Deal Castle's ingenious design of concentric rings of bastions round a central tower gave it the pattern of a Tudor rose, a nice piece of flattery.

Walmer Castle, Kent

N 51°12'02.0" E 1°24'07.0"
Grid Ref: TR378501 Map Ref: 3 L9

Walmer Castle is the most southerly of King Henry VIII's three 'Castles in the Downs'. They were built a double cannon-shot apart, so that they could enfilade a line of enemy troops advancing between them without danger of hitting each other. In the 18th century Walmer Castle became the official residence of the Lord Warden of the Cinque Ports (originally a medieval trading confederation). The most famous incumbent was the Duke of Wellington, hero of the Battle of Waterloo in 1815, who lived in Walmer Castle and died there in 1852. His body was escorted by torchlight from the castle to Deal railway station, and from there to London and a magnificent state funeral.

Kingsdown Cliffs, Kent *N 51°10'15.8" E 1°24'13.6" Grid Ref: TR380468 Map Ref: 3 L9*

Kingsdown Cliffs rise just south of Deal. Ian Fleming, creator of secret agent 007 James Bond, knew the area well and used it as a setting for his 1955 thriller *Moonraker*. It was from the top of these cliffs that dastardly Sir Hugo Drax launched the nuclear rocket with which he planned to wipe out London. A few days earlier Drax had almost succeeded in liquidating 007 and his love interest by bringing down the cliff face on them as they lay on the beach below. But our hero survived that scare, and managed to neutralize both rocket and villain. Bond had spotted that Drax was a wrong 'un, of course - the fellow had red hair, and he cheated at cards.

White Cliffs at South Foreland, Kent *N 51°08'19.5" E 1°22'22.5" Grid Ref: TR360431 Map Ref: 3 L9*

Ramparts of chalk two hundred feet tall, the white cliffs that buttress the south-east coast of Kent seem as solid and defiant as their world-renowned image suggests. This vast chalk wedge, formed of the shells and exoskeletons of countless tiny marine creatures, goes down many hundreds of feet below the sea. Yet the cliffs are fragile walls on uncertain foundations, battered by the sea, constantly subject to cracks and falls.

Ferry at Dover, Kent *N 51°07'15.2" E 1°20'35.3" Grid Ref: TR340411 Map Ref: 3 K9*

An iconic image, and a poignant and nostalgic one: a ferry entering the harbour at Dover, with the famous White Cliffs picked out in evening sunlight. More than any other piece of landscape around the British coast it was the White Cliffs of Dover that came to symbolise the nobility, steadfastness and moral purity of this island's resistance to Nazism and Fascism during the Second World War.

Dover Castle, Kent *N 51°07'42.4" E 1°19'23.6" Grid Ref: TR326418 Map Ref: 3 K9*

Perched on a hilltop 465 feet above sea level, Dover Castle has commanded its land and sea surroundings for more than 800 years. From its late Norman origins it grew over the centuries into a mighty, complicated fortress that withstood French attack, Civil War insurrection and German shelling and bombing. Yet what you see is only half the story, for beneath this and the other cliffs around Dover runs a labyrinth of tunnels and subterranean fortifications, some dug by French prisoners-of-war in Napoleonic times, many used as command posts, shelters and underground hospitals during the Battle of Britain and subsequent Blitz of 1940-1.

Folkestone, Kent

N 51°04'23.5" E 1°09'34.1"
Grid Ref: TR214352 Map Ref: 3 K10

Drawn up in self-confident ranks along the western cliffs of Folkestone, the handsome hotels and streets of respectable villas confirm the town's status as a Victorian seaside resort *par excellence*. Yet in 1842, the year the railway arrived in the town, Folkestone was a neglected fishing village in decline from the prosperity it had enjoyed during the Napoleonic wars as a base for smuggling golden guineas into war-torn Europe. It was the iron road that made the fortunes of Folkestone, as of so many other obscure seaside villages in Victorian Britain.

Dungeness, Kent (right)

N 50°54'45.5" E 0°57'47.0"
Grid Ref: TR084168 Map Ref: 3 J11

The enormous arrow-headed shingle spit of Dungeness is Europe's largest. Thousands of parallel lines score its shingle surface, each one a ridge formed during a storm. Dungeness is famous among botanists for its exuberant, hardy shore plants, and among birders all over Britain for its spectacular 'falls' of migrating birds and its sightings of passing sea duck and seabirds. The spit is treasured among discerning walkers and lovers of odd corners of landscape for the strangeness of the scene – two hulking nuclear power stations set in a desert of stones dotted with black-tarred fishermen's huts – and, paradoxically, for the sense of solitude it offers.

Rye, Kent

N 50°57'01.0" E 0°44'26.0"
Grid Ref: TQ926203 Map Ref: 3 I11

The ancient, red-roofed town of Rye clusters on its knoll overlooking the River Rother and the lush green flatlands that form the westernmost edge of Romney Marsh. The little town - a prosperous member of the medieval Cinque Ports trading league, a freemasonry of coast towns with enormous financial privileges – was the beneficiary of an enormous stroke of luck in 1287, when a ferocious storm forced the distant River Rother to change course and to flow right at the feet of Rye, offering a gateway to the sea. Neither privileges nor accidents of geography saved the town on the hill, however, when French marauders came raiding in 1377. They sacked Rye, and burned the whole place to the ground.

Sovereign Harbour, Eastbourne, East Sussex *N 50°47'18.4" E 0°20'00.2" Grid Ref: TQ646014 Map Ref: 3 G12*

Looking freshly laid – as indeed they are – the twin breakwaters of Eastbourne's Sovereign Harbour defend the narrow entrance to one of the most ambitious marina schemes on the South Coast. Since its inaugural year of 1993, shops, apartments, restaurants, housing schemes and dozens of yacht berths have been added to this large and ever-expanding development – at a price. Sovereign Harbour is founded on what was the beautiful vegetated shingle bank of The Crumbles, now obliterated beneath the new construction. Whether, in the face of rising sea levels, that name will prove prophetic remains to be seen.

Eastbourne Pier, East Sussex *N 50°45'57.4" E 0°17'42.6" Grid Ref: TV620988 Map Ref: 3 F12*

Opened in stages during the 1870s, Eastbourne Pier was built of Teesdale cast iron to a clever design – the legs stand untethered in special holders on the seabed which provide some 'give' during storms. The pier runs a thousand feet out to sea, and boasts some handsome Edwardian weather shelters complete with ornate dolphins. It is the only pier in the world with a working Victorian camera obscura, a brilliant way to survey the scene through 360° and admire the splendid hotels along Eastbourne's seafront, classics of the genre with their balconies, domes and pepperpot turrets.

Beachy Head, East Sussex *N 50°44'06.7" E 0°14'28.1" Grid Ref: TV582952 Map Ref: 3 F13*

Nothing could better illustrate the majesty and the fragility of chalk cliffs than this superb view of Beachy Head on the Kent/Sussex border. At 530 feet tall, the Head is the highest chalk cliff in Britain. It dwarfs the lighthouse at its feet – and that itself is 150 feet tall. Yet the great fans of fallen chalk that slope almost from top to bottom of Beachy Head illustrate the volume of material that is continually crumbling away from the cliff.

Seven Sisters, East Sussex *N 50°45′22.5″ E 0°09′27.7″ Grid Ref: TV523974 Map Ref: 3 F12*

Dry valleys run in a series of parallel ridges, so regular that they might be man-made, southward to the edge of the Seven Sisters cliffs, with the white whale's-jaw grin of Belle Tout cliff showing beyond. A walk from Beachy Head over Belle Tout and the Seven Sisters, returning at low tide under the giant white walls along a shore strewn with fallen chalk boulder and lumps of flint, is one to remember for ever.

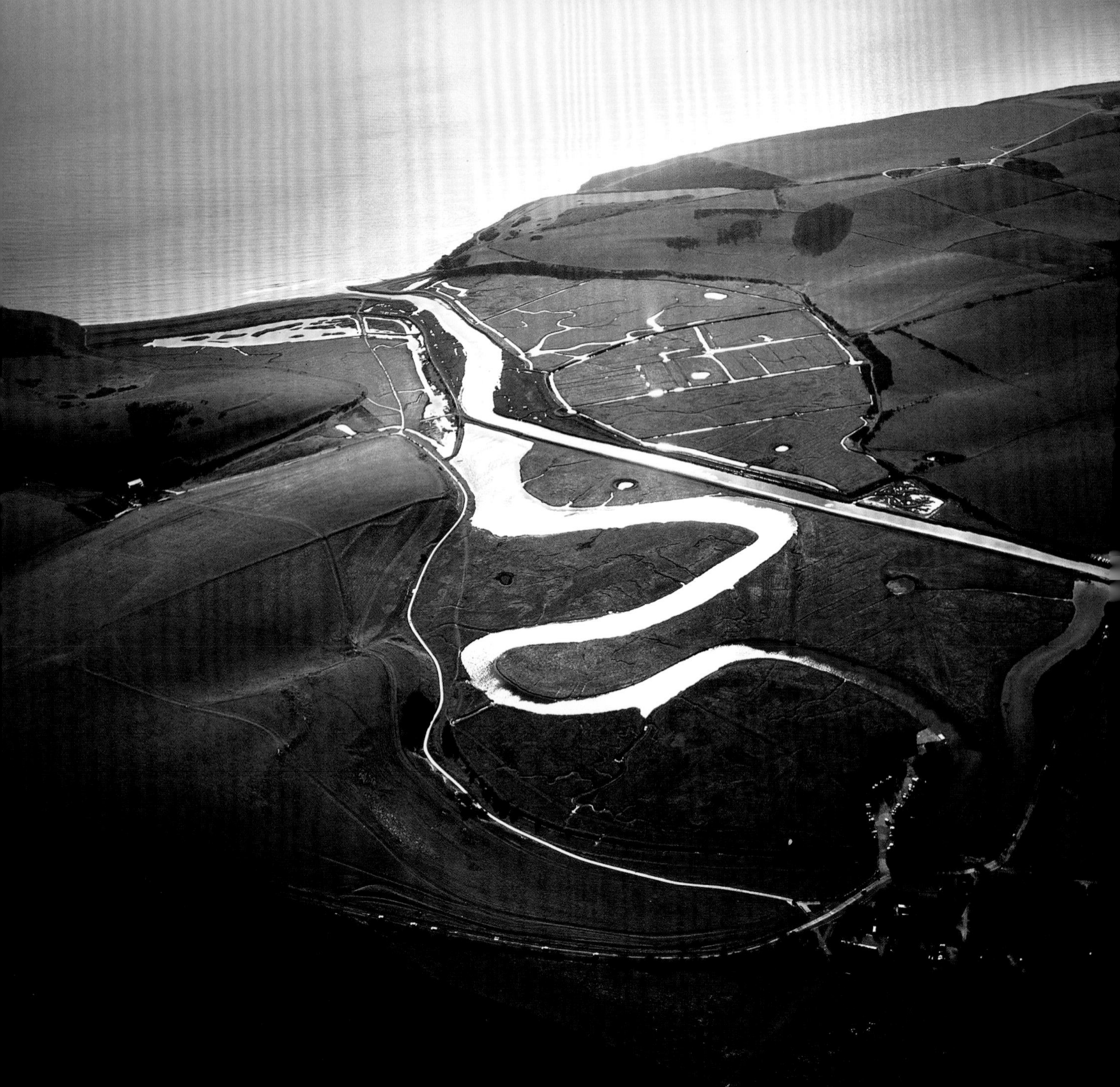

Cuckmere River, East Sussex *N 50°46'10.1" E 0°09'02.0" Grid Ref: TV517989 Map Ref: 3 F12*

Sinuous bends of the Cuckmere River gleam like a silver snake as they wind through the flat meadows towards Cuckmere Haven at the western end of the Seven Sisters cliffs. On the right runs the ruler-straight artificial channel cut in 1847 to bypass the meanders and ease the transportation of goods to and from the Haven. A shingle bank has been maintained for centuries along the shore to prevent sea flooding of the valley, but with the Environment Agency's new policy of 'managed realignment' in the face of rising sea levels, this defence looks set to be abandoned.

Brighton Marina, East Sussex *N 50°48'39.0" W 0°05'58.9" Grid Ref: TQ340030 Map Ref: 3 E12*

The irreconcilability of man and sea is beautifully illustrated in this magnificent shot of the marina at Black Rock on the eastern outskirts of Brighton. Thousands of apartments and houses, nearly 2,000 yacht berths, a host of retail outlets and offices have been built here over the past 30 years, and more are planned. The whole construction directly faces the sea, at the sea's current level – a position only made tenable by the enormous breakwater that shelters the development. Inside that guardian arm, a calm lagoon reflecting images of a confident consumer society; outside, the troubled tides of the rising sea.

Palace Pier, Brighton, East Sussex

N 50°48'54.6" W 0°08'13.6"
Grid Ref: TQ313034 Map Ref: 3 E12

Brighton's Palace Pier was a comparative late-comer to the Victorian seaside ball. It opened in 1899, just one year short of the new century that soon swept away the old order of things. Yet this pier is a survivor, still in business, still taking money in its slot machines and penny-falls, still whirling holidaymakers round on its rollercoasters and roundabouts. The Palace Pier spells fun - good old-fashioned, unsophisticated fun.

West Pier, Brighton, East Sussex

N 50°49'08.1" W 0°09'06.3"
Grid Ref: TQ303038 Map Ref: 3 E12

There could not be a more poignant contrast: Palace Pier, gaudy, rakish and lively, alongside the shrivelled, broken and colourless skeleton of Brighton's senior West Pier, collapsed into the indifferent arms of the sea. West Pier opened in 1866, and for more than 30 years she reigned unchallenged as queen of the seafront. She never recovered from the shock of gaining a rival. After closure in 1975, many and wonderful were the schemes for her future. She would be transformed, revitalised as a casino, a night club, a skating rink, a dance hall, a restaurant ... Meanwhile wind, rain, fire, salt and sea ate away at the old queen, until a storm broke her back and left her entirely redundant, to settle slowly beneath the waves.

Royal Pavilion, Brighton, East Sussex (right)

N 50°49'19.2" W 0°08'16.3"
Grid Ref: TQ313042 Map Ref: 3 E12

As a splendiferously over-the-top monument to princely egotism and bad taste, Brighton's Royal Pavilion stands alone. The Prince Regent, George-IV-in-waiting, had it built in 1815 as his own particular seaside pleasure-dome, and held fantastically extravagant receptions there amid its onion domes, minarets, jewelled dragons and trompe-l'oeuil carvings. Contemporary comments included 'Turnips and tulip bulbs' (William Cobbett), 'Pumpkins and pepper-boxes' (William Hazlitt), and 'One would think that St Paul's Cathedral had come to Brighton – and pupped!' (Sidney Smith). Or, as a local rhymer in 1830 put it:

> 'Well, Cockney, may you drawl, "What's there?"
> It is the Pavilion – see!
> The architecture's worth a stare,
> The order Cherokee!'

KEEP CLEAR

Worthing, West Sussex

N 50°48'34.9" W 0°22'12.8"
Grid Ref: TQ149024 Map Ref: 3 C12

Pushed by the prevailing south-west winds of the English Channel, the strong north-easterly set of the tide is well demonstrated as the sea wrinkles aslant on its journey to the shore around Worthing Pier. The pier, opened in 1862, has had a history typical of so many of these wonderful, ramshackle and vulnerable structures. It has been bashed by ships, damaged in storms and ravaged by fires. In 1913 an Easter Monday storm broke the pier in two, prompting locals to dub the severed seaward portion 'Easter Island'. A blaze twenty years later destroyed the Victorian pierhead pavilion. Yet Worthing Pier soldiers on - like all piers, a Heath Robinson contraption, endearing and faintly preposterous.

Bognor Regis, West Sussex

N 50°46'57.0" W 0°40'10.1"
Grid Ref: SZ939990 Map Ref: 3 B12

Like Brighton, like Hastings and Folkestone and many another south-east resorts, Bognor was a village absorbed in fishing and smuggling until the 18th century craze for sea bathing and sea air turned it into a resort. King George V, recovering from pneumonia, came to convalesce here in 1929, and allowed the town the dignity of suffixing its name with 'Regis' in his honour. On his deathbed on 30 January 1936 the King had Bognor Regis in his thoughts. When told he would soon be well enough to convalesce at the resort again, George uttered his final words: 'Bugger Bognor.' This was relayed to the waiting world as: 'How goes the Empire?'

Pagham Harbour, West Sussex (right)

N 50°45'48.8" W 0°45'44.8"
Grid Ref: SZ874967 Map Ref: 3 B12

Glinting and gleaming like a subtle piece of mirror sculpture, Pagham Harbour lies half drowned at high tide. This big marshy inlet in the east flank of the Selsey peninsula of West Sussex is inundated twice each 24 hours. Back at the turn of the 20th century the whole basin had been reclaimed for agriculture and was full of barley fields. An exceptionally high tide broke through the shingle bank at Christmas 1910 and re-flooded the harbour, returning it to its previous status of a tidal inlet. Rising sea levels will see Pagham Harbour permanently filled with seawater in the not too distant future.

Soft and Hard

Chichester Harbour to Poole Harbour

Where West Sussex and Hampshire incline west towards Dorset, the coast melts and spreads like sun-warmed camembert. This is a soft coast, low lying and sheltered, of rivers coming to the sea through a clay and chalk hinterland. Landforms are weather-smoothed, bulgy with downs inland, marshy and creek-ridden by the shore. The coast softens and splits into myriad channels in a succession of sizeable tidal harbours - Chichester Harbour which contains its own world of large flat peninsulas and causeway islands, Portsmouth Harbour and the long broad inlet of Southampton Water, marshy Newtown Harbour across the Solent on the north coast of the Isle of Wight, and then Christchurch Harbour and Poole Harbour, 'identical twins' except that Poole Harbour's 9,400 acres dwarf the modest six hundred of its easterly neighbour. Beyond Poole Harbour the landforms stiffen and the coastline hardens again into tremendous freestone cliffs at the eastern end of the Jurassic Coast (see Chapter 13).

It is a coast adapted through millennia by man for his own ends. Permanent reinforcement of naturally malleable sites have seen a bending of Nature's forces to man's will – for example, the shingly shore and soft, muddy western flank of the Portsmouth peninsula hardened for the founding of the great naval base, the marshy ridge at Yarmouth on the Isle of Wight stiffened with groynes and an enormous breakwater, the multiple groynes that consolidate the sandspits of Sandbanks and Mudeford Spit, or Hurst Castle on its rigid foundations at the seaward end of the crab's claw shingle spit of Hurst Beach. This sector of the south coast is especially rich in castles. Both King Henry VIII, in 16th-century fear of a French or Spanish Catholic invasion of the country he had declared a Protestant state, and the British Government of three centuries later, in less-justified paranoia over the threat of a French invasion under Napoleon Bonaparte's great-nephew, identified the Royal Navy's home base of Portsmouth as the most likely focus for any attack, and its approaches were larded with fortifications – Fort Cumberland, Hurst Castle, the Isle of Wight forts and Branksea Castle on Brownsea Island, to name but a few of the many.

Where tidal creeks, rivers and harbours might perhaps admit an enemy, they certainly offered a trading opportunity as outlets for exports and a means of entrance for foreign goods. Rivers and tidal waterways were the main transport highways, especially for heavy goods, until the 19th century and the coming of the railways, and many led inland to tiny centres of industry – the mills and wharves of Birdham Pool and Dell Quay on Chichester Harbour, for example, or the shipyards at Buckler's Hard up the Beaulieu River from which the hulls of wooden ships could be floated seaward after construction. At their mouths, too, industries made use of the estuarine surroundings – fishing, netting, smuggling, and the manufacture of sea salt, as witness the salt pans that still pit the marshes along the estuary of the River Yar at Yarmouth.

Birdham Pool Marina, Chichester, West Sussex *N 50°48'14.4" W 0°49'11.2" Grid Ref: SU833012 Map Ref: 2 M7*

Looking over serried ranks of yachts in Birdham Pool Marina, and on west along Chichester Channel as it snakes its way into the open reaches of Chichester Harbour. This 230-berth marina lies squirreled away in a backwater, one of many mazy ramifications of the huge tidal harbour, hung with three marshy peninsulas and the ragged tongue of Hayling Island, that extends ten miles westward to the shores of Portsmouth.

Dell Quay, Chichester, West Sussex *N 50°49'09.2" W 0°48'57.8" Grid Ref: SU835029 Map Ref: 3 A12*

Dell Quay was one of the busiest ports in England in medieval times, but you'd never suspect it now. Long gone are the years when outgoing salt fish and oysters, salt meat, corn and Sussex cheeses shared the quay with incoming timber, coal, wine and ironwork. Nowadays Dell Quay is a place to have your sailing boat mended at the Yacht Yard, or to sit outside the Crown & Anchor and contemplate the sunset over a glass of something nice.

Soft and Hard

Chichester Harbour to Poole Harbour

Over the centuries change has crept in, another progression from hard to soft as trade has leached into leisure. Where freighters tied up at Cowes, now it is sleek yachts and ocean cruisers. Dell Quay has moved from a prosperous working port to a profitable marina. Portsmouth's stern, centuries-old trade of victualling, repairing and equipping the Royal Navy is tucked away amid high security inside Her Majesty's Naval Base these days, and is rarely glimpsed by visitors or townsfolk. The practical business of the old waterfront is now diluted by leisure – Gunwharf Quays are a shopping mall, overlooked by the mock 'sail' of the Spinnaker Tower, a kind of homage to a naval heritage now encapsulated in the museums and the preserved ships within the former dockyard, re-christened 'Portsmouth Historic Dockyard'. The slim-built warships of the Royal Navy glide down Portsmouth Harbour from time to time, their practical matt grey paintwork and bristling hardware as menacing among the pleasure cruisers as sharks in a swimming pool.

There are problems along with all this leisure. The proliferation of marinas along the coast and up its creeks has resulted in pollution from anti-fouling paint and diesel, in the introduction of alien species of ship parasites, water weeds and marine animals, and in the hardening of muddy river banks and marshy coastal margins which would naturally act as buffers for the incursions of the sea. And the rash of holiday homes and exclusive developments that has followed a general rise in prosperity has led to tremendously inflated prices, the proliferation of an alien, pattern-book style of architecture, and an influx of well-off strangers – often second-home owners who are rarely in residence - who don't feel any obligation or desire to take part in local activities.

The mudflats, marshes and many miles of soft, convoluted coast incorporated within the wide natural harbours with which this coast is blessed will do a lot to absorb the impact of rising sea levels during the coming century. Some locals believe that the residents of such rarified developments as Sandbanks will simply step into their yachts and sail away from the whole tiresome business. In complete contrast to the white-hulled, graceful sailing palaces of such celebrity householders are the superannuated houseboats that lie in the muddy bay of The Kench at the south-western tip of Hayling Island. Some date back to the post-war years, when they supplemented the local housing stock at a time of national shortage. Full of idiosyncrasy and character, with toppling chimneys and home-made superstructures, they resemble a fleet of miniature Noah's Arks. Perhaps that is exactly what they will turn out to be.

Langstone Harbour entrance, Hampshire *N 50°47'24.5" W 1°01'39.2" Grid Ref: SZ686994 Map Ref: 2 L7*

Shaped like the heads of two mythical beasts – the rhinoceros proboscis of Eastney's spit on the west side, facing the horned sheep's head of The Kench promontory on the south-west tip of Hayling Island – the entrance to Langstone Harbour from the open sea is less than 200 yards wide at low tide. A ferry spans the gap in a minute. On the east, protected by the sharp spike of a small sandspit, the tidal bay of The Kench shelters thousand of seabirds along with a motley collection of houseboats – superannuated hulls with ramshackle miniature houses crammed on top.

Portsmouth, Hampshire *N 50°47'27.8" W 1°06'38.5" Grid Ref: SZ628994 Map Ref: 2 L7*

Like the cracks and bumps on a characterful old face, every nook and cranny of Portsmouth's waterfront tells a story – most of them concerned with fighting and seafaring. Here are the Square and Round Towers built to ward off French raids, the blunt-tipped peninsula of Spice Island where sailors flocked to booze and whore, the little beach from which Lord Nelson embarked for the Battle of Trafalgar, and the Historic Dockyard where his wooden battleship HMS *Victory* lies preserved.

Spinnaker Tower, Hampshire *N 50°47'43.1" W 1°06'30.6" Grid Ref: SZ629999 Map Ref: 2 L7*

The huge lattice-work bulge of its *faux* sail paying a kind of homage to those of the schooner moored below, Portsmouth's Spinnaker Tower soars 560 feet above the harbour waters. Opened in 2005, the topmost deck of the tower offers a stunning 23-mile prospect across port, harbour, sea and countryside, including dizzying foreshortened views down into the Historic Dockyard from a height four times that of the mainmast of a ship-of-the-line.

Portsmouth naval base, Hampshire *N 50°48'29.1" W 1°05'50.8" Grid Ref: SU637013 Map Ref: 2 L7*

As the 'home port' of the Royal Navy since medieval times, Portsmouth ('Pompey' to generations of sailors) enjoys a very close relationship with the Navy. Her Majesty's Naval Base, otherwise known as HMS *Nelson*, is one of three operating bases in the UK - the others are HMNB Devonport near Plymouth, and HMNB Clyde at Gare Loch west of Glasgow. HMNB Portsmouth builds, repairs and services the Royal Navy's ships, whose sleek grey shapes are often seen gliding to and from the base just beyond the Historic Dockyard.

Portchester Castle, Hampshire *N 50°50'13.2" W 1°06'49.7" Grid Ref: SU625045 Map Ref: 2 L7*

The Romans knew a good defensive site when they saw one. From its promontory at the innermost point of Portsmouth Harbour, many miles inland of present-day Portsmouth, the stronghold of Portchester Castle commands the channel from the open sea. The hollow square of walls that the Romans built here still stands to its full height, rounded bastions and all, cradling a moated Norman keep in its north-west angle. The keep dates back to the 12th century, an ancient building by any standards – but the walls that surround it are more than twice as old.

Buckler's Hard and Beaulieu River, Hampshire *N 50°48'02.3" W 1°25'25.4" Grid Ref: SU407003 Map Ref: 2 J7*

The Beaulieu River, named by the Normans in homage to this 'beautiful place', snakes lazily down to the sea at the edge of the New Forest. Nowadays the very picture of timeless peace and quiet, two centuries ago this was a scene of clangour, bustle and sharp industrial smells. It was on the Beaulieu River at Buckler's Hard that the Royal Navy built its warships. With the broad river at hand, the sea only three miles away and plenty of trees all around, Buckler's Hard was the ideal location. Visiting today you can still see the remarkably broad village street where shipbuilding timbers were stacked, and the ribs of the cradles in the river where ships-of-the-line were constructed.

Keyhaven salt marsh, Hampshire *N 50°43'10.6" W 1°33'22.8" Grid Ref: SZ314912 Map Ref: 2 J8*

Yachts moor up in line abreast along one of the sheltered channels in Keyhaven salt marsh. The extensive marsh, cut by creeks into a fractured jigsaw of islets, has developed eastward inside the crook of the shingle spit of Hurst Beach. Salt pans once pitted the face of the marsh, whose margins lie whitened by formations known as 'cheniers' – rough beaches of shell and shingle that act as buffers between the salt marsh and the sea.

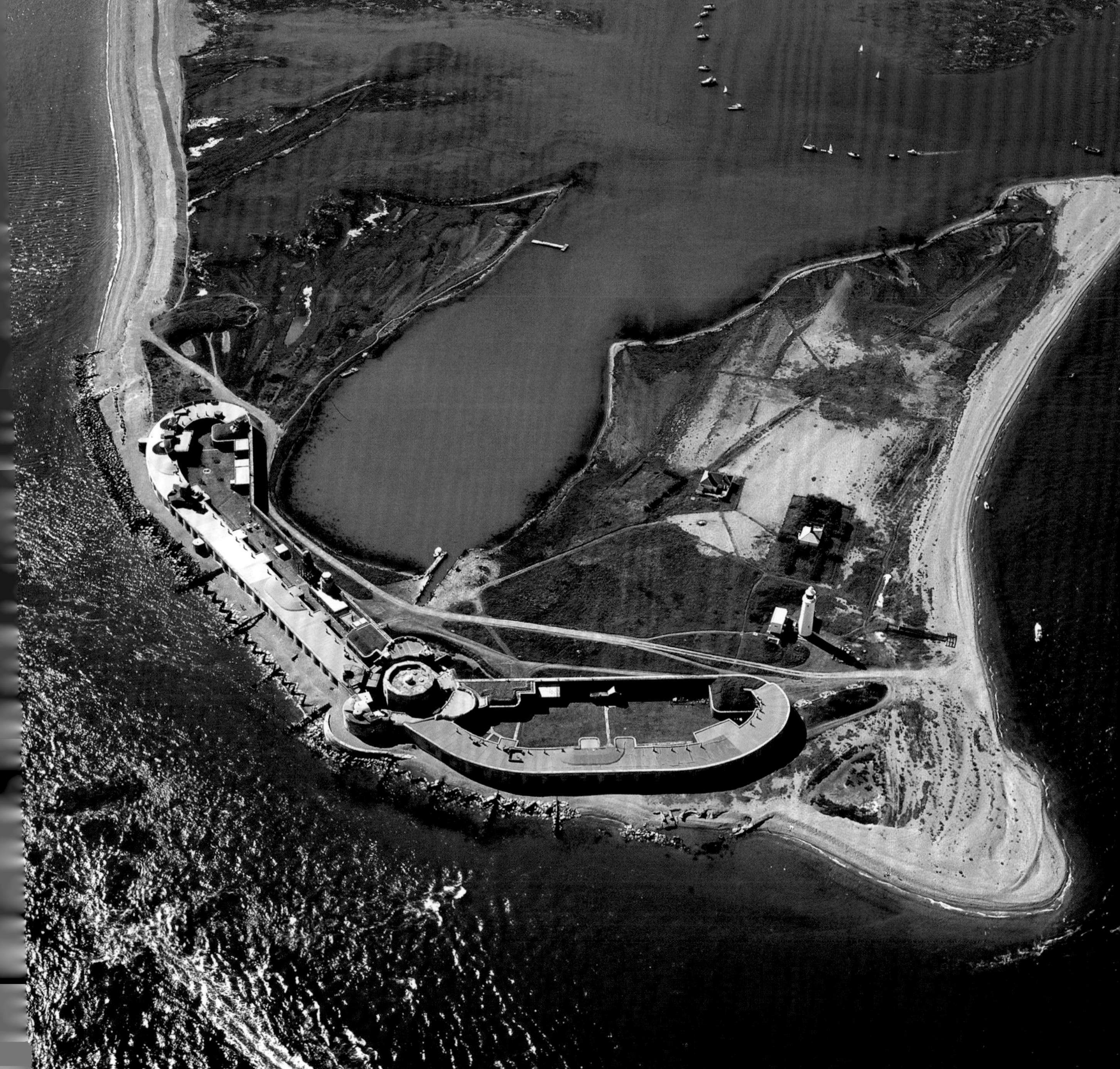

Hurst Castle, Hampshire *N 50°42′22.7″ W 1°33′05.3″ Grid Ref: SZ318897 Map Ref: 2 J8*

A remarkable piece of engineering, Hurst Castle crouches defiantly at the seaward end of its shingle spit, more than a mile from land. The original castle, seen in this picture as a round button at the centre of the 'wings', was one of the string of South Coast forts built in the 1540s by King Henry VIII to deter any invasion attempt by the French. The 'wings' were added in the 1870s during another French invasion scare, which also saw the massive stronghold of Fort Victoria built on the Isle of Wight coast immediately opposite. The channel between the two castles is only a mile wide, so any potential attacker would have had to run a particularly hot gauntlet.

Cowes, Isle of Wight *N 50°45'49.0" W 1°17'49.3" Grid Ref: SZ497962 Map Ref: 2 K8*

Looking south up the broad stream of the River Medina into the heart of the Isle of Wight. At the mouth of the Medina lies the little sailing town of Cowes – East Cowes on the left of the picture, opposite Cowes of the gin palaces, the Royal Yacht Squadron and the endless tides of sailing talk. The Royal Yacht Squadron, founded in 1815 and housed in a Tudor fort with pepperpot turrets and velvet lawns, is the centre of the social whirl associated with regatta-laden Cowes Week in August. The private members of the Royal Cruising Club, founded in 1880 'for persons interested in aquatic amusements', see themselves by contrast as more about sailing than socialising.

Yarmouth, Isle of Wight *N 50°42'04.3" W 1°30'07.1" Grid Ref: SZ353892 Map Ref: 2 J8*

A mosaic of marsh fragments and the remains of old salt pans fringe the channel of the River Yar as it snakes towards the marina and harbour at Yarmouth on the north-west coast of the Isle of Wight. Defended from French attack by one of King Henry VIII's castles at the harbour mouth, Yarmouth was the most important town in the island during the late Middle Ages, but had declined to a run-down borough by the turn of the 19th century. Napoleonic wartime paranoia was so strong in Yarmouth that the painter George Morley was arrested as a spy and accused of drawing a map of the island. It turned out to be a sketch of his pet spaniel.

The Needles, Isle of Wight *N 50°39'44.8" W 1°35'26.1" Grid Ref: SZ290848 Map Ref: 2 J8*

A dramatic view of The Needles, the three iconic sea stacks that project like shark teeth from the outer waters of Christchurch Bay off the westernmost tip of the Isle of Wight. A thick band of chalk runs through the middle of the island, and The Needles are its western full stops. In the days when the Needles lighthouse was manned, provisioning was by helicopter; landing on the flat pad on the cap of the tower, in the swirling and unpredictable winds that could suddenly gust from any quarter, was always a dicey business.

Tennyson Down, Isle of Wight *N 50°39'55.8" W 1°32'32.5" Grid Ref: SZ324852 Map Ref: 2 J8*

The great chalk cliff under Tennyson Down rises almost 500 feet to the granite Celtic cross on the green back of the down. The cross was erected in memory of the 19th century's best-remembered Poet Laureate, Alfred, Lord Tennyson, who lived nearby at Farringford in the 1850s. Tennyson loved to walk here in trademark cloak and broad-brimmed hat, sometimes pursued by ardent admirer and pioneer portrait photographer Julia Margaret Cameron.

Mudeford Spit and Hengistbury Head, Dorset *N 50°43'21.5" W 1°44'27.5" Grid Ref: SZ184915 Map Ref: 2 I8*

The eastward-trending, heathy promontory of Hengistbury Head, in its time an Iron Age settlement and a Roman trading port, forms a lower jaw that all but shuts the mouth of Christchurch Harbour. From its eastern tip protrudes the ever-growing sandbar of Mudeford Spit, once a line of tall dunes, but now eroded to a flat tongue of sand. Its beautiful, sculpted shape, like the dorsal fin of a fish, arises from the motion of longshore drift, which drags sand eastward to be trapped by the groynes and moulded into miniature bays by the tide.

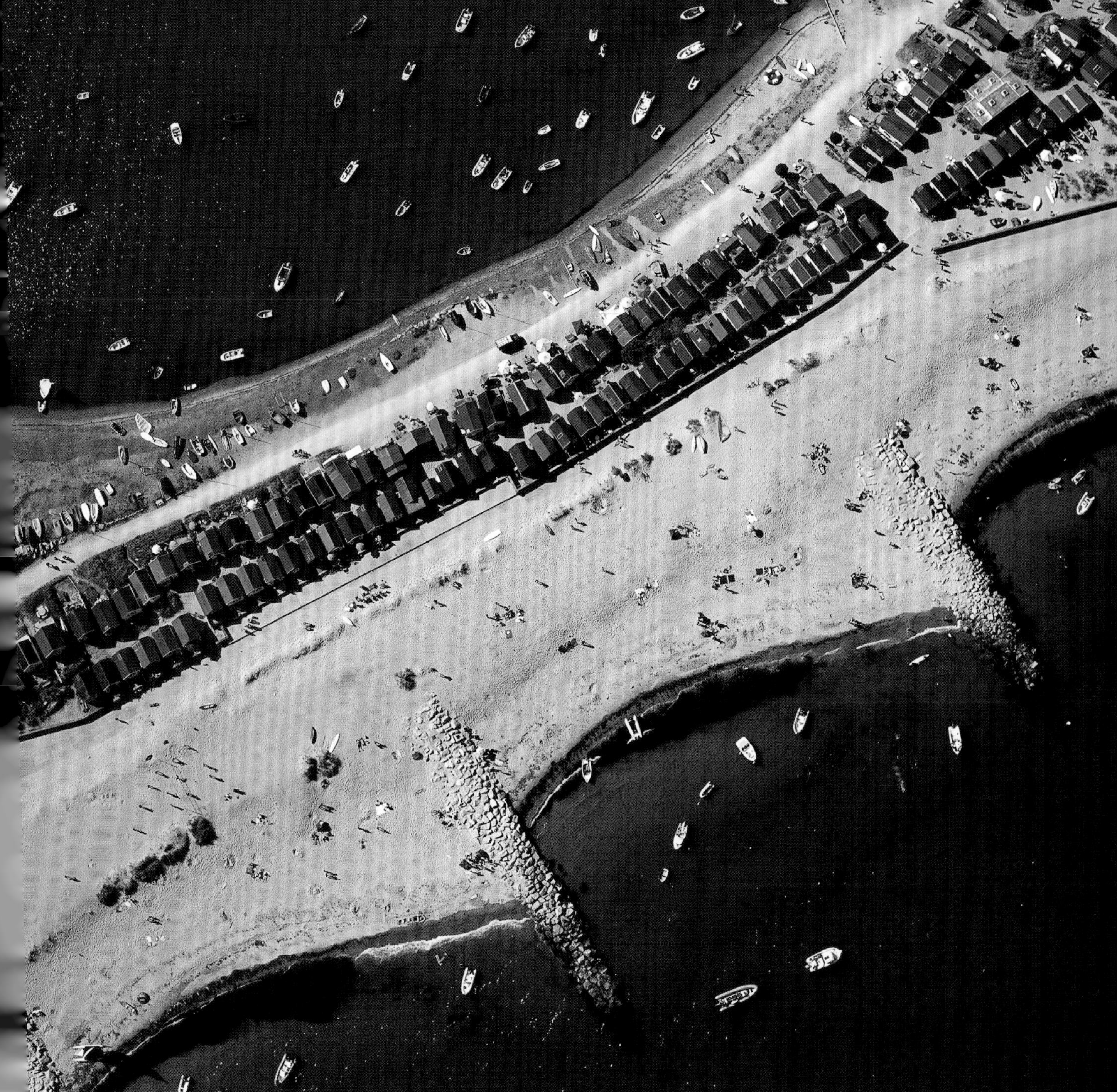

Mudeford Spit, Dorset *N 50°43'21.5" W 1°44'27.5" Grid Ref: SZ184915 Map Ref: 2 I8*

Mudefort Spit is a favourite place to lie out sunbathing on a sunny day, the sea on both sides and a warm breeze blowing uninterrupted across the spit. The famous black beach huts are worth a pretty penny – in 2006 they were changing hands for upwards of £100,000, and that figure has risen a long way since then.

Bournemouth seafront, Dorset *N 50°42'56.9" W 1°52'32.5" Grid Ref: SZ089907 Map Ref: 2 H8*

Two hundred years ago Bournemouth was a tiny cluster of coastal hamlets getting by on fishing and smuggling. Having come through an early 19th-century phase of extreme gentility (no shops – everything was brought to the door by tradesmen), and a rollicking Victorian and early 20th-century heyday as a popular seaside resort, the town is now one of Britain's premier conference venues. But its superb beach still sees a good turnout of sunbathers and sand sculptors on sunny weekends.

Sandbanks, Dorset *N 50°41'02.2" W 1°56'58.6" Grid Ref: SZ037871 Map Ref: 2 H8*

The Sandbanks peninsula lies secluded at the mouth of Poole Harbour, the rich blue glint of swimming pools gleaming from its well-hidden gardens. Its beaches are warm and golden, its woods deep and shady, and its houses some of the most expensive in Britain – in 2008, £3.5 million for a 3-bedroom bungalow, £6.5 million for a 4-bedroom split-level house, and £8 million for a 5-bedroom residence in an 'exclusive beach-front location.' Like a golden city in a fable, however, Sandbanks in its exposed, low-lying location may not last much longer if climate change brings the anticipated rise in sea levels and worsening of storms.

The Jurassic Coast
Isle of Purbeck to Exe Estuary

The Dorset and East Devon coast that runs west from Poole Harbour to the Exe Estuary is nicknamed the 'Jurassic Coast', thanks to its extraordinary richness of geology. In 2002 it was designated a UNESCO World Heritage Site, equal in world heritage value to the Grand Canyon and the Great Barrier Reef. There is a magnetic attraction to the odd-shaped cliffs of this coast, their multi-coloured pointed heads, their crazily tilted strata and multiple collapses, their caves, arches and ledges. Extensively quarried and dug into, they have only very selectively been built on, because of their propensity – deadly to man in his fixed abodes, endlessly renewing to nature in its nomadic fluidity – to topple and fall into the sea.

The geological history of the Jurassic Coast spans some 185 million years. The non-specialist mind tends to boggle at the concept of so much raw time – the period between 250 and 65 million years ago when this coast was being created. There are bewildering varieties of geological forms on display here. But one simple fact underpins all the complications. The various layers of rock – originally stacked horizontally, the oldest at the bottom, the youngest on top – were tilted to the east by ancient subterranean upheavals. So the oldest material now rises high and exposed along the western end of the coast; while the youngest layers are what you see in the east, where the older stuff underneath lies angled down out of sight below the sea.

The oldest rocks, near Exeter in the west, are dusky red sandstones laid down in the Triassic period when southern England was one huge sun-baked desert. Most of the Jurassic-era material – dark clays and pale limestones, deposited between 200 and 140 million years ago in a warm sea that flooded the old red desert – lies towards the middle of the coast. And the young Cretaceous chalk, formed of the bodies of countless minuscule forms of marine life settling on the bed of a clear, shallow sea, is seen mostly in the east of the region.

It is a coast of fantastic physical beauty, a run of endless curves and hollows, ups and downs, with perfectly semi-circular coves, wave-worn arches, folded and squeezed sandwiches of rock strata all unrolling one beyond the next, the cliffs falling to a sea whose colour reflects the composition of their rocks – a Mediterranean island turquoise at the feet of the more easterly freestone and chalk, a deep velvet blue below the sandstone ramparts of the west. The coast is best appreciated from a boat, or from the undulating cliff-top rollercoaster of the South-West Coast Path National Trail.

Quarrying has scarred the cliffs, especially towards the eastern or Dorset end where the freestone stands exposed. This hard limestone, in which many fossil footprints of giant dinosaurs have been found, is easily cut and polished. Sir Christopher Wren built St Paul's Cathedral and half of post-Great Fire London with it. The quarry industry here has been on the go since Roman times, and the cliffs stand riddled and burrowed with

Old Harry Rocks, Dorset *N 50°38'34.7" W 1°55'21.1" Grid Ref: SZ056826 Map Ref: 2 H9*

From the southern point of Studland Bay extends the slender promontory of Handfast Point, its unstable chalk being steadily whittled away by the waves into semi-circular coves and thick sea stacks. Off the tip stands the slender chalk column of Old Harry, wading to his white knees in the water that separates him from his parent stack. Old Harry once had a wife, who stood seaward of him, but the waves have beaten her almost to invisibility.

The Jurassic Coast
Isle of Purbeck to Exe Estuary

square-mouthed quarry caverns and geometrically cut ledges. The Isle of Portland has been so profoundly altered by quarrying that from some angles it looks like nothing so much as a giant offcut left in the sea by a monstrous sculptor.

Writers have found romantic inspiration along this moody, strangely shaped and often stormy coast - Thomas Hardy in the Isle of Portland, John Meade Falkner along Chesil Beach in his smuggling yarn *Moonfleet*, Jane Austen at Lyme Regis in *Persuasion* – and at Sidmouth in her own personal life, some say – and John Fowles on the wave-lashed Cobb at Lyme Regis where his enigmatic heroine Sarah Woodruff stood and gazed seaward in *The French Lieutenant's Woman*. But the hard facts of everyday existence along the Dorset and Devon coasts of past centuries were always a lot grittier than fiction. Quarrymen led a rough life, and so did the subsistence fishermen of this harsh, often storm-bound coast. No wonder so many of them turned to smuggling, a trade for which Dorset and Devon were just as notorious as Cornwall in 18th-century England.

Wrecks were common, terrifyingly so. The shingle bar of Chesil Beach, fifty feet high and unclimbable with rolling storm waves snatching at your heels, was the death of tens of thousands of seafarers. So many wreck victims were pounded and drowned on Chesil in the 18th and 19th centuries that they fill two large graveyards around Wyke Regis church at the eastern end of the bar. One of thousands who lie here in unmarked graves is William Wordsworth's seafaring brother John, drowned along with 300 passengers when the *Abergavenny* - of which he was captain - was wrecked off Portland in 1805.

Sudden destruction reared his giant form
Black with the horrors of the midnight storm.

So announces the church wall plaque that carries details of 140 passengers and crew of the East Indiaman *Alexander*, wrecked in Chesil Bay in 1815, that lie buried here. Even that disaster, and the wreck of the *Abergavenny*, pale beside the calamity of 18 November 1795, when three military transports came to grief in the bay with the loss of over 1,000 soldiers and crew members. Two hundred were buried where they were washed up on the beach; the rest were brought up the hill, like so many others, to lie in Wyke churchyard.

Wrecks still occur hereabouts, and sometimes they attract the attention of wolfish men, as in the case of the wholesale plundering of the cargo of MSC *Napoli* as she lay beached in Branscombe Bay after a January storm in 2007. But today's Jurassic Coast is largely given over to holidaymakers, to coast path wanderers, to admirers of geological wonders, and to collectors of the extraordinary riches of fossils that fall from the crumbling cliffs and lie for sharp eyes to spot among the shingle stones.

Swanage, Dorset *N 50°36′33.0″ W 1°57′21.2″ Grid Ref: SZ032788 Map Ref: 2 H9*

The quarrying of Purbeck stone, so workable and durable, brought prosperity to Swanage through the building of medieval cathedrals and the rebuilding of post-Great Fire London. It also made the fortune of local stonemason George Burt in the late 19th century when London was rebuilt once again. Keen to show his home town how well he'd done, Burt salvaged from Old London and installed around Swanage a gallimaufry of statues, columns, gargoyles, obelisks, ornate gates, and – his masterstroke – the entire, fabulously ornate 17th-century façade of the Mercers' Hall in Cheapside. He had it erected as the frontage of Swanage's Town Hall, where it still stands in overblown opulence.

Purbeck cliffs, looking east from Blacker's Hole, Dorset *N 50°35'27.2" W 1°59'01.7" Grid Ref: SZ012768 Map Ref: 2 H10*

Beyond Swanage you meet the Jurassic Coast proper along the great freestone cliffs of the Isle of Purbeck, whose broad, sloping back has been quarried since at least Roman times. Just beyond Blacker's Hole (in the foreground) rises a pair of Measured Distance Marker Posts, with their twins precisely one nautical mile to the east beyond the lighthouse on Anvil Point (seen in distance). Ships use them to calculate their speed, timing their run from when the first pair appears in line to the moment the second pair is aligned. A nautical mile (6,080 feet) is slightly longer than a statute mile (5,280 feet), and is equal to one minute of latitude along any meridian.

Chapman's Pool, Dorset *N 50°35'36.2" W 2°03'53.4" Grid Ref: SY956771 Map Ref: 2 G9*

The instability of the cliffs hereabouts, shown in the ledges caused by landslips, means that the sea finds plenty of weaknesses in the rocks to break through, smoothing out beautiful hollow coves such as Chapman's Pool beyond St Alban's Head. The zigzag descent is steep and tricky, and not many walkers brave it; those that do find their reward on a quiet, unfrequented beach of sand and shingle with only the blue water and occasional seal for company.

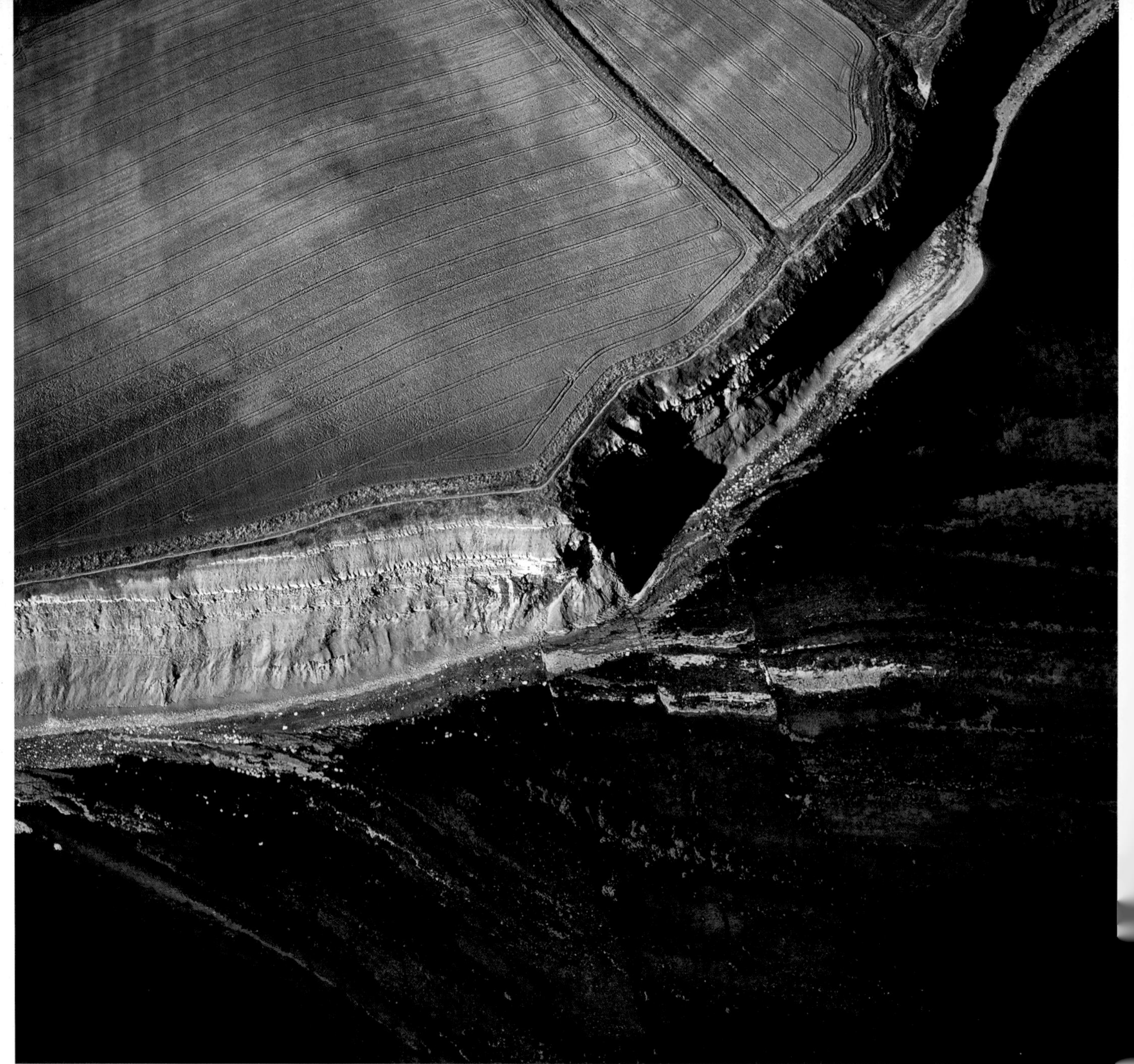

Kimmeridge Ledges (left) and Kimmeridge Bay (right), Dorset

N 50°35'49.7" W 2°06'19.0" Grid Ref: SY926775 Map Ref: 2 G9 (left) *N 50°36'38.6" W 2°08'22.1" Grid Ref: SY902790 Map Ref: 2 G9 (right)*

Bathers splash, kayakers paddle and rock-poolers fossick under the cliffs of Kimmeridge Bay, where shore ledges run out from land to drop into clear blue water. Who would guess that such a green and rural piece of Dorset coast has an oil industry? The two-foot-thick ledge of bituminous shale that stretches along the cliffs east of Chapman's Pool yields 100 barrels of oil a day to a 'nodding donkey' pump in Kimmeridge Bay – only the latest in a long line of efforts to squeeze economic gain out of the shale, from bracelets made by Iron Age farmers to a Victorian company that briefly lit the streets of Paris with gas made from Kimmeridge shale oil.

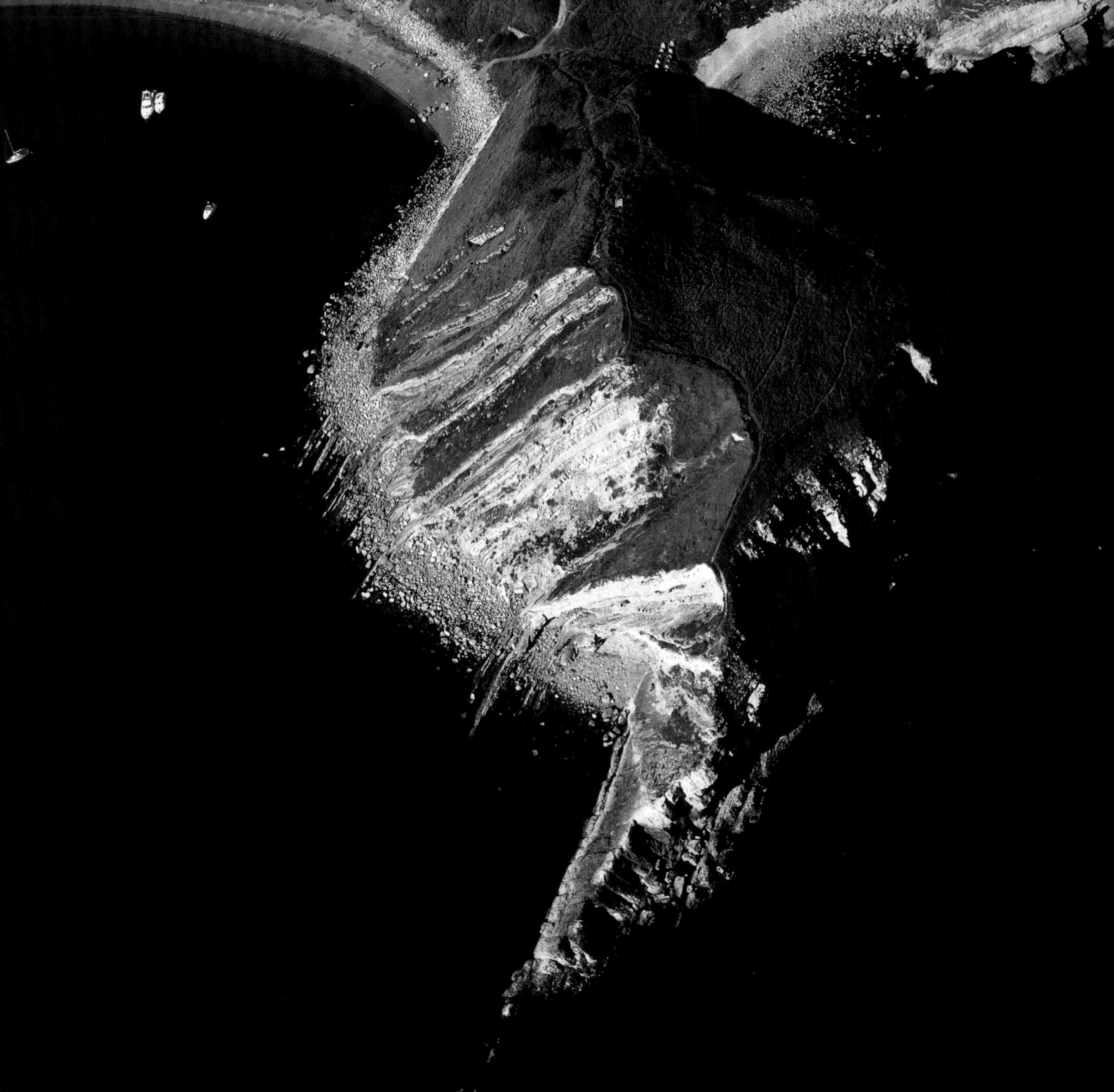

Worbarrow Tout, Dorset *N 50°36'56.4" W 2°11'08.4" Grid Ref: SY870796 Map Ref: 2 G9*

'Tout' signifies a lookout place, and the promontory of Worbarrow Tout that pokes its snake head out from the western end of Gold Down must always have been a favoured place from which to keep an eye on comings and goings by sea and along the Purbeck coast. The Tout is one of the best fossil-hunting spots on the Jurassic Coast, yielding dinosaur footprints, bivalve shells, sea snails and seed shrimps.

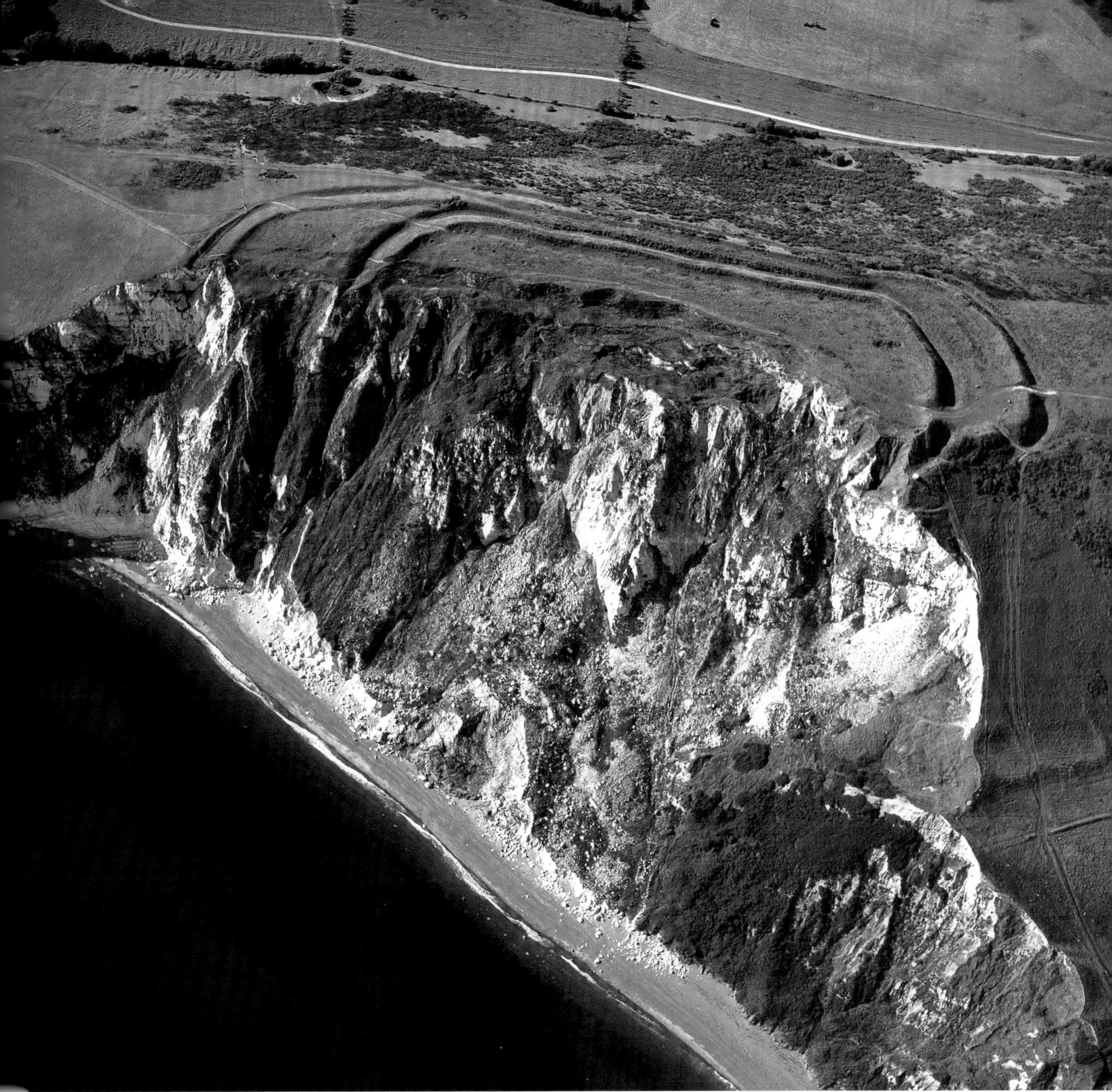

Flowers Barrow Hill Fort, Dorset *N 50°37'28.7" W 2°11'38.9" Grid Ref: SY864806 Map Ref: 2 G9*

Sprawled at the very rim of Worbarrow Bay lies the Iron Age hillfort of Flowers Barrow, its concentric horseshoe of ramparts enclosing several round hut foundations. Perhaps it once formed a circular enclosure, of which the whole southern half has gradually crumbled into the sea; or maybe, like the great stone forts of the Aran Isles in Galway Bay, it was built in semi-circular shape right up to the cliff edge, with the 550-ft drop to the sea providing all the protection needed.

Lulworth Cove, Dorset *N 50°37'08.0" W 2°14'48.5" Grid Ref: SY826799 Map Ref: 2 F9*

The peace of the Jurassic Coast around Lulworth Cove is sometimes disturbed by the thudding of heavy guns from the MoD range at Lulworth Camp. As you come down the narrow road to Lulworth Cove, you find the limestone bands in the cliffs spectacularly crumpled and bent into sinuous folds by ancient subterranean convulsions. Not only that – the sea has nibbled through weak points in the rampart of hard freestone and scoured out the softer chalk and clay behind, forming the remarkable, perfectly circular bay of Lulworth Cove.

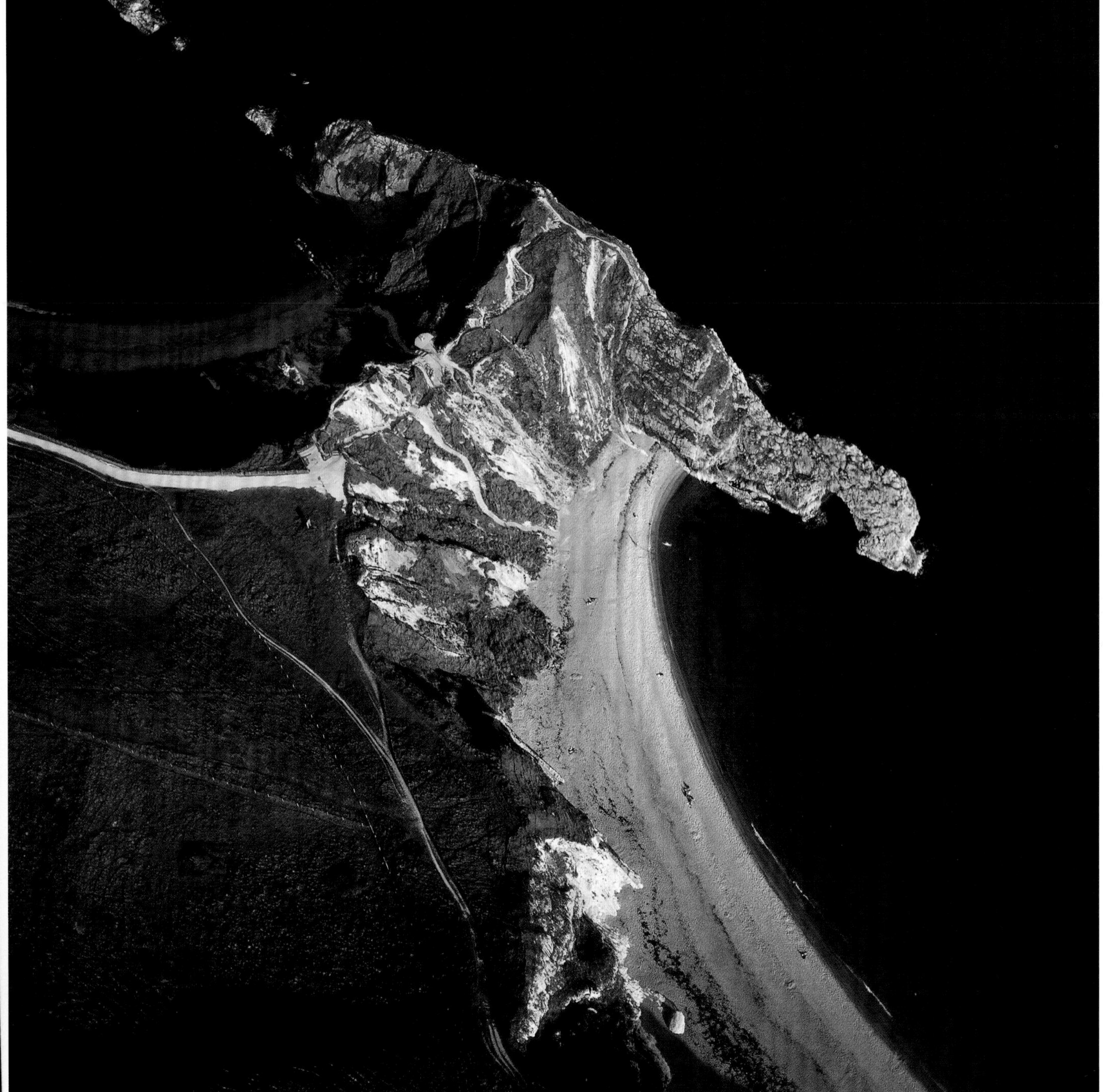

Durdle Door, Dorset *N 50°37'16.2" W 2°16'37.4" Grid Ref: SY805802 Map Ref: 2 F9*

The Purbeck stone promontory of Durdle Door, a mile to the west of Lulworth Cove, has been pierced through by the sea to form an arch big enough to sail a fair-size boat through. The term 'durdle' derives from the Old English term 'thirl', meaning 'to pierce a hole' – as Chaucer's Knight so graphically illustrated in his battle story:

> 'Al were they sore y-hurt, and namely oon
> That with a spere was thirled his breastboon.'

Bat's Head, Dorset *N 50°37'21.2" W 2°17'27.9" Grid Ref: SY796804 Map Ref: 2 F9*

The sea-shaped chalk promontory of Bat's Head, a mile west along the coast from Durdle Door, once had a similar arch - or perhaps a series of arches, for a whole line of chalk stacks stands evenly spaced a little way offshore between the two promontories. These former cave pillars possess evocative names: The Bull, The Blind Cow, The Cow and The Calf. Now the sea is in the process of 'thirling' Bat's Head with another arch, known as the Bat's Hole.

White Nothe cliffs, Dorset *N 50°37'33.0" W 2°18'22.3" Grid Ref: SY784807 Map Ref: 2 F9*

White Nothe cliffs rear skyward at the east end of secluded Ringstead Bay, and this striking exposure of chalk continues eastward in the direction of Bat's Head and Durdle Door. Partly vegetated, the undercliff is a haven for wildlife. Fossils such as sea lilies, tightly curled ammonites, bullet-shaped belemnites and rounded, faintly segmented sea urchins can be picked up at low tide along the narrow beach, which is scalloped with delicate, lace-like indentations by the sea.

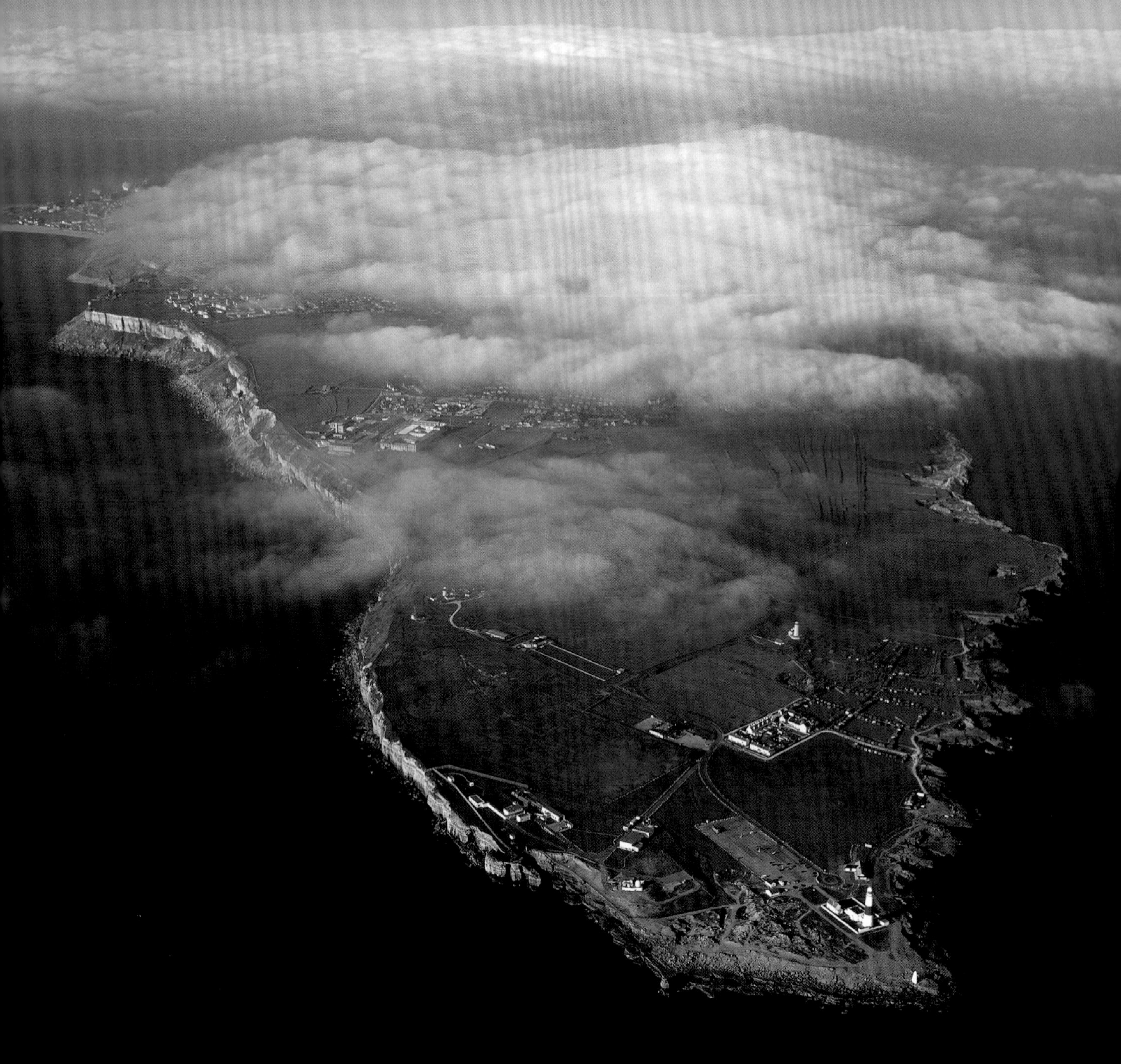

Isle of Portland, Dorset *N 50°30'56.0" W 2°27'24.6" Grid Ref: SY678685 Map Ref: 2 E9*

Thomas Hardy's 'Gibraltar of Wessex' lies out in the sea at the end of its shingle promontory, not quite an island, yet in no way part of the mainland. The Isle of Portland seems always to have been a place apart; mentally disturbed people were incarcerated there during the Dark Ages, and today the island plays 'host' to a large prison and a Young Offenders' Institution. Its fortunes have rested for 2,000 years on the quarrying of its durable yet workable freestone, which Sir Christopher Wren used almost exclusively when rebuilding London after the Great Fire of 1666. Quarrying has given a geometric sharpness to the pale cliffs, which rise from a wide-spreading skirt of grey scree – many centuries-worth of quarry spoil, tipped over the cliff edge.

Chesil Beach, Dorset *N 50°36'20.1" W 2°31'05.0" Grid Ref: SY634786 Map Ref: 2 E9*

A sensational prospect looking east along the entire 10-mile length of Chesil Beach, the longest and most deadly shingle bar in Europe. Countless ships were smashed and sailors drowned on Chesil in days of sail. The brackish Fleet lagoon separates the bar from the mainland, whose string of villages – Abbotsbury, Rodden, Langton Herring, East Fleet, Chickerell – were up to their elbows in smuggling during the 18th and early 19th centuries.

Abbotsbury Swannery, Dorset *N 50°39'11.2" W 2°36'00.5" Grid Ref: SY577839 Map Ref: 2 E8*

At Abbotsbury Swannery on the edge of the Fleet a thousand nesting swans pack the shores, squealing and grunting, flapping and fussing. The Abbot of Abbotsbury established the Swannery back in the 11th century with the object of putting something appetising on his table. No-one these days, of course, would dream of taking knife and fork to the big white birds, though the local foxes always maintain a keen interest in their welfare.

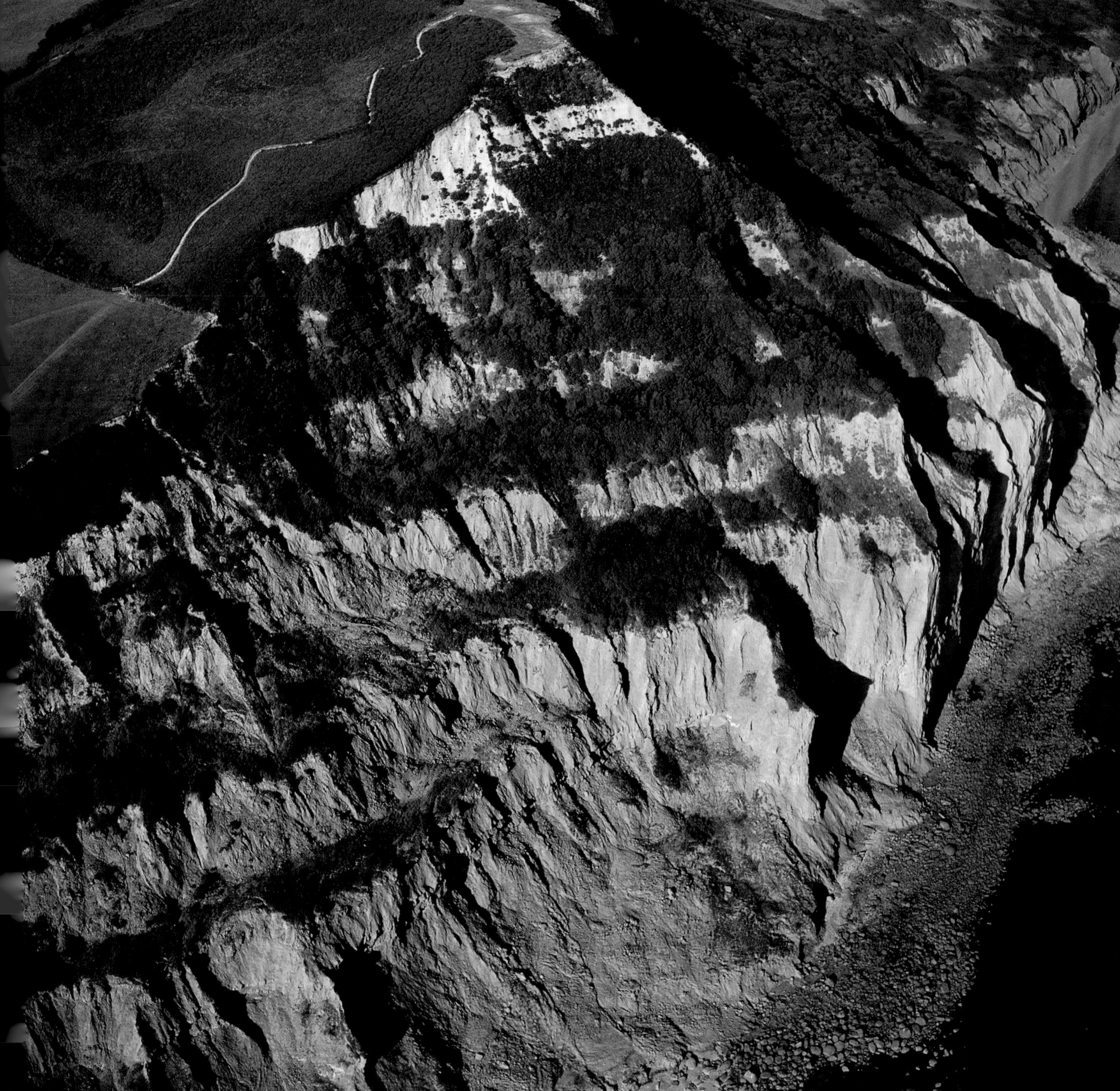

Wear Cliffs at Golden Cap, Dorset *N 50°43'29.5" W 2°50'39.7" Grid Ref: SY405920 Map Ref: 2 D8*

Chalk-surfaced and dusty, the South West Coast Path National Trail winds in a thin ribbon of white over the 617-ft summit of Golden Cap a couple of miles east of Charmouth. The tiers of vegetated ledges below the peak bear witness to the instability of this coast, whose cliffs are forever collapsing, sliding seaward and halting again. Golden Cap gets its name from its topping of Upper Greensand, whose exposed face rarely remains stable long enough for weathering to dull its golden hue.

Eroding cliffs at Cain's Folly, Charmouth, Dorset *N 50°43'59.2" W 2°53'00.8" Grid Ref: SY377930 Map Ref: 2 C8*

As they near the Dorset/Devon border, the cliffs of the Jurassic coast become progressively more sloping, eroded and prone to falls. The cliffs around Charmouth and Lyme Regis, in particular, are some of the wobbliest in Britain. Their pointed or flat-crowned heads of golden and green sand and white chalk are carried on shaky shoulders of older, profoundly unstable grey lias clays. These clays are the villains of the piece. Impervious to water, they become slippery skating mats for the chalk and sand cappings - sodden and heavy with rain and natural springs - that rest so precariously above them. They slope far back from the beach in a muddle of ledges, outflows, rock falls and fresh tumbles of material.

Lyme Regis and the Cobb, Dorset *N 50°43'10.9" W 2°56'16.8" Grid Ref: SY339915 Map Ref: 2 C8*

The little seaside resort of Lyme Regis, lying where Dorset meets Devon at the innermost point of the great half circle of Lyme Bay, is cradled by steep hills and shielded from storms by the protective arm of the Cobb. This ancient breakwater, its stones studded with fossils, is a beautiful sinuous thing, shaped like an open-mouthed sea beast coiling for a strike to the east. Halfway along the Cobb are 'Granny's Teeth', a set of weatherbeaten stones sticking out of the breakwater wall. It was up these steps that Jane Austen made Louisa Musgrove run in *Persuasion*, turning at the top to leap down into her lover's arms – or rather, clean through them, knocking herself unconscious on the hard stone walkway. Out at the seaward end of the Cobb stood another literary figure, John Fowles's wind-blown emblem of a tough-minded modern woman, Sarah Woodruff, captivating heroine of *The French Lieutenant's Woman*.

Beer Head, Devon (left)

N 50°41'09.1" W 3°05'46.5"
Grid Ref: SY227879 Map Ref: 2 B8

Over the county boundary in Devon, the western flank of Seaton Bay is closed by the sharp right-angle of the promontory of Beer Head. This panoramic view looks east over the headland's Hooken Cliff and its wide jungle of undercliff. The great rampart of jumbled rock below the vegetation was thrust outwards from the main cliff during a massive landslip in March 1790. That was not the biggest slip along this shaky coast, though. Beyond Beer Head, on the far side of Seaton Bay, a wide arc of pale rock above the woods of the distant cliffs shows the site of the epic slip of Christmas Eve, 1839, when an estimated eight million tons of land dropped 200 feet all at once.

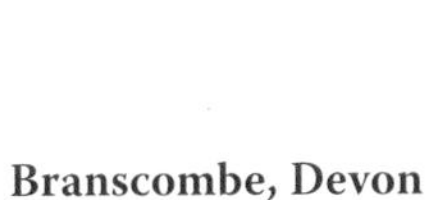

Branscombe, Devon

N 50°41'11.0" W 3°06'49.4"
Grid Ref: SY214880 Map Ref: 2 B8

Cargo containers scattered along the beach below Branscombe cliffs (**above right**), a mile west of Beer Head, are the legacy of the much-disputed salvage operation attempted on the Mediterranean Shipping Company's container vessel *Napoli* (**below right**) after she was holed in a storm in the English Channel in January 2007. Notwithstanding the international ecological and geological importance of the Jurassic Coast as a UNESCO World Heritage Site, *Napoli* was beached at Branscombe on 20 January. Oil leaked, seabirds died, and a crowd of plunderers descended on the tiny coast village to steal the cargo of motorbikes, wine casks, personal possessions and whatever else they could lay their hands on.

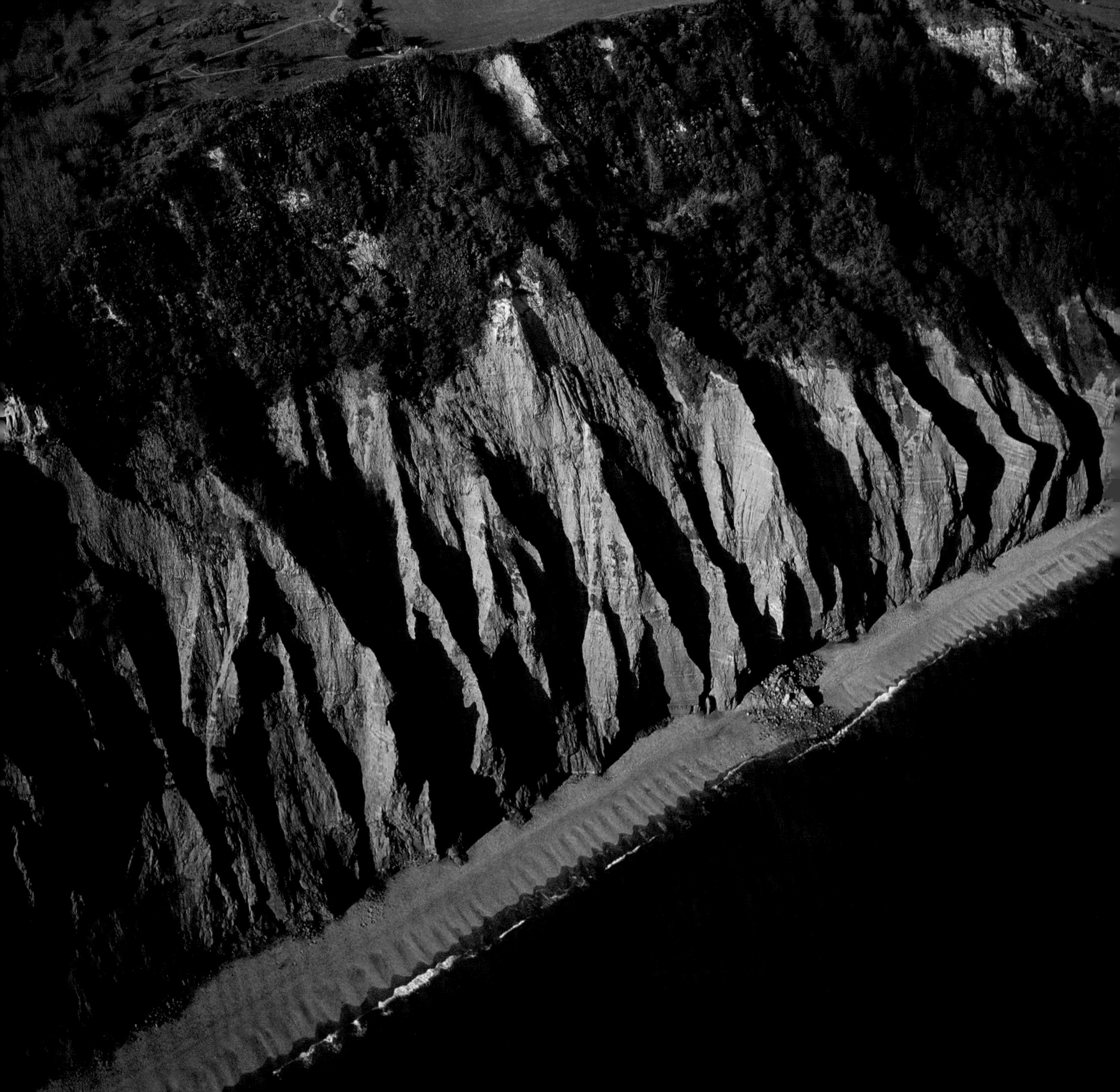

Salcombe Hill Cliff, Devon *N 50°40'51.5" W 3°13'19.2" Grid Ref: SY138875 Map Ref: 2 B8*

Vegetation grows thickly on the caps of Salcombe Hill Cliff just east of Sidmouth – this summit layer is of lime-rich chalk and greensand, and its propensity to crumble and fall away has lent it a slope on which shrubs and small trees can get purchase for their roots. Below this plant-friendly stratum the underlying sandstone, acid and bare, falls steeply away in craggy fissures worn by rainwater and frost.

Ladram Bay, Devon *N 50°39'33.0" W 3°16'38.0" Grid Ref: SY098852 Map Ref: 2 B8*

The western or Devon end of the UNESCO World Heritage Coast is all beautiful red sandstone some 250 million years old. The sandstone in Ladram Bay has no blanketing layer of chalk or greensand – it stands naked, finely layered and deeply eroded, with dramatic rock stacks rising offshore. Dawn is the time to view Ladram Bay, sitting on the cliff at Smallstones Point to watch the sunrise strike hues of mauve, crimson, orange and finally rich gold out of the cliffs and sea stacks.

Sandstone to the West
Dawlish Warren to Isles of Scilly

On the last leg of our great sweep around the sea margins of the British Isles, things change. As we go west towards the toe of the South West peninsula the rocks get older, darker, more rugged, more indented. The agricultural hinterland grows higher and wilder, the fields smaller, the headlands more heathery and bracken-brown. The dynamic processes of the sea cause coves and cracks to furrow the old red sandstone of Devon and East Cornwall, the immensely ancient olivine, augite and hornblende that form the beautiful serpentine rocks of the Lizard Peninsula, and the primitive granite of Penwith out at the western tip of Britain.

The south coast of the West Country is cut through by the snaking estuaries of Exe, Teign and Dart, of Kingsbridge, Erme, Tavy and Tamar, of Fowey, Fal, Carrick Roads and Helford River. These wide rivers offer sheltered anchorages; castles were built at their mouths to protect the fleets, the houses and the townspeople of Dartmouth and Plymouth, Fowey and Falmouth, and other such trading and fishing towns that grew up along the estuary banks. In the *Canterbury Tales* Geoffrey Chaucer's tanned toper of a 'Shipman of Dertemouth' was based on John Hawley, the chief Dartmouth ship-owner of the late 14th century, and Dartmouth offers a good example of how a well-guarded estuarine town could thrive on seafaring. The little South Devon port on the River Dart sent warships to the Crusades and the Siege of Calais, fishing boats to the Grand Banks of Newfoundland, wine-importing ships to France, exploring vessels under Walter Raleigh, Humphrey Gilbert and John Davis to discover the world, and buccaneering craft to all points of the compass to grab whatever was going.

The naval history of this coast, from the Channel Fleet's storm anchorage in Torbay to the cadets of the Royal Naval College at Dartmouth and the wretched Second World War GIs drowned off Slapton Sands, is breathtaking. The fishing history is epic: the development in Brixham of the trawlers that revolutionised the trade, the huge fishmarkets at Newlyn, Plymouth and Brixham, the hardship and danger of the fisherman's calling, the little home villages such as Polperro, Mevagissey, Porthleven and Mousehole, crammed in anywhere they could get a toehold and access to a scrap of sheltered harbour among the harsh sandstone and granite cliffs of the coast. These cliffs held the key to livelihoods other than the pursuit of the 'silver darlings'; they contained tin for mining and smelting, granite for the quarrying of roadstone and armourstone. Hard, wearying livelihoods all, as were the domestic callings of the fish and mine and quarry wives with huge

Sandstone to the West
Dawlish Warren to Isles of Scilly

families to raise on meagre means. No wonder that smuggling, with all its potential to lead a man to dance the hangman's jig, proved so popular and so long-lasting throughout the 18th and 19th centuries.

The wild Atlantic waves, powered by the prevailing westerlies, roll in to thump up against rocks and stacks, just-concealed reefs and tall, unforgiving cliffs. Shipwreck was a persistent threat to seafarers in fogs or storms, a continual source of raw materials and comforts to those who lived along these coasts. The plundering may have died down, but the dangers of the south Devon and Cornwall coasts remain very real. Nowadays it is mostly volunteer members of the National Coastwatch Institution who keep a vigilant eye on what is going on along their patch of coast - an essential job that used to be carried out by the lighthouse keepers and coastguards who no longer man the lonely towers and cliff-top lookouts.

For all its harshness, hardships and dangers, this is the most romantic coast in England. Early travellers loved the clear light, the mild climate and the rugged landscape, the picturesquely poised villages, the vigorous sea bathing accompanied by the universal sound of the crash and boom of waves. Later arrivals by coach and train, by bus and car, fell in love with all these elements too. Small resorts developed everywhere there was a sandy beach and a means of access. The coast became the country's favourite seaside holiday destination, a status it still maintains.

It is the tiny islands off South Devon and Cornwall, in particular, that seem to exert a magnetic pull, though in very different ways. The fairy-tale attraction of the Art Deco hotel on Burgh Island off Bigbury lured the beautiful people between the wars; the self-contained sparseness of St George's Island off Looe captivated the hardy spinster sisters Babs and Evelyn Atkins. Legends drift like sea fog around the islands: the boy Jesus coming to St Michael's Mount, the grizzled warrior Arthur finding a royal grave on a tiny Scilly islet. Truth can seem stranger than fiction here. The isles of the Scilly archipelago, nearly 30 miles into the wide ocean from Land's End, were all one piece of land only 1500 years ago, and the sea floor between them is so near the surface that a tall adventurer can walk between them on rare low tides. Such facts make the mind reel. But in the end it is pure romance that holds the ring as you sweep across fabled Lyonesse, the kingdom beyond Land's End, on towards the deep Atlantic, and out into the wide blue yonder.

Dawlish Warren, Devon (left)

N 50°36'41.6" W 3°25'31.9"
Grid Ref: SX992801 Map Ref: 1 M8

Curling in a graceful arc like a motif in a modern stained glass window, the two-mile-long sandspit of Dawlish Warren shows off its subtlety of form and beauty of colour to the 'eye in the sky' in a way it never does to mere mortals seeing it from ground level. The Warren has been building north-eastwards for some 7,000 years, and has already almost closed the mouth of the Exe Estuary. With over 600 plant species in spring and summer, and 25,000 wildfowl in winter, it is a major refuge for hard-pressed nature along the holiday coast of the English Riviera.

Torquay, Devon

N 50°27'33.1" W 3°31'39.8"
Grid Ref: SX917633 Map Ref: 1 M9

The big east-facing bight of Torbay was the home anchorage for ships of the Royal Navy's Channel Fleet during the Napoleonic Wars, and it was the wives and families of the serving officers, waiting for their men to return, who first gave the coastal village of Torquay its air of a fashionable resort. Business took place down on the harbour (today a marina); family life was conducted in villas up on the wooded slopes behind the town. When the railway arrived in 1848, Torquay boomed into a most satisfactorily genteel watering hole.

Brixham, Devon

N 50°23'56.9" W 3°30'36.4"
Grid Ref: SX928566 Map Ref: 1 M10

In its sheltered position facing north into Torbay, Brixham was always well placed for commercial fishing. The beam trawler, a craft that shot nets from its sides and gathered them in, was developed in Brixham in the 19th century and revolutionised fishing at the time of the great herring boom. Three hundred sailing trawlers were built in the town at this time. Nowadays the trawlers that operate out of Brixham are stubby, powerful vessels; but their crews still appreciate the shelter of the harbour, protected against storms from almost any quarter by the loom of the land behind the town, and by the half-mile-long breakwater - a famous spot for sea angling.

Dartmouth, Devon *N 50°20'59.8" W 3°34'27.6" Grid Ref: SX881512 Map Ref: 1 L10*

Dartmouth lies well up in the throat of the Dart, a superbly sheltered location that ensured the prosperity of the little port (on the right of the picture, facing Kingswear across the river). It came into being eight centuries ago as a port of embarkation for the Crusades, and throve on cross-Channel trade and the Newfoundland cod fisheries when they were opened up in Tudor times. The Pilgrim Fathers took refuge from storms here in 1620 before setting out in *Mayflower* for the New World. Dartmouth has preserved its handsome old houses and cobbled quays; no wonder it is a favourite spot to linger and photograph the tall ships that often pay a visit to the salty old town.

Slapton, Devon *N 50°16'35.6" W 3°39'05.1" Grid Ref: SX824432 Map Ref: 1 L11*

The beautiful lagoon of Slapton Ley, sheltered from the seas of Start Bay by the protective shingle bar of Slapton Sands, is the biggest freshwater lake in the West Country. This National Nature Reserve plays host to the UK's largest population of Cetti's warbler, a little dark brown bird of wetlands and marshes with a tremendous, vigorous burst of song. Slapton Sands was the scene of a Second World War tragedy, long hushed up. On 28 April 1944, German E-boats got amongst US forces training for the forthcoming D-Day assault on Utah Beach in Normandy, and killed 749 of them.

Salcombe, Devon *N 50°14'21.4" W 3°45'41.4" Grid Ref: SX745392 Map Ref: 1 K11*

Looking south down the Kingsbridge Estuary in South Devon. The green headland of Snapes Point curls out from the right of the picture, sending the river round a long eastward curve towards Salcombe huddled on its hill slope in the middle distance. The narrowness of the estuary, its promontories and its steep high banks offer sheltered sailing and anchorage in all wind conditions, and have made Salcombe a paradise for small-boat sailors.

Burgh Island, Devon *N 50°16'45.2" W 3°54'03.1" Grid Ref: SX647439 Map Ref: 1 K11*

Burgh Island is small, beautiful and other-worldly, but this tiny tidal island off Bigbury-on-Sea is famous for just one thing: the splendid Art Deco hotel that faces the mainland across its causeway. Noel Coward, Winston Churchill, Agatha Christie and the Duke and Duchess of Windsor are just some of the celebrity names in the guestbook. Nowadays you can walk, ride or sail to Burgh Island, or come ashore by antique hydraulic sea tractor.

Royal Albert Bridge and Tamar Bridge *N 50°24'29.3" W 4°12'11.0" Grid Ref: SX436588 Map Ref: I 110*

Twin bridges leap the thousand-yard width of the Hamoaze, a narrow stretch of the River Tamar west of Plymouth. The Tamar Road Bridge was opened in 1961; but handsome though it is, all heads are turned when trains pass from Devon into Cornwall across the neighbouring Royal Albert Bridge, one of the finest of the many engineering triumphs of Isambard Kingdom Brunel. The great Victorian engineer had nowhere to anchor the tension chains of the suspension bridge he wished to build; so he made the bridge itself do the job, by hanging the deck from chains which themselves hung from an immense pair of cast-iron tubular trusses arching overhead. On 6 May 1859, two days after the official opening, the mortally sick Brunel was drawn ceremonially across the bridge in an open wagon. Four months later, he was dead.

Tregantle Fort, Cornwall *N 50°21'27.9" W 4°16'11.0" Grid Ref: SX387533 Map Ref: 1 I10*

Low-lying Tregantle Fort was built on Antony Tor Point in 1858-66, during the great French invasion panic, to command Whitsand Bay and the western approaches to the Royal Navy Dockyard a few miles eastward up the River Tamar at Devonport. Tregantle's grim grey stone walls look seaward at the head of long, sloping cliffs seeded with rifle ranges that are still in use.

Looe Island, Cornwall *N 50°20'12.1" W 4°27'02.1" Grid Ref: SX258514 Map Ref: 1 H10*

Babs and Evelyn Atkins were quintessentially English, a pair of humorous, eccentric and tough spinster sisters who didn't care a jot what people thought when, in 1965, they bought and set up home on Looe Island a mile off the Cornish coast. The remote and amenity-free island, otherwise known as St George's Island, has a coastline you can walk round in fifteen minutes. Here on this tiny slip of rock the sisters lived until they died, Evelyn in 1997 at the age of 87, Babs in 2004 at eighty-six, having bequeathed the island to the Cornwall Wildlife Trust.

Polperro, Cornwall *N 50°19'50.1" W 4°30'56.2" Grid Ref: SX211509 Map Ref: 1 H10*

In many ways Polperro is the archetype of a Cornish fishing village. Immensely picturesque, it tumbles down its narrow cleft in the cliffs, the lanes twisting and turning until broadening out on a tiny cove whose beachfront is reinforce with harbour walls. The old stone-built fishermen's cottages, the tall ground-floor lofts where they kept their gear and the cellars where they stored their catch are mostly in service as holiday accommodation these days.

Polruan Boatyard, Cornwall *N 50°19'45.5" W 4°38'03.9" Grid Ref: SX126510 Map Ref: 1 G10*

Yachts laid up for winter huddle like frightened sheep into a corner of Alan Toms's boatyard at Polruan on the estuary of the Fowey, a river with a strong tradition of boatbuilding. Jane Slade, a widow who ran this yard early in the 20th century, was the model for the heroine of Daphne Du Maurier's first novel, *The Loving Spirit*. Nowadays the largest working boatbuilder on the river, the Polruan boatyard turns out meticulously crafted trawlers and other small vessels.

St Catherine's Castle, Fowey, Cornwall *N 50°19'41.7" W 4°38'40.3" Grid Ref: SX119509 Map Ref: 1 G10*

Small coastal castles, silent witnesses to the invasion fears of Tudor England, stand all along the south coast, and Fowey, too, possesses one - St Catherine's Castle, built on its rocky headland just south of the port in 1536 to deter the French. The foundations of the blockhouse that lay seaward of the keep, fortified with bastions, can easily be made out. Another invasion scare of the 1850s – this one, too, involving the French – saw the blockhouse converted into a two-gun battery, and a gun emplacement was built here during the Second World War to dominate the river mouth.

Chapter Point, Portmellon, Cornwall *N 50°15'23.7" W 4°46'07.7" Grid Ref: SX027433 Map Ref: 1 F11*

Thrusting east from the craggy coast near St Austell, the crocodile snout of Chapel Point protects the tiny, perfect curve of Colona Beach. The three houses on the Point were built of the promontory's own rock in 1933-8, to the Arts & Crafts designs of architect John Campbell. This man of strong and passionate vision died in 1947, aged nearly 70, after falling from a cliff near his beloved Chapel Point.

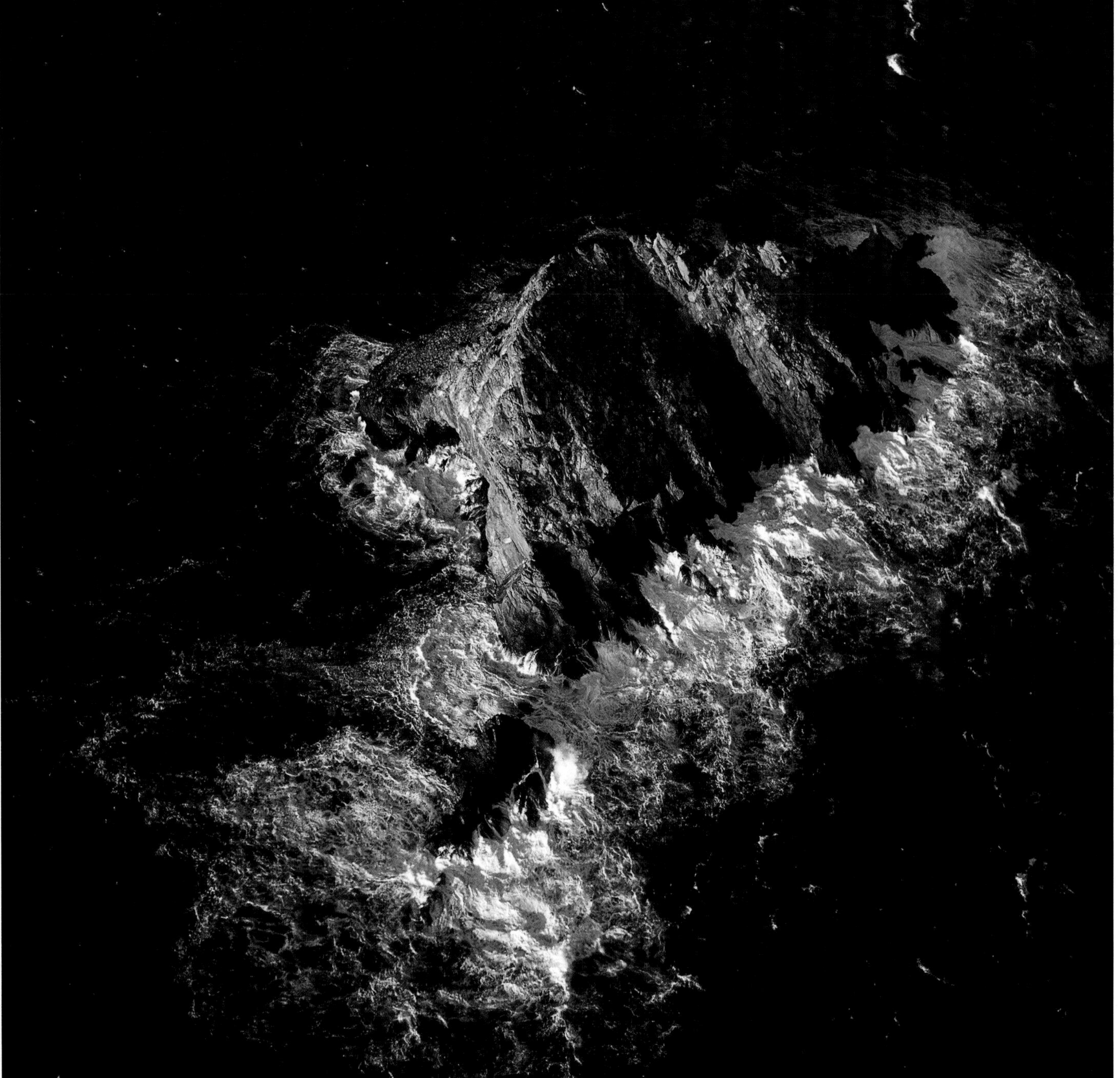

Gull Rock, near Nare Head, Cornwall *N 50°11'43.0" W 4°54'17.6" Grid Ref: SW928369 Map Ref: 1 F11*

Spiky, rugged and shaped in profile like a sea castle sprouting many spires, Gull Rock lies off Nare Head a little north-east of Falmouth. The rock is aptly named – herring gulls haunt it, along with guillemots and razorbills, shags and cormorants, and the kittiwakes that wheel on black-tipped wings as they cry their name, '*ee-wake*! '*ee-wake!* South-west of Gull Rock rises a line of rock teeth, the Inner, Middle and Outer Stones, while below the surface lurks the Whelps reef. In February 1914 the 2,000-ton German barque *Helvetia* ran onto the reef. Twelve men were swept away to their deaths when she struck the Whelps. Seven others refused help from the Falmouth lifeboat and decided to stay with the wrecked ship, a deadly decision – within ten minutes, both wreck and men had vanished.

Zone Point, Cornwall *N 50°08'23.8" W 5°00'33.4" Grid Ref: SW851310 Map Ref: 1 E12*

The ragged bear's paw of Zone Point appears to stroke the agitated sea in this remarkable image. This southernmost point of the Roseland Peninsula is all ancient sandstone, topped by heathy slopes too steep to have been cultivated. Atlantic grey seals are often seen on the adjacent beaches, which are so difficult of access that the mothers come ashore to give birth to their pups with no fear of human disturbance.

St Anthony's Lighthouse, Cornwall *N 50°08'28.0" W 5°00'56.9" Grid Ref: SW846311 Map Ref: 1 E12*

Squeezed precariously between the steep slope of St Anthony Head and the sea, St Anthony's Lighthouse stands immediately west of Zone Point (see opposite) at the entrance to the broad estuary of Carrick Roads. Built in 1835, the light was originally provided by eight oil lamps. Until 1954 the fog warning consisted of a large bell. Archaisms aside, however, St Anthony's Lighthouse has always fulfilled a vital rôle beside that of marking the mouth of Carrick Roads; it warns seafarers that they are entering the sea area of The Manacles, one of Cornwall's deadliest reefs, which lies off the east coast of the Lizard peninsula some 7 miles to the south.

St Mawes Castle, Cornwall *N 50°09'19.4" W 5°01'25.5" Grid Ref: SW842328 Map Ref: 1 C12*

St Mawes Castle near Falmouth is another of the anti-invasion forts built in the late 1530s and 40s on the orders of King Henry VIII. In spite of its strong central tower and three clover-leaf bastions, its roof-mounted cannon and defensive rock-cut ditch, in 1646 St Mawes Castle was surrendered to Roundhead besiegers without a shot being fired by its pragmatic Royalist garrison, who realised their chances of holding out in such an isolated location were nil.

Quarry near St Keverne, Cornwall *N 50°02'33.7" W 5°04'07.0" Grid Ref: SW804204 Map Ref: 1 E12*

Among the ancient rocks of the Lizard Peninsula is gabbro, an adamantine dark volcanic composition highly suitable for roadstone and for building sea defences. Near Porthoustock on the eastern side of the Lizard, Dean Quarry extracts large chunks of gabbro, known to the construction trade as 'armourstone'. Concerns over quarry dust, noise and road traffic have seen the company urged to ship out the stone by sea – a tricky proposition in such a location, as this picture clearly shows.

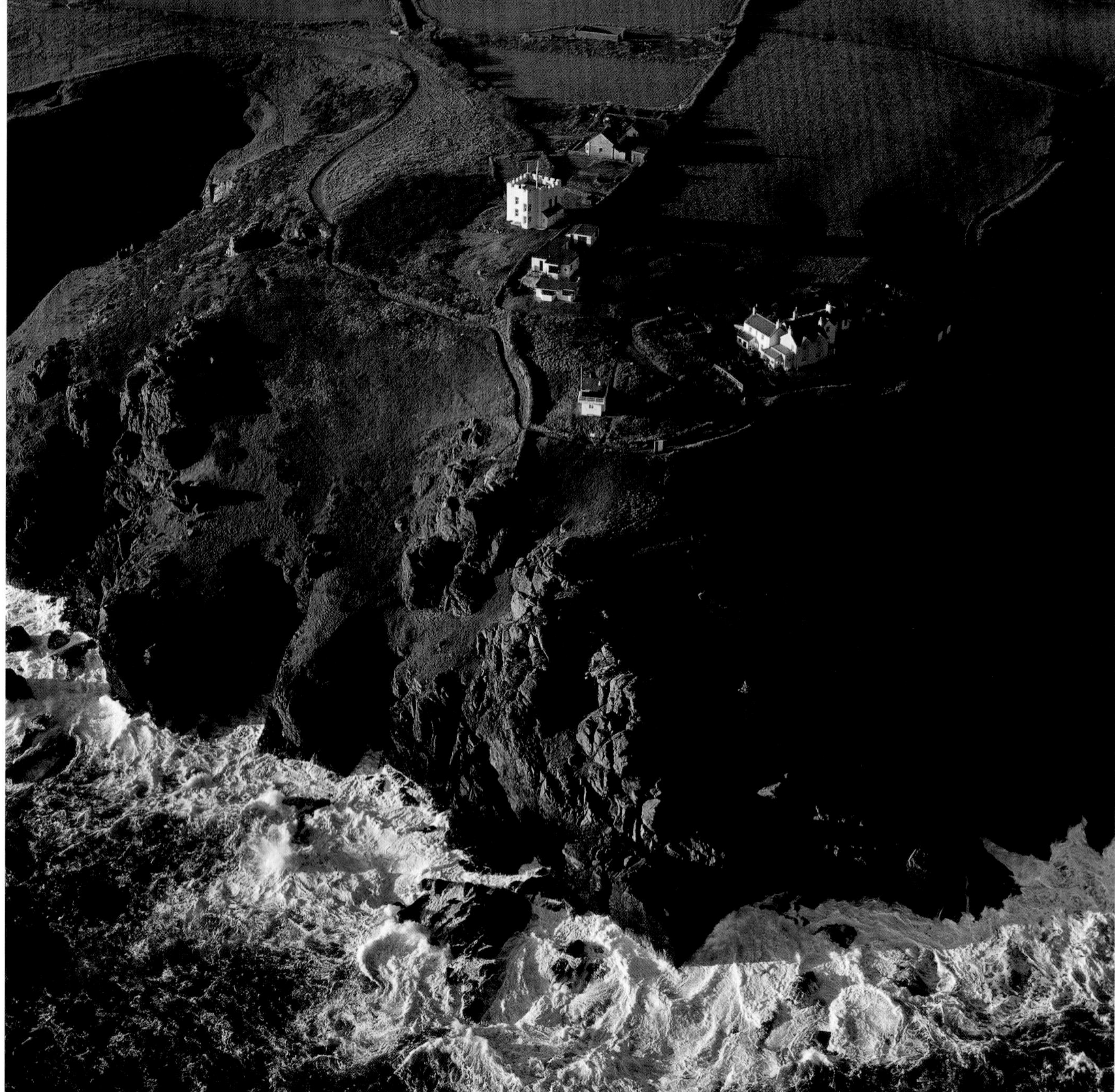

Bass Point, Cornwall *N 49°57'49.4" W 5°11'12.8" Grid Ref: SW715119 Map Ref: 1 D13*

High on the bluff back of Bass Point stands a cluster of buildings, each with its own remarkable story. The castellated miniature castle is a Lloyd's Signal Station, built on the cliff in 1878 to communicate with passing ships by semaphore. Nearby stands the house where the station crew lived, and here also are the restored huts of the Lizard Wireless Station, set up by radio pioneer Guglielmo Marconi in 1900 to experiment with transmitting across the Atlantic. The modest white-fronted building near the cliff edge is a lookout station manned by volunteer members of the National Coastwatch Institution, the ever-open eyes and ears of the rescue services on this dangerous coast. The catalyst for the opening of the Bass Point lookout in December 1994 was a tragic accident in which two fishermen from nearby Cadgwith drowned within sight of the official coastguard lookout, which was unmanned because of job cuts.

Polpeor Cove, Cornwall *N 49°57'32.1" W 5°12'22.0" Grid Ref: SW701115 Map Ref: 1 D13*

Creaming waves around the point of Polpeor Cove cover the deadly reef of Vellan Drang as the tide sets in at Britain's most southerly point. With the Lizard lifeboat now housed over at Church Cove, the fishermen use the redundant lifeboat shed in Polpeor Cove as a net store. The former lifeboat station saw some desperate rescues. The greatest was on 17/18 March 1907 when the White Star liner *Suevic*, with 524 souls on board, ran onto the Mên Hyr rocks a mile offshore in thick fog. Four local lifeboats, working together, saved everyone; the Lizard boat, making six trips into the fog, rescued 167 people.

Porthleven, Cornwall

N 50°04'57.0" W 5°19'01.7"
Grid Ref: SW628255 Map Ref: 1 D12

High in the north-west 'armpit' of the Lizard Peninsula, Porthleven presents the classic view of a Cornish fishing village. Massive storm walls and a sturdy breakwater keep the sea at bay, so that when surfing waves driven in from the west are thundering on the beach below the town, all is calm in the inner harbour. Seafarers seeking shelter in a storm look for the landmark tower at the harbour entrance – not a church tower, in spite of appearances, but the clock tower of the scientific and literary institute founded here in 1882 by local philanthropist William Bickford-Smith.

Wheal Trewavas, Cornwall (right)

N 50°05'25.3" W 5°21'22.8"
Grid Ref: SW600265 Map Ref: 1 D12

Perched in a very hazardous situation on East Rinsey cliff at the eastern edge of Mounts Bay, the engine house and chimney of Wheal Trewavas stand among the scars and lumps of mine spoil. Opened around 1834, the mine extracted copper from four lodes. Some ten years after Wheal Trewavas began operating it was employing 200 locals, one of the shafts had reached a depth of 600 feet, and levels were being run far out under the sea. Things looked good for Wheal Trewavas. But – typically of so many Cornish mining ventures of the time – within a couple of years the whole enterprise had gone bust amid talk of financial shenanigans and whispers of fraudulent dividend payouts. Altogether the mine produced £100,000 worth of copper ore in its decade of existence. The stark ruins remain on the cliff to remind onlookers of the grimness, danger and insecurity of the Cornish miner's working life.

Prussia Cove, Cornwall

N 50°06'01.2" W 5°24'55.0"
Grid Ref: SW559278 Map Ref: 1 C12

King's Cove lies to the right of the headland, Bessy's Cove to the left – yet Prussia Cove is the name by which everyone knows these indentations in the coastline on the eastern side of Mount's Bay. Originally known as Portleah, Prussia Cove took its title from local smuggler chief John Carter, styled 'The King of Prussia' because of his admiration for Frederick the Great. Active around the turn of the 19th century, Carter and his brother Henry led the Excisemen a merry dance for a few years. Non-swearing Methodists, they were not afraid to fight – in 1788 Henry Carter had his nose slashed in two and several lumps knocked out of his skull during a battle. Around 1807 the King of Prussia abdicated his smuggler throne and disappeared; his brother gave up the game, too, and became a preacher.

St Michael's Mount, Cornwall *N 50°06'59.1" W 5°28'41.8" Grid Ref: SW514298 Map Ref: 1 C12*

Was this fairy-tale hillock in the sea the Isle of Ictis, fabled centre of the ancient tinning industry? Did the tin-trader Joseph of Arimathea bring his young great-nephew Jesus with him on a trip to Cornwall and land with him on the Mount? And did those feet in ancient time walk upon England's mountains green? Certainly there are accounts of all this, and of the Archangel Michael appearing on the Mount that bears his name. More verifiably, a Norman abbey of the Benedictine order was built on St Michael's Mount; so was one of King Henry VIII's castles against the French. After the St Aubyn family bought the isle in 1659 the fort became their magnificently furnished house; but mystery and magic continued to cling to this spellbinding rock.

Minack Theatre, Cornwall *N 50°02'27.3" W 5°39'03.8" Grid Ref: SW387220 Map Ref: 1 B12*

The smooth, regular tiers of seating at the Minack Theatre present an eyecatching contrast to the jumbled, rugged rocks of Minack Point in which they are set. The theatre dates from the heady, optimistic days of the 1930s arts scene in west Cornwall, when painters Ben Nicholson and Christopher Wood were becoming entranced with the area and Bernard Leach was producing his innovative pottery at nearby St Ives. The Minack Theatre was the brainchild of Rowena Cade, a formidably determined woman who bought Minack Point for £100, built her own house from its stones, and then designed and built the classical-style open-air theatre, much of it with her own hands.

The Eastern Isles, Isles of Scilly

N 49°56'32.5" W 6°15'47.6"
Grid Ref: SV942134 Map Ref: 1 C3

Tiny and mysterious, opalescent in a cobalt blue sea, the uninhabited Eastern Isles float like a flock of sea beasts, 28 miles from Land's End at the eastern entrance of the Scilly archipelago. Great and Little Ganinick are seen in the foreground; beyond rises the round blob of Little Ganilly. To its right lies torc-shaped Great Arthur with its chambered cairn where, some say, King Arthur lies awaiting his call to rise and save Britain from some unnamed calamity of the dark future. In the distance is the long-backed sprawl of Great Ganilly; from its western headland of Nornour, Roman jewellery was recovered.

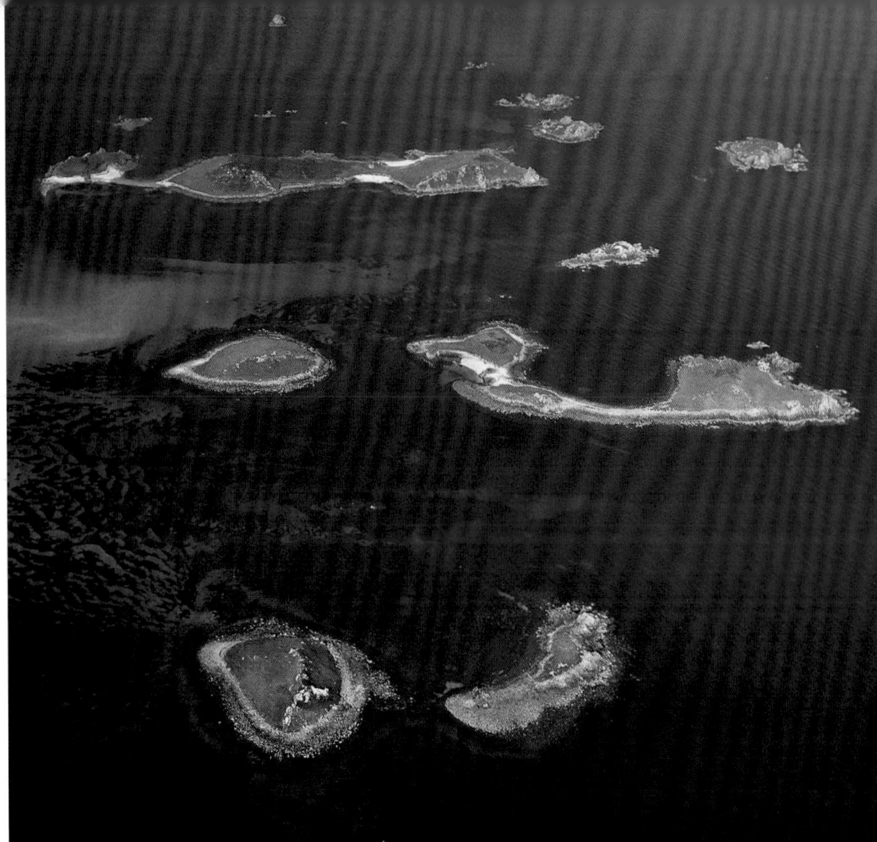

Tresco, Isles of Scilly (left)

N 49°56'47.9" W 6°19'21.9"
Grid Ref: SV900141 Map Ref: 1 C3

Looking northwards over the rugged granite outcrops of Crow Point towards the wide pools and lush tree cover at the centre of the island of Tresco. In contrast to the other Scilly isles Tresco is a miracle of fertility and spectacular plant growth – all thanks to Augustus Smith, an autocrat as energetic as he was dictatorial, who in 1834 took on the lease of the whole archipelago and the title of Lord Proprietor of the Isles of Scilly. Smith built himself a residence, Tresco Abbey, and proceeded to create a marvellous garden of sub-tropical plants which has been cared for and added to by successive generations of the family ever since.

Round Island Lighthouse, Isles of Scilly

N 49°58'32.4" W 6°19'00.3"
Grid Ref: SV906173 Map Ref: 1 B3

Built on its lonely rock in 1887, Round Island lighthouse was one of the most remote in Britain. It was also one of the most difficult of access. Food and supplies had to be winched up along a 400-ft wire cable to the keepers in the tower at the edge of its sheer granite cliffs. What passed through those men's minds as they gazed out from their lonely station at the rim of the Scilly archipelago? Beyond that hazy blue horizon it is all rumour - of the 'Green Fields of Amerikay', of Tir-na-nOg, the Land of the Young, and of Atlantis, the once and future realm.

Land's End, Cornwall *N 50°04'07.8" W 5°43'00.2" Grid Ref: SW341254 Map Ref: 1 B12*

At the end of our 9,000-mile journey is Land's End. Perched on top of the cliffs is the 'first and last house in England' and beyond, the white buildings of the attraction centre. The outermost toe-tip of south-west Britain has been the scene of many shipwrecks, the harsh, blocky rocks of the promontory and treacherous reefs encircled by white foam and an indigo sea that bears the merciless swell of the Atlantic Ocean.

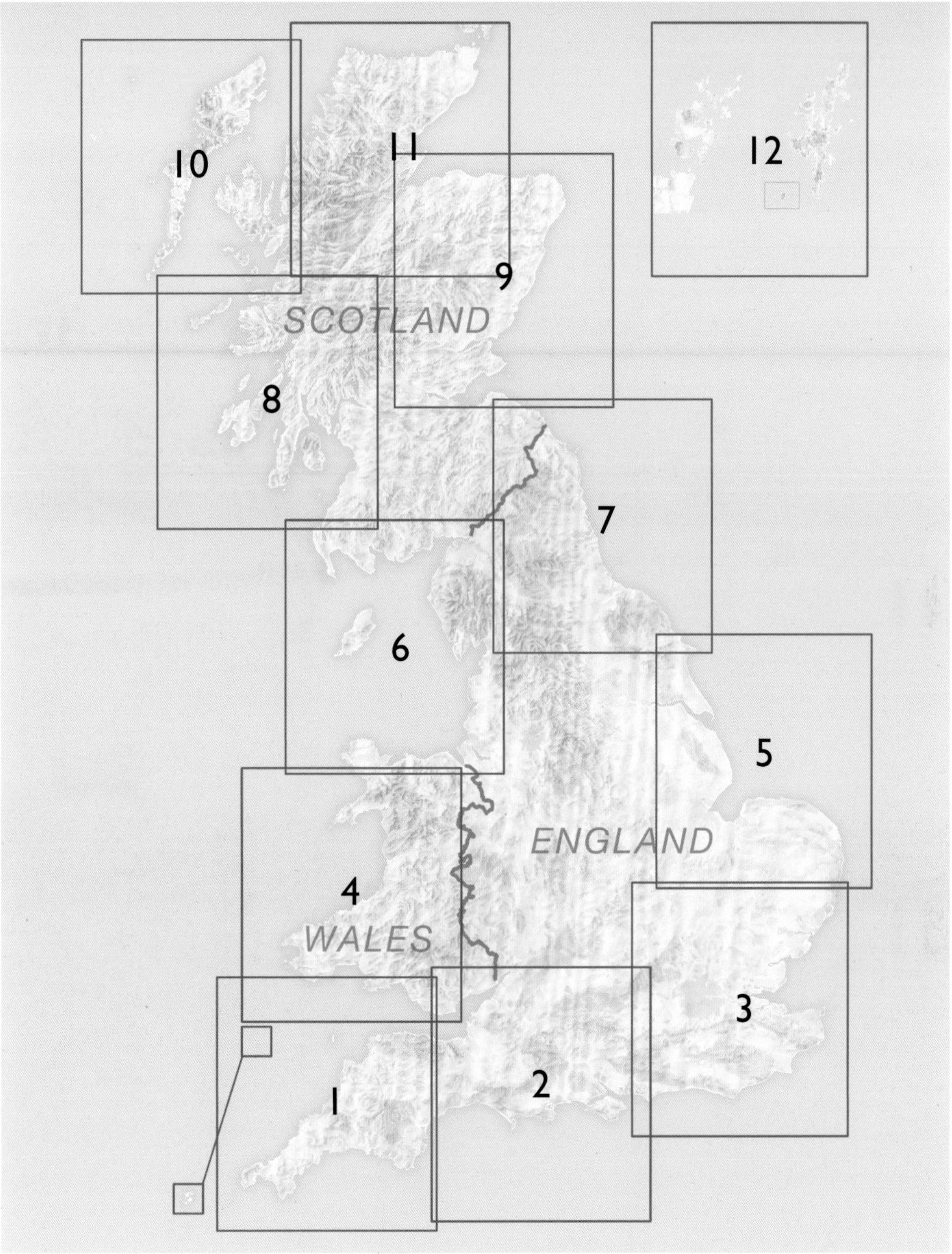

The Living Coast - Maps of photographic locations

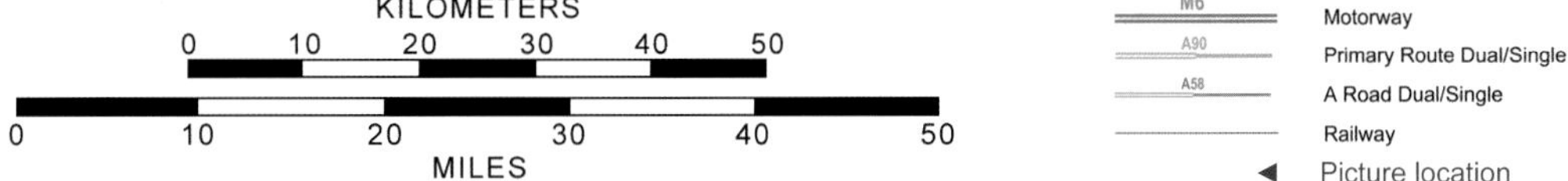

All maps © mapsinternational.co.uk. Updated from Collins Bartholomew mapping

A
B
C
D
E
F
G
H
I
J
K
L
M
ISLES OF SCILLY
Round Island Lighthouse
Tresco
St. Martin's
Bryher
Eastern Isles
Hugh Town
St. Mary's
St. Agnes
St. Just
Newlyn
Land's End
Lundy
Rhossili
Worms Head
The Mumbles
Port Talbot
Swansea Bay
Pyle
Bridgend
Porthcawl
Cowbridge
Nash Point
Bristol Channel
Little Hangman
Widmouth
Great Hangman
Ilfracombe
Foreland Point
Old Burrow Fortlet
Bull Point
Lynton
Combe Martin
Morte Point
Woolacombe
Lynmouth & Lynton
Minehead
Croyde
Braunton
Barnstaple or Bideford Bay
Taw & Torridge Estuary
Barnstaple
Hartland Point
Northam
Appledore & Instow
Hartland
Bideford
Torridge Bridge
Buck's Mills
Torrington
South Molton
Dulverton
Lower Sharpnose point
Chulmleigh
Chawleigh
Tiverton
Bude Bay
Bude
Stratton
Holsworthy
Hatherleigh
DEVON
Cullompton
Crackington Haven
Crediton
Roadford Res
Okehampton
Boscastle
Tintagel Castle
Exeter
Rumps Point
Camelford
Launceston
Moretonhampstead
Port Isaac
Dawlish Warren
Trevose Head
Padstow
Polzeath
Bovey Tracey
Park Head
Colliford Reservoir
Tavistock
Kingsteignton
Bedruthan Steps
Wadebridge
Yelverton
Ashburton
Newton Abbot
Towan Head
Bodmin
Pentire Point
Newquay
Liskeard
Tamar Bridge
Saltash
Buckfastleigh
Torquay
CORNWALL
Lostwithiel
Looe
Plymouth
Plympton
Totnes
Paignton
Fowey
Polperro
Torpoint
Tregantle Fort
Ivybridge
Brixham
St. Agnes
St. Austell
Polruan
Plymstock
Dartmouth
Mevagissey
Whitsand Bay
St Ives
Redruth
Truro
Chapel Point
Burgh Island
Kingsbridge
Slapton
Gurnard's Head
Gull Rock
Start Bay
Camborne
Levant tin mine
Penryn
St Mawes
Salcombe
Start Point
St Michael's Mount
Bigbury Bay
Prawle Point
Falmouth
Penzance
Zone Point & St Anthony's Lighthouse
Land's End
Helston
Falmouth Bay
Porthleven
Quarry near St Keverne
Minack Theatre
Prussia Cove
Mount's Bay
Wheal Trewavas
Lizard
Bass Point
Polpeor Cove
Lizard Point
1
2
3
4
5
6
7
8
9
10
11
12
13
14

A
B
C
D
E
F
G
H
I
J
K
L
M
Caldicot Castle
Second Severn Crossing
CARDIFF
Mouth of the Severn
Cardiff waterfront
BRISTOL
Flat Holm
Weston-Super-Mare
Brean Down
Bridgwater Bay
Kilve Beach
Watchet
SOMERSET
WILTSHIRE
HAMPSHIRE
DORSET
Swindon
Reading
Salisbury
Southampton
SOUTHAMPTON
PORTSMOUTH
BOURNEMOUTH
Lyme Regis
Golden Cap
Charmouth
Salcombe Hill Cliffs
Beer Head
Branscombe
Ladram Bay
Lyme Bay
Abbotsbury Swannery
Chesil Beach
Isle of Portland
Bill of Portland
White Nothe
Bats Head
Durdle Door
Lulworth Cove
Flowers Barrow
Worbarrow Tout
Kimmeridge Bay
Kimmeridge Ledges
Chapmans Pool
St. Aldhelm's or St. Alban's Head
Blackers Hole
Swanage
Old Harry Rocks
Sandbanks
Bournemouth
Hengistbury Head
Hurst Castle
Yarmouth
The Needles
Tennyson Down
Cowes
Bucklers Hard
Portchester Castle
Gosport & Portsmouth
Langstone harbour
Birdham Harbour
St. Catherine's Point
ISLE OF WIGHT

A B C D E F G H I J K L M
SUFFOLK
ESSEX
HERTFORDSHIRE
BEDFORDSHIRE
SURREY
KENT
EAST SUSSEX
WEST SUSSEX
Slaughden
Aldeburgh
Orfordness
Orford Ness
Orfordness Mouth
Orford Beach
Felixstowe
Harwich
Harwich Harbour
The Naze
Walton-on-the-Naze
Frinton-on-Sea
Clacton-on-sea
Clacton-on-Sea
Brightlingsea
West Mersea
Abberton Res
Tiptree
Colchester
Wivenhoe
Maldon
Northey Island
South Woodham Ferrers
Burnham-on-Crouch
Foulness Island
Rochford
Coryton Oil Refinery
Southend-on-Sea
Canvey Island
Shoebury Ness
Thurrock Oil Depot
Grays
Tilbury
Isle of Grain
Car Depository
Sheerness
Warden Point
Isle of Sheppey
Dartford Crossing
Colemouth Creek
Gillingham
Chatham
Sittingbourne
Faversham
Whitstable
Herne Bay
Reculver
Margate
Kingsgate
North Foreland
Broadstairs
Ramsgate
Sandwich
Canterbury
Deal Castle
Deal
Walmer Castle
Sandwich Bay
Kingsdown
South Foreland
Dover Castle
Foreland lighthouse
Dover
Folkestone
Hythe
Channel Tunnel
Dymchurch
New Romney
Dungeness
Rye
Rye Bay
Hastings
Bexhill
Battle
Sovereign Harbour
Eastbourne
Eastbourne Pier
Beachy Head
White Cliffs - Seven Sisters
Cuckmere River
Seaford
Newhaven
Peacehaven
Rottingdean
Brighton
BRIGHTON
Hove
Shoreham-by-Sea
Worthing
Littlehampton
Bognor Regis
Arundel
Chichester
Dell Quay
Selsey
Selsey Bill
Pagham Harbour
LONDON
Cambridge
Bury St. Edmunds
Newmarket
Ipswich
Chelmsford
Basildon
Maidstone
Tonbridge
Royal Tunbridge Wells
Ashford
Crawley
Guildford
Luton
Bedford
Northampton
Milton Keynes
3

A
B
C
D
E
F
G
H
I
J
K
L
M
1
2
3
4
5
6
7
8
9
10
11
12
13
14
15
Caernarfon Castle
Caernarfon
Bethesda
Llanrwst
Betws-y-Coed
Denbigh
Ruthin
Caernarfon Bay
Blaenau Ffestiniog
Ffestiniog
Nefyn
Criccieth
Porthmadog
Corwen
Llangollen
Pwllheli Harbour
Pwllheli
Criccieth Castle
River Dwyryd
Llyn Tegid
Bala
Abersoch
Harlech Castle
Llyn Efyrnwy
Bardsey Island
Barmouth
Dolgellau
Llanfyllin
Welshpool
Cardigan Bay
Tywyn
Machynlleth
Montgomery
Newtown
Nant-y-moch Res
Llyn Clywedog
Llanidloes
Aberystwyth
WALES
Claerwen Res
Aberaeron
New Quay
Llandrindod Wells
Caban-coch Res
Llyn Brianne
Builth Wells
Lampeter
Dinas Head
Cardigan
Newcastle Emlyn
Llanwrtyd Wells
Strumble Head
Strumble Head Lighthouse
Bryn Henllan
Goodwick
Fishguard
Llandovery
Abercastle
Porthgain
St. David's Head
Carreg Rhoson
St. David's
Brecon
Penpleidiau
South Bishop
Ramsey Island
Llandeilo
Carmarthen
Whitland
St. Clears
Crickhowell
Haverfordwest
Narberth
Glanaman
Ammanford
Skomer Island
Milford Haven
Neyland
Taf Estuary
Kidwelly
Ystalyfera
Glynneath
Merthyr Tydfil
Tredegar
Rhymney
Stack Rock Fort
Fort Hubberstone
Saundersfoot
Pontardawe
Skokholm Island
Fort Popton
Pembroke Dock
Burry Port
Pontarddulais
Aberdare
Tenby
Loughor
Milford Haven Oil Refinery
Pembroke
Carmarthen Bay
Llanelli
Gorseinon
Blackwood
Ferndale
Gelligaer
Neath
SWANSEA
Swansea
Rhondda
Maesteg
Linney Head
St Margaret's Island
Caldey Island
St. Govan's Head
Worms Head
Rhossili
Port Talbot
Pontypridd
Porth
Caerphilly
Worms Head
Paviland Cave
The Mumbles
Oxwich Bay
Mumbles Head
Swansea Bay
Llantrisant
Pyle
Bridgend
Porthcawl
Cowbridge
Nash Point
Sully
Barry
Rhoose
Bristol Channel

A B C D E F G H I J K L M

1 2 3 4 5 6 7 8 9 10 11 12 13 14 15

Bempton Cliffs
Flamborough Head
Bridlington
Flamborough Head
Bridlington
Bridlington Bay
Driffield
Hornsea
Weighton
Beverley
Kingston upon Hull
KINGSTON UPON HULL
Hessle
Withernsea
Barton-upon-Humber
Humber
Immingham
Grimsby
Spurn Head
Cleethorpes
Grimsby
Brigg
Market Rasen
Louth
Mablethorpe
Alford
Lincoln
Washingborough
Chapel St. Leonards
Horncastle
Ingoldmells Point
North Hykeham
Woodhall Spa
Spilsby
Waddington
Skegness
Coningsby
LINCOLNSHIRE
Gibraltar Point
Ruskington
Boston Deeps
Lynn Deeps
Wells-next-the-Sea
Blakeney Point
Tibby Head
Scolt Head Island
Sheringham
Cromer
Sleaford
Boston
Hunstanton
Cromer
Wells-next-the-sea
Blakeney Point
Overstrand
Frampton Marsh
Hunstanton
The Wash
Fakenham
North Walsham
Happisburgh
Pinchbeck
Sutton Bridge
Mouth of Great Ouse
Aylsham
Bourne
Spalding
Holbeach
King's Lynn
NORFOLK
Market Deeping
East Dereham
Stamford
Wisbech
Norwich
Swaffham
Brundall
Great Yarmouth
Downham Market
Peterborough
Whittlesey
March
Wymondham
ENGLAND
Oundle
Lowestoft
Lowestoft
Bungay
Beccles
Ramsey
Chatteris
Littleport
Thetford
Harleston
Ely
Diss
CAMBRIDGESHIRE
Thrapston
Little Stukeley
Haddenham
Mildenhall
Eye
Halesworth
Southwold
St. Ives
Soham
Huntingdon
Higham Ferrers
Brampton
Godmanchester
Burwell
Bury St. Edmunds

A
B
C
D
E
F
G
H
I
J
K
L
M
1
2
3
4
5
6
7
8
9
10
11
2
3
4
5
Clatteringshaws Loch
New Galloway
Loch Ken
Dumfries
Locharbriggs
Cargenbridge
A74(M)
River Esk
Longtown
Newton Stewart
Caerlaverock Castle
Annan
Gretna Green
Brampton
Stranraer
Gatehouse of Fleet
Castle Douglas
Dalbeattie
Solway Firth
Carlisle
Wigtown
Silloth
Wetheral
Portpatrick
Wigtown Bay
Kirkcudbright
Auchencairn
Wigton
Luce Bay
Solway Firth
Allonby Bay
Whithorn
Wigtown Bay
Maryport
M6
Cockermouth
Burrow Head
Mull of Galloway
Penrith
Workington
Keswick
Whitehaven
Crummock Water
Derwent Water
Appleby-in-Westmorland
Ullswater
St. Bees Head
Ennerdale Water
Thirlmere
Haweswater
Egremont
Grasmere
Point of Ayre
Ambleside
Ramsey Bay
Seascale
Windermere
Bowness-on-Windermere
ISLE OF MAN
Ramsey
Kendal
Coniston Water
Windermere
Peel
Duddon Estuary
Millom
Milnthorpe
Morecambe Bay
Ulverston
Grange-over-Sands
Dalton-in-Furness
Douglas
Port Erin
Carnforth
Barrow-in-Furness
Barrow-in-furness
Castletown
Morecambe
Roa Island
Morecambe
Heysham
Hilpsford Point
Lancaster
Piel Island
Morecambe Bay
River Lune
Fleetwood
Cleveleys
Thornton
Poulton-le-Fylde
Longridge
BLACKPOOL
Blackpool Tower
M55
Irish Sea
Kirkham
Lytham St. Anne's
Freckleton
River Ribble
Southport
Chorley
Ormskirk
Liverpool Bay
Formby
Skelmersdale
Crosby
Kirkby
St. Helens
Bootle
Wallasey
LIVERPOOL
Amlwch
ANGLESEY
Dulas Bay
Great Orme's Head
Prestatyn
Birkenhead
Puffin Island
Llandudno
Prestatyn
West Kirby
Widnes
Holyhead
Benllech
Colwyn Bay
Rhyl
Rhyl
River Dee Estuary
Runcorn
Llangefni
Beaumaris
Conwy
Heswall
Holy Island
Beaumaris Castle
Conwy
Abergele
Holywell
Frodsham
Menai Bridges
Menai Bridge
Bangor
Llanfairfechan
St. Asaph
Flint Castle
Ellesmere Port
Connah's Quay
Northwich

A
B
C
D
E
F
G
H
I
J
K
L
M
1
2
3
4
5
6
7
8
9
10
11
12
13
14
15
Dunbar
East Linton
Dunbar
Eyemouth
Duns
Berwick-upon-Tweed
Berwick-upon-Tweed
Lidisfarne Priory & Castle
Holy Island or Lindisfarne
Coldstream
Earlston
Farne Islands
Bamburgh Castle
Farne Islands
Kelso
Dunstanburgh Castle
Craster
Jedburgh
Alnwick
Alnmouth
Warkworth Castle
Amble
Kielder Water
NORTHUMBERLAND
Lynemouth
Ashington
Newbiggin-by-the-Sea
Morpeth
Bedlington
Blyth
Blyth
Whitley Bay & St Mary's Island
Whitley Bay
Ponteland
North Shields
Tynemouth
Tynemouth
NEWCASTLE UPON TYNE
South Shields
Haltwhistle
Hexham
Ryton
Blaydon
Whickham
Gateshead
Sunderland
Sunderland
Derwent Reservoir
Washington
Stanley
Seaham
Seaham
Consett
Chester-le-Street
Alston
Hetton-le-Hole
Durham
Peterlee
Tow Law
Brandon
Hartlepool
Hartlepool
Crook
Spennymoor
DURHAM
Bishop Auckland
Tees Mouth
Tees Bay
Shildon
Sedgefield
Seal Sands
Redcar
Middlesbrough
Marske-by-the-Sea
Newton Aycliffe
Saltburn-by-the-Sea
Appleby-in-Westmorland
Stockton-on-Tees
Barnard Castle
Skelton
Loftus
Darlington
Thornaby-on-Tees
Guisborough
Kirkby Stephen
Whitby
Whitby
Richmond
Catterick Camp
Northallerton
Leyburn
Scalby
Scarborough
Scarborough
Thirsk
Helmsley
Pickering
Kirkby Lonsdale
Skipton-on-Swale
Filey
Reighton Sands
Flamborough Head
Malton
Norton
Ripon
YORKSHIRE
7

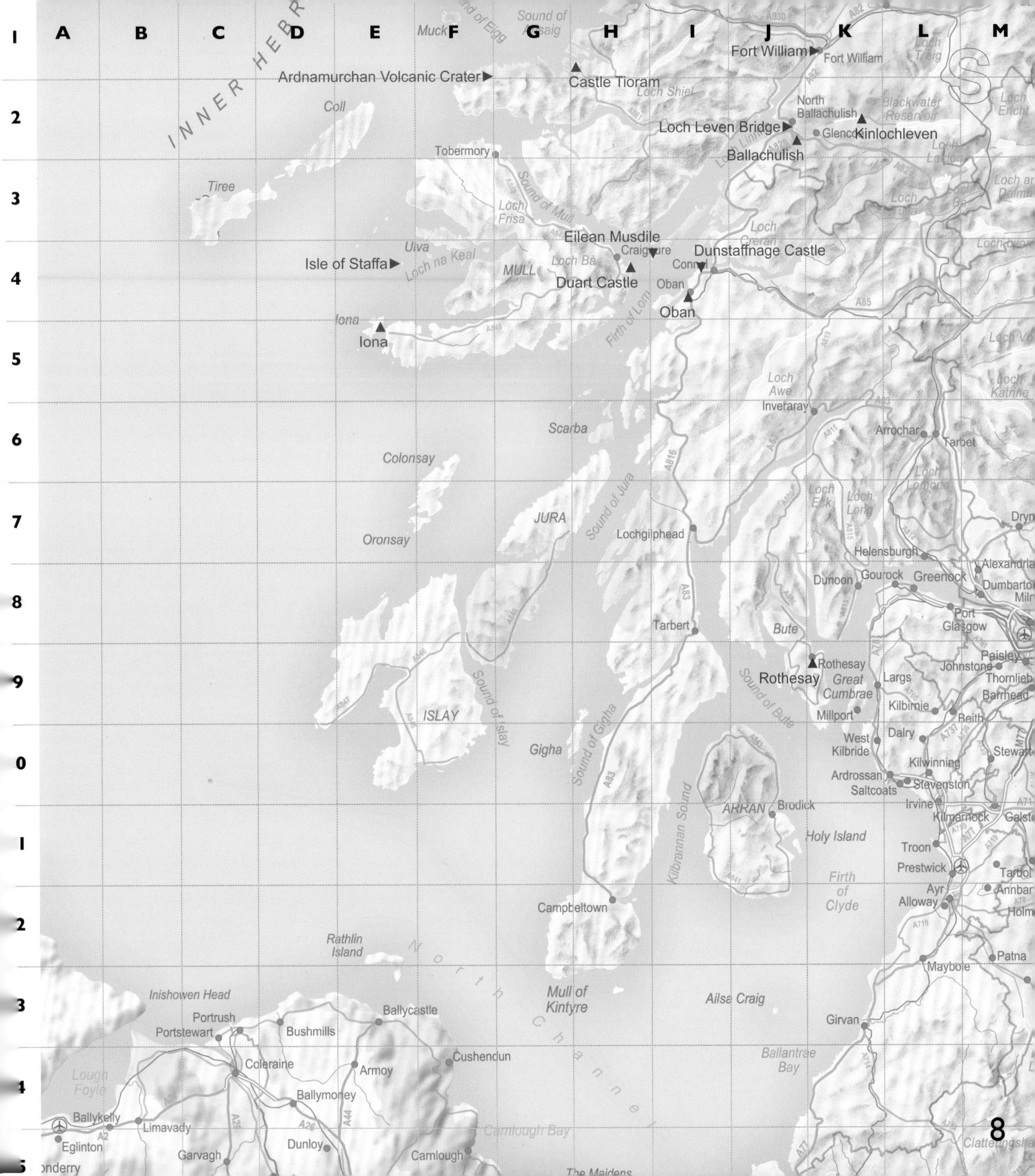

A
B
C
D
E
F
G
H
I
J
K
L
M
Ardnamurchan Volcanic Crater
Castle Tioram
Fort William
Loch Leven Bridge
Kinlochleven
Ballachulish
Tobermory
Isle of Staffa
Eilean Musdile
Dunstaffnage Castle
Duart Castle
Oban
Iona
Coll
Tiree
MULL
Scarba
Colonsay
JURA
Oronsay
ISLAY
Gigha
Lochgilphead
Inveraray
Arrochar
Tarbet
Helensburgh
Dunoon
Gourock
Greenock
Port Glasgow
Tarbert
Bute
Rothesay
Largs
Millport
West Kilbride
Ardrossan
Saltcoats
Stevenston
Irvine
Kilmarnock
ARRAN
Brodick
Holy Island
Troon
Prestwick
Ayr
Alloway
Campbeltown
Rathlin Island
Mull of Kintyre
Ailsa Craig
Girvan
Maybole
Patna
Inishowen Head
Portrush
Portstewart
Bushmills
Ballycastle
Coleraine
Armoy
Cushendun
Ballymoney
Limavady
Ballykelly
Eglinton
Dunloy
Garvagh
Carnlough
Carnlough Bay
Lough Foyle
Ballantrae Bay
Firth of Clyde
North Channel
Sound of Jura
Sound of Islay
Sound of Gigha
Sound of Mull
Kilbrannan Sound
Sound of Bute
Firth of Lorn
Loch Shiel
Loch Awe
Loch Lomond
Loch Eck
Loch Long
Loch na Keal
Loch Frisa
Great Cumbrae
Kilbirnie
Dalry
Kilwinning
Johnstone
Paisley
The Maidens
1
2
3
4
5
6
7
8
9
0
1
2
3
4
5
8

A B C D E F G H I J K L M
1 2 3 4 5 6 7 8 9
Tain
Invergordon
Cromarty
Moray Firth
Burghead
Lossiemouth
Findochty
Buckie
Cullen
Portsoy
Whitehills
Rosehearty
Kinnaird Head
Fraserburgh
Findhorn
Elgin
Banff
Macduff
Rattray Head
Fortrose
Fort George
Nairn
Forres
Aberchirder
New Pitsligo
Culloden
Rothes
Keith
Turriff
Peterhead
Craigellachie
Aberlour (Charlestown of Aberlour)
Dufftown
Huntly
Lochindorb
Grantown-on-Spey
Ellon
Oldmeldrum
Collieston
Rhynie
Carrbridge
Inverurie
Kintore
Aviemore
Aberdeen
Kingussie
Ballater
Banchory
Braemar
Stonehaven
Dunnottar Castle
Loch Muick
Todhead Point Lighthouse
Laurencekirk
Inverbervie
OTLAND
Edzell
Loch Tummel
Brechin
Montrose Basin
Montrose
Pitlochry
Kirriemuir
Aberfeldy
Alyth
Forfar
Dunkeld
Blairgowrie
Rattray
Loch Tay
Coupar Angus
Arbroath
Loch Freuchie
Dundee & Tay Bridges
Dundee
Carnoustie
Monifieth
Tayport
Newport-on-Tay
Perth
Firth of Tay
St. Andrews Bay
Crieff
Ballinbreich Castle
Newburgh
Muthill
St. Andrews
St Andrews
Auchtermuchty
Cupar
Fife Ness
Auchterarder
Ladybank
Crail
Falkland
Doune
Dunblane
Kinross
Glenrothes
Anstruther
Loch Leven
Leven
Bridge of Allan
Methil
Earlsferry
Pittenweem
Isle of May
Alloa
Tillicoultry
Buckhaven
Stirling
Clackmannan
Kelty
Lochgelly
Firth of Forth
Bass Rock
Kirkcaldy
Dunfermline
Cowdenbeath
North Berwick
Grangemouth
Kincardine
Burntisland
Tantallon Castle
Forth Bridge
Inverkeithing
Gullane
Falkirk
Leith Docks
Dunbar
Linlithgow
EDINBURGH
Prestonpans
East Linton
Cumbernauld
Broxburn
9

A B C D E F G H I J K L M
Butt of Lewis (Rubha Robhanais)
Cellar Head
Gearrannan Blackhouse Village
Isle of Lewis
Carloway Broch
Spade Cultivation, Lewis
Flannan Islands
Gallan Head
East of Berraglom
Great Bernera
Stornoway
Eye Peninsula (An Rubha)
Callanish Standing Stones
Mangersta sands
OUTER HEBRIDES
Scarp
North Harris (Ceann a Tuath Na Hearadh)
Kebock Head
Boreray
Hirta, St Kilda
St Kilda
Taransay (Tarasaigh)
Talbert
Corran Ra, Taransay
Isle of Scalpay
Shiant Islands
Losgaintir Sands
Scalpay (Eilean Scalpaigh)
South Harris (Ceann a Deas Na Hearadh)
Stockinish Island
THE MINCH
Pabbay
Leverburgh
Haskeir Island
Rodel
Boreray
Isle of Berneray
Haskeir Eagach
Vallay Strand
Berneray Bridge
Gairloch
North Uist (Uibhist Atuath)
Basalt Cliffs
Kilt Rock Waterfall
Loch Obasaraigh, North Uist
Eigneig Bheag, North Uist
Monach Islands
Grimsay, North Uist
Rona
Basalt Cliffs Bearreraig Bay
Ronay, North Uist
Hornish Point
SKYE
Old Man of Storr
Raasay
Portree
Inner Sound
Rudha Hallagro
Skye Bridge Kyleakin
South Uist (Uibhist a Deas)
Broadford
Kyle of Lochalsh
SEA OF THE HEBRIDES
Barra (Barraigh)
Eriskay
Canna
Soay
Mallaig
Vatersay (Bhatarsaigh)
Rum
Sandray (Sanndraigh)
Eigg
Mingulay (Miughalaigh)
Pabbay (Pabaigh)
Ardnambuth Beach
Muck

A
B
C
D
E
F
G
H
I
J
K
L
M
Cape Wrath
Whiten Head
Strathy Point
Dunnet Head
Pentland Firth
Island of Stroma
South Walls
Brough Ness
SOUTH RONALDSAY
Flotta
St. Margaret's Ho
John O' Groats
Duncansby Head
Thurso
Keiss
Sinclair's Bay
Water of Wester
Noss Head
Loch Calder
Loch Watten
Wick
Sinclair & Girnigoe Castle
Kyle of Tongue
Torrisdale Bay
Tongue
Loch Hope
Loch an Dherue
Loch Stack
Loch Meadie
Loch Naver
Eddrachillis Bay
Point of Stoer
Loch More
Achmelvich & beach
Soyea Island
Lochinver
Enard Bay
Loch Assynt
Loch Merkland
Loch nan Clár
Loch Choire
Lybster
Helmsdale
Loch Shin
Loch Brora
Summer Isles
Lairg
Brora
Golspie
Loch Fleet
Ullapool
Bonar Bridge
Dornoch
Dornoch Firth
Tarbat Ness
Little Loch Broom
Loch na Sealga
Fionn Loch
Loch Glascarnoch
Loch Morie
Tain
Lochan Fada
Loch Fannich
Loch Glass
Alness
Invergordon
Moray Firth
Burghead
Lossiemouth
Findochty
Portsoy
Cromarty
Findhorn
Buckie
Cullen
Elgin
Loch Luichart
Dingwall
Fortrose
Nairn
Forres
Loch a' Chroisg
Orrin Reservoir
Fort George
Muir of Ord
Beauly
Culloden
Rothes
Keith
Inverness
Craigellachie
Aberlour (Charlestown of Aberlour)
Dufftown
Huntly
Loch Monar
Lochindorb
Eilean Donan Castle
Loch Mullardoch
Grantown-on-Spey
Loch Ness
Rhynie
Carrbridge
Loch Cluanie
Loch Mhór
Aviemore
Barrisdale Bay
Fort Augustus
Caledonian Canal
Loch Loyne
Loch Quoich
Loch Nevis
Loch Garry
Kingussie
Ballater
Loch Arkaig
Loch Lochy
Loch Morar
Braemar
Spean Bridge
Loch Laggan
Loch Muick
11

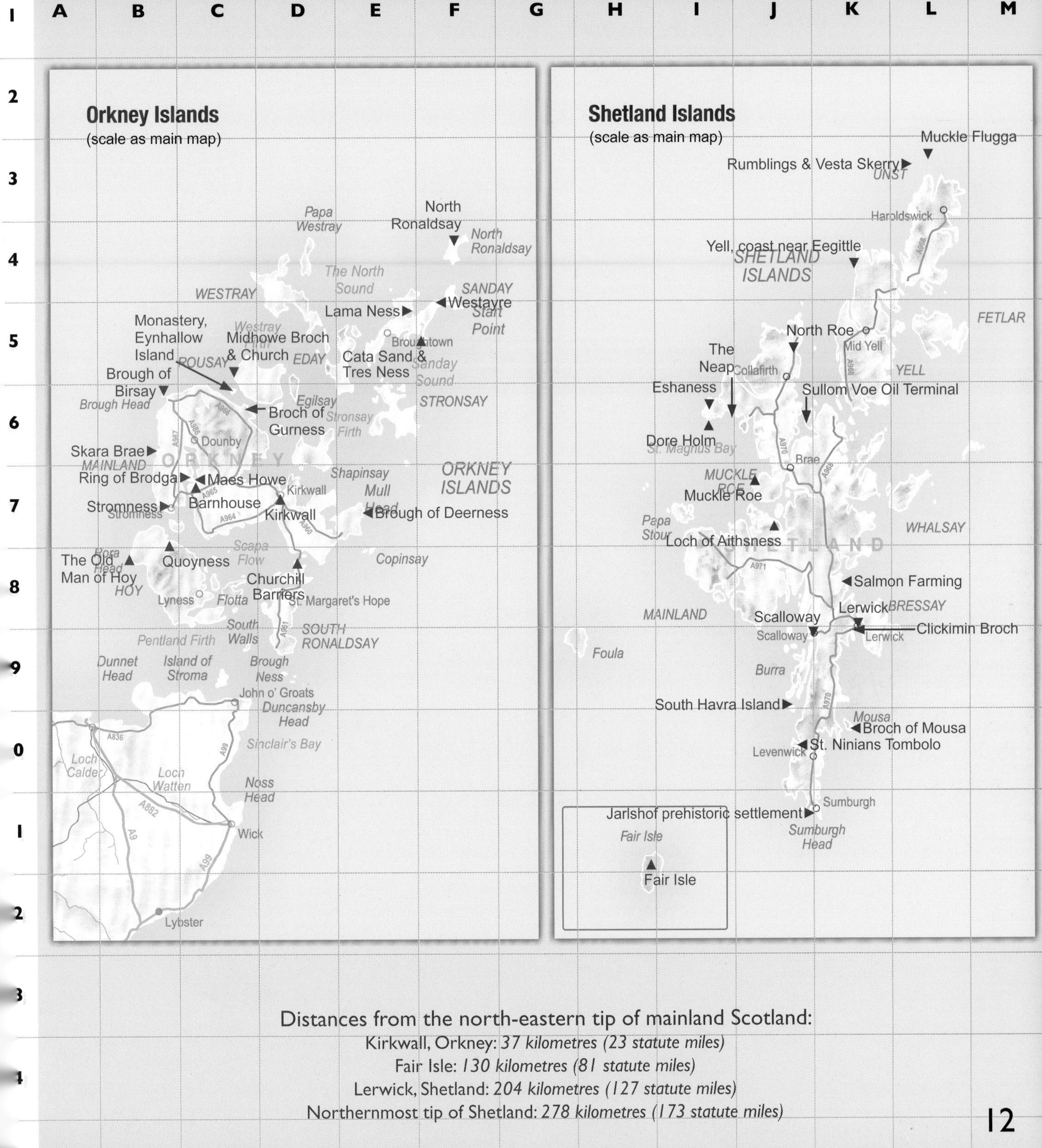

Distances from the north-eastern tip of mainland Scotland:
Kirkwall, Orkney: *37 kilometres (23 statute miles)*
Fair Isle: *130 kilometres (81 statute miles)*
Lerwick, Shetland: *204 kilometres (127 statute miles)*
Northernmost tip of Shetland: *278 kilometres (173 statute miles)*

List of photographs with page numbers & map references

List of photographs with page numbers & map references

INDEX

The Authors

CHRISTOPHER SOMERVILLE is one of Britain's best-known travel writers. He specialises in exploring the coasts and countryside of these islands at slow pace, usually on foot. He has written the Daily Telegraph's Walk of the Month feature since its inception nearly 20 years ago, and contributes travel articles to the Telegraph, Times, Sunday Times, Daily Express, Observer and other national newspapers and magazines. He is the author of more than 30 books, including the best-selling **Coast** books associated with the popular BBC2 TV series, and has had two collections of his poems published.

ADRIAN WARREN has been making wildlife and environmental films worldwide for over thirty years, for the BBC, IMAX large format and National Geographic, and as an independent for his own company, Last Refuge Ltd. As a professional pilot, he specialises in aerial photographic work, and has devised a special wing mounted system for film and video cameras. His many awards include a Winston Churchill Fellowship; the Cherry Kearton Medal from the Royal Geographical Society; and film awards include the Genesis Award from the Ark Trust for Conservation; an International Prime Time Emmy; and the Golden Eagle Award from New York.

DAE SASITORN is from Thailand. She came to England to do a postgraduate study in chemistry many years ago, then had a change of heart to follow her love of nature into the natural history film-making world. She manages Last Refuge Ltd, together with its photographic archives and website. In addition to aerial photography, she undertakes scanning, post-production of images and designs these books.

ADRIAN and **DAE** are currently building a comprehensive aerial photographic archive of Britain. They have published several books including **England: An Aerial View** (2004), **England: The Mini-Book of Aerial Views** (2005) and **Britain: The Mini-Book of Aerial Views** (2007), with new titles on Scotland, Wales and London planned for 2009.

LAST REFUGE Ltd was established in 1992 to document and archive the natural world through films, images, and research, and to play an educational role in raising public awareness in conservation. The company started publishing books in 2004, and regularly supplies images and film from its growing archives to other publishers, broadcasters and interested parties worldwide.

Other aerial titles available from Last Refuge

– England: An Aerial View, ISBN: 0-9544350-2-8, publication date: December 2004
– England: The Mini-Book of Aerial Views, ISBN: 0-9544350-5-2, publication date: November 2005
– Britain: The Mini-Book of Aerial Views, ISBN: 978-0-9544350-8-0, publication date: November 2007

Also available from Last Refuge

– Unseen Companions: Big Views of Tiny Creatures, ISBN: 0-9544350-4-4, publication date: May 2007

All photographs in these books are available as high quality prints from www.lastrefuge.co.uk